The Gospel According to Mark

The Gospel According to Mark

A COMMENTARY

By Sidney L. Poe

The Gospel According to Mark
A Commentary

by Sidney L. Poe

©1994, Word Aflame Press
Hazelwood, MO 63042-2299

Cover Design by Tim Agnew

All Scripture quotations in this book are from the King James Version of the Bible unless otherwise identified.

Printed in United States of America

Printed by

Library of Congress Cataloging-in-Publication Data

Poe. Sidney L.
    The Gospel according to Mark : a commentary / Sidney L. Poe.
        p.   cm.
        Includes bibliographical references.
        ISBN 1-56722-024-X
        1. Bible. N.T. Mark—Commentaries.   I. Bible. N.T.   Mark
    English. Authorized. 1994. II. Title.
    BS2585.3.P64 1994
        226.3'07—dc20   94-15350
                                                                             CIP

Contents

To Darla Rene'
who, through all the grueling hours of work, has
again proven what a great little trooper she is
when the going gets rough

Introduction

Introduction

Introduction

Of the books included as Gospels of Jesus Christ, Mark is generally accepted to be the earliest and it certainly is the shortest. In art and sculpture of antiquity depicting the Gospels as creatures (see Ezekiel 1:10; Revelation 4:7), Mark is symbolized by a lion. The lion designation was given to Mark because of the manner in which the book opens: John the Baptist preaching like the roaring of a lion out of the wilderness.

The theme of this Gospel is more akin, however, to the gentleness of Isaiah 42:1: "Behold my servant, whom I uphold; mine elect, in whom my soul delighteth; I have put my spirit upon him: he shall bring forth judgment to the Gentiles."

The Gospel of Jehovah's servant is the good news of the meek and lowly man full of good deeds. Mark's treatise forms a synoptic part of the history of the life and works of Jesus Christ. It provides both detailed close-ups and broad outlines of events. The book contains over thirty prophecies, fulfillment of eleven Old Testament prophecies, twenty-one promises, twenty-three commands, innumerable lessons and sermons, and the new covenant made by our Lord.[1] It is a compendium of a man's short life, presented with the freshness of an independent observer. The book is noted for its brevity but also for the span of time covered in its pages—from John the Baptist's preaching to the Twelve's commission. Only a single verse depicts the Ascension (16:19) and the early activities of the church in fulfilling their charge (16:20).

Influence of the Apostle Peter

Mark is unique among the Gospels because of downplaying the role of the apostle Peter. This fact along with other evidence suggests that the writer was influenced by the great apostle.

For example, the Gospel of Mark notes that Jesus changed the name of Simon to Peter (3:16). It does not mention Peter by name as one of the disciples sent to prepare the Passover (chapter 14). It records in detail a strong rebuke (8:33) with only brief mention of the great revelation that immediately preceded it (8:29). In the garden Jesus upbraids Peter for sleeping: "Simon, sleepest thou?" (14:37). Further, the book presents the denial of Christ with great detail but the forgiveness and restoration with only a brief note.

Most scholars believe that II Peter 1:15 reflects the apostle's desire to leave a trustworthy record of an eyewitness to the majesty of Christ. All this evidence indicates that the writer of Mark was a reliable recorder of what the great apostle Peter had seen and heard. Undoubtedly the writer was himself also an eyewitness and in some cases a participant. The mention of an otherwise insignificant young man in 14:51-52 leads many scholars to conclude that this man was Mark.

Evidence of Authorship

About the author of the Gospel of Mark, several characteristics are evident. (1) The writer was intimately familiar with the country of Palestine and the city of Jerusalem as deduced from the detailed reference of two specific locations about one mile apart (11:1). (2) The author was familiar with languages of the day. He supplied interpretations for Aramaic words used by the Lord (5:41; 7:34), suggesting an awareness that readers would not be able to comprehend as well as he the intent of these words. This would be true of a man writing in Greek, especially if he were a Palestinian Jew. Another clue to authorship lies in the similarity in text outline with Peter's sermon given at Caesarea (Acts 10:34-43), indicating that Peter might have been a major source of information for the writer. Add to this the fact that Peter called Marcus his son (I Peter 5:13), and one has the intimacy requisite to an author.

Both a divine commission and an eyewitness account of Jesus Christ were necessary for inspired writings in the New Testament canon.[2] Mark was almost certainly an eyewitness, and with the force of Peter's apostolic authority, this writing was never excluded from the New Testament canon or even questioned.

The earliest Christian writers subsequent to the Bible identified Mark as the author. First Papias (c. A.D. 90), then Irenaeus, Clement of Alexandria, Origen, and Jerome, as well as the Anti-Marcionite Prologue of the second century, named Mark as author.[3] Eusebius indicated that the Gospel was written under the eye of Peter.[4]

About the Author

Mark was the son of the Mary in whose home was held the prayer meeting that miraculously delivered Peter

11

from prison (Acts 12:12). This is the first New Testament mention of Mark.

The name Mark is derived from the Latin *Marcus*, meaning a hammer. The name was commonly ascribed to the firstborn of a family. In a spiritual sense Mark was the son of Peter (I Peter 5:13). Some have suggested that he was a Hebrew of the tribe of Levi and a priest after the order of Aaron.[5] This would account for the wearing of linen (Mark 14:51-52). He is the John whose surname is Mark (Acts 12:12, 25), John being the Jewish name, Marcus the Roman. In Acts he is called John Mark until 15:39, where John is dropped altogether. The epistles use the surname exclusively.

As the owner of a large house in Jerusalem, Mary was probably a woman of some wealth and position and undoubtedly provided Mark with sound educational training. Her house was open to church members and disciples. It is possible that here the Lord kept the Passover and here the disciples gathered on the eve of the Resurrection.[6] Their home became a center of Christian worship after Pentecost, maybe the first Christian church in Jerusalem.

Mark's association with the church may stem from an incident in Mark 14:51-52. In this passage a young man with a linen cloth about his body followed Jesus to His arrest. When he himself was accosted, he fled, leaving behind the linen cloth. Quite possibly Mark related what happened to himself.

In character Mark appears to have been sincere and kindhearted but timid and impulsive. The events of the arrest, crucifixion, and resurrection of Christ followed by Pentecost and early persecutions must have left a vivid impression upon the young man. As nephew to Barnabas (Colossians 4:10) and because of his position and calling, he was selected to accompany Paul and Barnabas as an attendant or minister on their first missionary journey.

The purpose for his departure from the journey is only speculation, but Pamphylia with its wild and rowdy manners was hardly the place for a young man of noble birth and genteel upbringing. Yielding to impulse, he departed when the opportunity came at Perga (Acts 13:5, 13). Because of this premature departure, Paul denied him passage on the second journey (Acts 15:36-41). Instead, Mark accompanied Barnabas on an evangelistic effort to Cyprus (Acts 15:39).

He later appeared with Paul at the time of Paul's first Roman imprisonment (Philemon 23-24), then with Peter in Babylon (I Peter 5:13). Paul wrote of Mark in Colossians 4:10, instructing the church to receive him. If they had heard of the dissent between Barnabas and Paul (described in Acts 15:36-40), any question as to the standing of Mark was absolved by Paul in this epistle. Still later he was an acknowledged asset to Paul in his ministry (II Timothy 4:11; Philemon 24) and was requested to travel to Rome with Timothy.

The summary of scriptural references to Mark is as follows: Acts 12:12, 25; 13:5, 13; 15:37-39; Colossians 4:10; II Timothy 4:11; Philemon 24; I Peter 5:13. It appears that Peter's note occurred about five years before that of II Timothy 4:11, which is the final personal reference to Mark.

Qualifications of Mark to Write a Gospel

Mark had to his credit a close and intimate relationship

with Peter, Paul, Barnabas, and Timothy. He was privileged to travel to Cyprus with Barnabas, to Rome with Paul, and to Babylon with Peter.

Jerome said that Mark was not only the interpreter for the apostle Paul but also the first bishop of the church in Alexandria. Eusebius quoted Papias as saying, "Mark, being the interpreter of St. Peter, wrote down exactly whatever things he remembered, yet not in the order in which Christ either spoke or did them; for he was neither a hearer nor a follower of our Lord, but he was afterward a follower of St. Peter."[7]

Eusebius said Mark was the first bishop and the founder of the catechetical school at Alexandria, Egypt. This information, along with the idea that there he died a martyr's death, is not reliably documented.

Last Twelve Verses—Which Ending?

The book, although brief, is not without controversy in biblical history. The inclusion of the final twelve verses of Mark has been the subject of sharp contention for decades.

It is not possible to consider here all evidence and manuscripts, but we can briefly state the problem as follows: in certain early manuscripts the full text of Mark 16:9-20 is lacking, either missing or omitted; the chapter terminates rather abruptly with verse 8. Verses 9-20 are lacking in many older Greek manuscripts, including Codex Sinaiticus (Aleph), Codex Vaticanus (B), Old Latin Manuscript K, Sinaitic Syriac, Old Armenian manuscripts, and many Ethiopic manuscripts; other ancient texts include these verses as Scriptures.

The weight of evidence against inclusion rests with the

old uncial (capital-letter) manuscripts Codex Vaticanus (c. A.D. 325-50) and Codex Siniaticus (c. 340). Codex Regius (L) contains the traditional ending but adds a truncated third ending as well. Codex Washingtonianus I (W) has the traditional ending but inserts after verse 14 a fourth ending.

The familiar long ending of the King James Version from the Majority Text is found in uncials C, D, L, W, most miniscules (small-letter manuscripts), most Old Latin manuscripts, and Jerome's Vulgate (Latin translation), as well as in some Syriac and Coptic manuscripts.

Many early church writers indicated no knowledge of the passage. Jerome stated that "almost all the Greek copies do not have this concluding position." Those who include it usually do so with a notation of its addition to the text.[8] On the other hand the *Shepherd of Hermas* (c. A.D.) refers to Mark 16:16, Justin Martyr (c. A.D. 160) quoted the last two verses, and Irenaeus (c. A.D. 177) quoted Mark 16:19. At the time of Irenaeus there was no doubt of the genuineness of the passage in Asia Minor, Gaul, or Italy.[9]

The most ancient versions, both Eastern and Western, without exception recognize the longer passage. In the East, the second-century Syriac Peshitta, the Philoxenian, and the Curetonian Syriac bear witness to the traditional ending, and all those manuscripts predate the Sinaitic and Vatican Codices. Coptic versions also recognize its authenticity.

In the Western church, the earliest version of the Vulgate, the Old Italic, records it. Jerome in preparing the Vulgate admitted it while noting objections to it. The Gothic Version of Ulphelas (fourth century) includes only verses 8-12.

The internal evidence favors the longer ending of Mark. If the chapter terminated with verse 8, the abrupt conclusion would be so striking that it is highly unlikely that any author would have ended at this point. The abruptness of Mark in beginning his Gospel might suggest an equally abrupt conclusion stated with the terse conciseness of other factual reporting throughout the book. However, in few instances do Bible writers or any writers summarize and conclude in the fashion of a beginning. Abruptness in the beginning might be permissible; abruptness in the end is not.

Date and Circumstances of Writing

The book gives no specific date as to its writing. Scholars generally date the Gospel from A.D. 50-80 or from A.D. 65-70.

The latter is based on a reference made by Irenaeus that places the writing after the death of Peter. The Anti-Marcionite Prologue likewise says, "After the death of Peter himself he wrote down this same Gospel."

Those who deny the predictive nature of prophecy (i.e., 13:2), say the date must fall after A.D. 70. On the other hand, if Acts is dated at A.D. 61 and Luke's companion volume was earlier than Acts, then Mark was presumably written before A.D. 61, because most scholars hold that Luke had access to Mark's manuscript when writing his own book. This might even push the date as far back as mid to late A.D. 50s. The strongest lines of evidence support the conclusion that Mark was written after Peter died (A.D. 67) but before the fall of Jerusalem (A.D. 70).

The book was apparently written from Rome, although

John Chrysostom said Egypt. It was written in Greek to Gentiles, principally Romans. Several observations support this conclusion: (1) The candid explanations of particular Jewish terminology and customs (5:41; 7:2-4, 11, 34; 15:22) were unnecessary if writing to Jews. (2) Clement of Alexandria said the Romans requested that Peter's preaching be written down for them to study. (3) A Christian audience is suggested by the assumption of prior understanding and familiarity with earlier events. For example, Mark made no attempt to identify John the Baptist and treated his imprisonment as common knowledge. "Baptism" (1:4) and "Holy Ghost" (1:8) are given without explanation.

The striking absence of any genealogy of Christ (a must to convince any Jew but not necessarily given for a servant), the omission of any mention of the Sermon on the Mount, and the lack of serious condemnation of the Jewish sects all add weight to the evidence that Mark wrote to Gentile Christians. Moreover, as already noted, Mark interpreted Aramaic words (5:41; 7:34; 15:22), and he injected Latin terms absent from the other gospels, such as "executioner" (6:27) and *quadrans* ("farthing"; 12:42).

Purpose for Writing

First, Mark was undoubtedly inspired by the Holy Spirit to record an authentic written text of the life and works of Jesus for the edification and instruction of saints.

Second, the early church depended upon many saints' eyewitness accounts by "oral tradition," especially the apostles. However, as persecution arose and the apostles scattered, the secondary and tertiary nature of the testimonies weakened the proclamation and undoubted-ly gave rise to much embellishment of true stories. Mark sensed, as did Luke (1:1), the need for an enduring record free of distortions inculcated by constant retelling. A written word could be consistently copied and made available to groups who had no eyewitness within the assembly.

Third, this Gospel was put into writing at a time when Christians were generally undergoing persecution. To circulate the story of Jesus' suffering at a time like this would encourage steadfastness among the fledgling group. The first imperial persecution of Christians began in Rome by Emperor Nero following the great fire of A.D. 64. Mark's Gospel came shortly thereafter.

Untold saints could take courage from the bold example of Christ, who not only came to die (10:45) but also chose death over compromise of truth. He endured hatred, rejection, cruelty, and eventually crucifixion to establish His gospel and the way of Christians. That way meant self-sacrifice and suffering (8:31; 9:31; 10:32-34), but it also meant reigning with Him victoriously.

Finally, Mark was so impressed with the deeds of Christ that he spent little time on what was actually said. He deemed these actions worthy of recording for all people to know.

The Plan of Presenting the Gospel

Mark included a brief introduction (1:1-20) that links the story with the Old Testament messenger (John), omitting any references to the birth, genealogy, or childhood of Jesus. After the general introduction, Mark's presentation follows a geographical arrangement of Christ's ministry spreading from His home province of Galilee to

Jerusalem, as the following divisions show.

"The Great Galilean Ministry" (1:21-6:13) describes about one-and-a-half years of miracle-filled preaching and teaching in Galilee and the calling and preparation of disciples. "The Ministry Outside Galilee" (6:14-10:52) follows due to rising opposition at home. From the northern areas Jesus journeyed to Jerusalem through Galilee, Perea, and into Judea. "The Final Ministry in Jerusalem" (11:1-14:42), initiated in a dramatic and triumphal entrance, recounts long days of conflict and controversy with religious leaders. "The Crucifixion and Resurrection" (14:43-16:20) sets out the arrest, mocking trial, murder, and resurrection of Jesus.

Mark's Gospel is characterized by the simplicity, deity, and humanity of Jesus Christ. It is written to and for Gentile believers.

To analyze the Gospel of Mark, this commentary follows the outline presented by D. Edmond Hiebert in *An Introduction to the New Testament*, with added subdivisions.

In summary, the Gospel of Mark was written by John Mark of Jerusalem, a disciple of Peter, nephew of Barnabas, companion of Paul, and contemporary of Timothy. The book was heavily influenced by the apostle Peter and is dated A.D. 67-70. Mark's Gospel is the shortest of the four narratives but contains a realistic and uncensored reporting of facts without exhaustive interpretation. There is an elaboration of terms considered difficult for the Gentile audience to whom it was addressed. Events are reported as by an on-the-spot eyewitness (more than a mere scribe) with an urgency incumbent upon the writer. This is indicated by the key word *euthys*, translated "straightway," used forty-one times in the sixteen chapters. This term also serves to underscore the servant theme, which results in emphasis on our Lord's works and deeds rather than His words. The Gospel of Mark is the story of Jesus according to Peter, written and preserved by Mark under the leadership of the Holy Ghost. It is the inspired Word of God.

Notes

[1]Finis Jennings Dake, *Dake's Annotated Reference Bible* (Lawrenceville, GA: Dake Bible Sales), Mark endnote.

[2]Norman L. Geisler and William E. Nix, *A General Introduction to the Bible* (Chicago: Moody, 1986), 283.

[3]*Pulpit Commentary, Mark and Luke*, H. D. M. Spence and Joseph S. Exell (eds.) (Grand Rapids: Eerdmans, 1950), vii.

[4]*Ibid.*, v.

[5]*Ibid.*, iv.

[6]*Ibid.*, v.

[7]*Ibid.*, vii.

[8]*Ibid.*, viii-ix.

[9]*Ibid.*, ix.

I.
Coming of the Servant
(1:1-13)

I.

Coming of the Servant (1:1-13)
A. Title of the Book (1:1)

(1) The beginning of the gospel of Jesus Christ, the Son of God.

Verse 1. The gospel, the good news (Greek *euangelion*), did not begin with Bethlehem or with John the Baptist. Moses and the prophets envisioned Christ's coming and His work as far back as Genesis 3:15. God knew Him as His Son, the Lamb slain from the foundation of the world (Revelation 13:8). Mark chose the point of John the Baptist (cf. Acts 1:22; Matthew 11:12; Luke 16:16; John 1:6) to begin his gospel story of the identity, words, and activities of Jesus Christ.

B. Ministry of the Baptist (1:2-8)
(Matthew 3; Luke 3:1-22; John 1:6-34; 3:23;
Isaiah 40:3; Malachi 3:1)

(2) As it is written in the prophets, Behold, I send my messenger before thy face, which shall prepare thy way before thee. (3) The voice of one crying in the wilderness, Prepare ye the way of the Lord, make his paths straight. (4) John did baptize in the wilderness, and preach the baptism of repentance for the remission of

23

sins. (5) And there went out unto him all the land of Judaea, and they of Jerusalem, and were all baptized of him in the river of Jordan, confessing their sins. (6) And John was clothed with camel's hair, and with a girdle of a skin about his loins; and he did eat locusts and wild honey; (7) and preached, saying, There cometh one mightier than I after me, the latchet of whose shoes I am not worthy to stoop down and unloose. (8) I indeed have baptized you with water: but he shall baptize you with the Holy Ghost.

Verse 2. Mark cites two prophets who declared that a messenger was to be sent before the Messiah. The first prophet was Malachi (3:1), who stated that a messenger would prepare the way. This was a threat to the unfit priesthood in Malachi's day. The messenger was to cleanse and purify the Temple worship, which from time to time fell into a shameful condition. When the Lord came, certain conditions had to be met; people needed to repent and purify themselves from foul deeds and embrace a sanctity acceptable to a holy God.

Verse 3. Second, Isaiah (40:3) declared that a voice in the wilderness would cry to prepare the way. The cry of the herald was to make a straight path in anticipation of the coming of the Lord. The phrase "in the wilderness" comes from Israel's experience in departing from Egypt and occupying the Promised Land. Spiritually it connotes a dry, barren, testing, trying place where the flesh learns submission to the Spirit through trials but through which, as Moses faithfully led Israel, Jesus faithfully leads those who follow Him.

Verse 4. John the Baptist (Baptizer) was that messenger, as signified by his appearing in the wilderness as prophesied. His message called for a baptism of repentance for the remission of sins. His method was to preach or proclaim the requirements to make "his paths straight" and then to baptize (dip by immersion) all believers. John worked in and out of the wilderness (Greek *eremos*), often meaning uncultivated, barren lands, frequently pasture lands lying outside the towns. Although he might have been acquainted with Jewish monastic groups near the Dead Sea wilderness, it is more likely that until the day he appeared publicly (Luke 1:80), he maintained a solitary existence in the wilderness.

Verse 5. People of Judea and the city of Jerusalem flocked to hear John. Many believed his message and obeyed, accepting baptism in the Jordan River and confessing their sins. The use of "all" is a figure of speech in which the whole represents a great part.

The baptism of John has been debated and still generates questions in the mind of scholars. Jesus Himself asked the Pharisees about its origin and meaning: was it of God or man? Several things about John's ministry are clear. First, his message was to the Jews; second, it announced a baptism of repentance or moral reform; and third, John made a proclamation that One infinitely greater was to come (verse 7). Several meanings of John's baptism are possible.

1. The ritualistic Jews washed and bathed themselves repeatedly because they believed they were daily defiled by touching various items (Leviticus 11-15).

2. Proselytes to the Jewish faith (Gentiles) were required to (a) be circumcised, which marked the Abrahamic Covenant, (b) have a sacrifice offered for them by the

priest, and (c) undergo a baptismal cleansing. This baptism was no mere ritual of sprinkling but a literal bath (immersion), plunging the entire body into the water. As a forerunner, it appears that John asked the pious Jews to confess their sins and to be baptized (*baptizo*, dipped, plunged) after the manner of a Gentile in anticipation of Him who was to appear.

3. Baptism was accompanied by confession—an acknowledgment of sin and wrongdoing—as part of repentance. Three confessions were required of the candidate: first, to himself as an admission of being a sinner; second, to those he had wronged, misled, hurt, injured, or grieved; third, to God. If pride ends where forgiveness begins, there can be no forgiveness without humiliation. When a man humbly admits, "I have sinned; I am a sinner," then God willingly extends mercy unto forgiveness. Baptism represents a dramatic and visible expression of inner remorse and contrition.

Verse 6. John's dress and diet, described in simple yet vivid terms, were after the tradition of solitary prophetic figures. Perhaps because of his lifestyle as much as the content of his message, people came to hear him. He was different from the religious sects who instructed others how to live but exempted themselves from the rules. John lived a life of religious protest. His domicile was rural areas that also housed wild beasts. John shunned the cities filled with corruption and the sin of man's failing efforts to govern himself.

In dress, John was most humble: camel's skin girdle covering the loins, tied with a leather belt around the waist after the style of Elijah (II Kings 1:8). He excited no envy as a fashionable orator of the day; his dress avoided the soft and effeminate luxuries that fail to challenge manhood and kill the soul with ease. In food, he was also consistent—nature provided roughage of locusts and wild honey. The locust of John's diet was probably a beanlike pod produced by the carob tree and gathered by the poor as food for themselves or their livestock. However, the grasshopper (*Locustidae*), an herb-feeding insect, was permitted as food (Leviticus 11:22-23). The honey in John's diet was either the sticky resinous exudate from the cambium of certain trees, or as more commonly believed, the condensed nectar gathered from flowers by the wild honeybee. No one questioned that John lived his message; for this reason people desired to hear his words.

William Barclay suggested that John was effective for four reasons.[1] First, he lived his message, unlike the Pharisees and other religious leaders of his day. He preached a simple antimaterialistic message, and his lifestyle was consistent in where he lived, what he wore, and what he ate.

Second, John was effective because he told people what they knew about themselves. The people had heard no prophet's voice for four hundred years, and John's had the ring of authenticity that their longing hearts craved.

Third, John was effective because of his humility. He viewed himself as unfit to be even a slave to the Master. He was yielded, a vessel, a forerunner of Messiah.

Finally, John was effective because he pointed to Someone greater than himself. All great persons have a burning cause with which they are consumed. John baptized in water; the One coming would submerge them in the Holy Ghost. Water might cleanse the body; the Holy Ghost would cleanse and purify the heart and life of a person. John did not attempt to gather a following to himself; rather he drew people for Jesus Christ.

Verses 7-8. Luke 3:10-14 specified sins that John called on the Jews to confess and abandon: greed, fraud, violence, false accusation. Not only did he require a turning from sin, but John preached the coming of a great One to whom he was not even a worthy servant. This One would baptize converts with the Holy Ghost. Mark contrasted the baptism of water, a complete submersion, with the equally complete deluge of the coming Spirit.

Baptism of the Holy Spirit presented a new concept even for the Jews. The Holy Spirit overshadowed Mary and wrought conception (Matthew 1:20); here it is the Spirit of God at work among people. The Spirit cannot literally be poured as liquid over one, nor can a person be dipped in the Spirit as in water. The One to come would pour out His Spirit in such a great flood that a deluge of the very presence of God would be at work purifying, purging, and sanctifying the people. Acts 1:5 uses the conjunction "*but* ye shall be baptized with the Holy Ghost" (emphasis added). This promise and its fulfillment are essential to be Christian, for the Spirit dwells (resides) within the believer and without the Spirit there can be no claim of belonging to Christ (Romans 8:9). The beginning of the church (Acts 2:1-4) was marked by the active influence of the Holy Spirit come to dwell in the believer as prophesied in Joel 2:28.

Like Moses who saw the Promised Land but did not enter in, John the Baptist stood on the threshold and declared that the kingdom of God had come but did not himself enter in. The least in the kingdom of heaven is greater than he (Matthew 11:11; Luke 7:28). John's baptism marked the threshold of this great kingdom.

C. Baptism of Jesus (1:9-11)
(Matthew 3:13; Luke 3:21)

How was Jesus prepared for ministry mentally, physically, and spiritually? First came baptism by John, then a testing in the wilderness. Proven worthy, He then began a ministry of supernatural power, miraculous healings, and deliverance designed to demonstrate that Jesus was indeed the Holy One of God, the Messiah.

(9) And it came to pass in those days, that Jesus came from Nazareth of Galilee, and was baptized of John in Jordan. (10) And straightway coming up out of the water, he saw the heavens opened, and the Spirit like a dove descending upon him: (11) and there came a voice from heaven, saying, Thou art my beloved Son, in whom I am well pleased.

Verses 9-11. Jesus departed Nazareth (His home place in Galilee), sought out John, and began His public ministry in a most humble manner—by submitting to baptism in the Jordan River.

Perhaps by this time John had baptized thousands of ordinary men with no special signs. "Straightway" (Mark's word for "at once" or "immediately") an unusual experience occurred when Jesus was baptized. Upon emerging from the water, three things happened: the heavens (the atmosphere or regions overhead) opened, the Spirit like a dove descended upon Jesus, and a voice from heaven spoke, proclaiming Him the beloved Son "in whom I am well pleased" to dwell. These events in a unique way signaled that here at last stood the Messiah. John, after the manner of Old Testament priests, declared Him manifest to all Israel: "Behold the Lamb of God, which taketh away the sin of the world" (John 1:29). The baptism of Jesus both confirmed to John and made manifest to Israel their Messiah.

John's baptism represented a cleansing for the penitent sinner who wished to be purged of his sins, but this purpose did not apply to the sinless Jesus. Even the devil acknowledged that Jesus is the "Holy One of God" (Mark 1:24). For Jesus the baptism represented something more.[2]

First, Jesus' baptism represented a marker event of His moment of decision. After thirty years of typical Jewish upbringing and manhood, He needed to mark a time to launch into public ministry. The appearance of John baptizing in Jordan must have served as a clarion call for Jesus. Baptism was a response to the summons of the Spirit—the appointed time had come, and there would be no retreat.

Second, baptism for Jesus singled Him out as one of those associated with a move back to God. He was not part of the rebellious crowd who defied Rome or the hypocritical religious system who defied the law and God.

Third, baptism provided divine approval and sanction for Jesus. Scripture is silent about Jesus' prayer life before this time, but now there was a relationship with God for all to see. Jesus prayed frequently and the transcendent God of Israel, silent for four centuries, now spoke directly through the man Jesus. God was in Christ, reconciling the world to Himself (II Corinthians 5:19).

Fourth, baptism represented a yielded commitment to the urging and dictates of the Spirit. It was a moment of surrender; from this point on the Spirit commanded, dictating and driving steadily and assuredly toward the final resolution of man's sin problem.

The gentle and peaceful descending dove provided a sharp contrast to the preaching of John about One coming who would sift, purge, fan, burn and condemn (Matthew 3:7-12; Luke 3:7-13). It was good news that Jesus would conquer not by force of violence but by love.

Finally, the words of John take on deeper significance in light of Old Testament sacrifices. John announced to the world the Lamb of God who takes away their sin. The Lamb was now placed under observation and intense scrutiny for flaw, defect, illness, or injury to determine its suitability to be the paschal lamb sacrificed at Passover. It was a death sentence, because such lambs died to provide a blood atonement.

D. Temptation by Satan (1:12-13)
(Matthew 4:1; Luke 4:1)

(12) And immediately the Spirit driveth him into the wilderness. (13) And he was there in the wilderness forty days, tempted of Satan; and was with the wild beasts; and the angels ministered unto him.

Verses 12-13. Jesus, surrendered to the dictates of the Spirit, was driven into the wilderness, the solitary, lonely reaches outside urban centers where no one but beasts were His companions. In the wilderness for "forty days" (a Hebrew idiom referring to a span of time), He was open to opposition by Satan. The devil (slanderer, one who lies or misrepresents) confronted Jesus, challenging what had

31

been established at baptism. Luke 4 indicates that Jesus was tempted to prove or doubt His identity, misuse His position as the Son of God, and compromise the method to accomplish God's will.

Jesus chose a response that bridged the gap to humans—not power to coerce them, fearful fire from heaven to destroy them, nor dictatorial power to enslave them, but love to appeal, allure, and bind the crushed, defeated human will to Himself. In resisting all these temptations—lust of the flesh, lust of the eye, and pride of life (I John 2:16)—Jesus became an unwavering example of dedication to the will of God. After the experience, the angels, helpers of God, ministered to Him.

Notes

[1]William Barclay, *The Gospel of Mark* (Philadelphia: Westminster Press, 1956), 7-8.

[2]*Ibid.*, 9-1

II.
Ministry of the Servant
(1:14-13:37)

A.
Ministry in Galilee
(1:14-4:34)

4

Ministry in Galilee

II.

Ministry of the Servant (1:14-13:37)
A. Ministry in Galilee (1:14-4:34)
1. Summary of the Preaching (1:14-15)
(Matthew 4:12; Luke 4:14)

(14) Now after that John was put in prison, Jesus came into Galilee, preaching the gospel of the kingdom of God, (15) and saying, The time is fulfilled, and the kingdom of God is at hand: repent ye, and believe the gospel.

Verse 14. Jesus entered Galilee, preaching the gospel of the kingdom of God only after John the Baptist's imprisonment. The disciples of John were leaderless, the people needed direction, and no rivalry would ensue between the bands of followers. John's work as forerunner had been accomplished at this point and a successor was needed.

Verse 15. Powerful words of Christianity are here attributed to Jesus in His preaching. People are either reminiscent and nostalgic or futuristic in their hope; they are reluctant to accept and act in the present. But the time had arrived, Messiah was here, this was the day, the kingdom was at hand. Jesus gave God's timely call: Repent and believe the good news.

A change of mind, repentance *(metanoia)*, is necessary

if directions are to be reversed. People need to change their minds from doubt, skepticism, and contentment with sinfulness to hope, expectancy, and sinless belief.

Israel's ideal future called for the reign of a delivering Messiah; God's reign in the Anointed One (Greek, *Christ*) would see a theocratic government ruled by One who had received the sacred oil (Psalm 93:1; 97:1; 99:1). Once anointed, He could never be unanointed, although He could be either rejected or accepted by the people. A change of thinking was called for to erase the mistaken Jewish ideas of a warlike, delivering Messiah and to change their way of life from self-centeredness to God-centeredness. We must accept at face value what the Synoptic Gospels illustrate by word, action, doctrine, and character: Jesus, the Son, brought God's kingdom within the reach of ordinary humans.

2. Call to Four Fishermen (1:16-20)
(Matthew 4:18; cf. Luke 5:8-11)

(16) Now as he walked by the sea of Galilee, he saw Simon and Andrew his brother casting a net into the sea: for they were fishers. (17) And Jesus said unto them, Come ye after me, and I will make you to become fishers of men. (18) And straightway they forsook their nets, and followed him. (19) And when he had gone a little farther thence, he saw James the son of Zebedee, and John his brother, who also were in the ship mending their nets. (20) And straightway he called them: and they left their father Zebedee in the ship with the hired servants, and went after him.

Verses 16-18. Having announced that the kingdom of God was come, Jesus began to select disciples as leaders for kingdom subjects. His eye fell on two brothers: Simon and Andrew, fishermen busy at casting their nets. Galilee was noted for its fish and had many fishermen. Josephus records that in his day more than three hundred boats were involved in the fish harvest. The average person of Palestine ate more fish than meat (Matthew 7:10; Luke 11:11; Mark 6:32-44), and fish were salted for preservation and exported. Fresh fish became a delicacy in inland cities. Names of cities along the lake indicated the importance of the fishing industry: Bethsaida (house of fish) and Tarichaea (the place of salt fish).

Nets were of two kinds. One, the *sagene*, was a trawl net or seine. Weights on one edge and floats on the opposite edge caused this net to stand upright in the water. It was plied from the end of a boat, and as the boat moved forward the net was drawn through the water like a great scoop to enclose the fish. A much smaller net, the *amphiblistron*, was cast by hand into the water and drawn like an umbrella to enclose the fish. Andrew and Simon used this latter type of net, which they immediately ("straightway") left to follow Jesus.

Verse 19. Jesus proceeded along the lake shore of Galilee where He saw two other fishermen, also brothers, in their boat mending nets. This net was probably the *sagene*, which being dragged through the water might more readily be snagged and torn. After a night of fishing, they needed to mend any rips or tears in anticipation of the coming night of work.

Verse 20. Jesus called them; James and John left their father Zebedee with the hired servants to follow after Jesus.

"Fishers of men" is a unique metaphor to relate to the saving of people by spreading the gospel. The action of fishing, whether for fish or people, is similar; albeit the purpose differs.

It is noteworthy that while these men were asked to leave their occupation to follow Him (as were other disciples), not everyone was asked to do so. In Mark 5:18-19, Jesus expressly required a man to remain at home as a witness. The masses were not to give up ordinary labors to live and work for Christ, although everyone must be willing to do so. The uncompromising claims of discipleship are spelled out in 8:34-35. Sound Christian men and women will find a ministry of service in the local community and in their own family. They provide a strong example for others who keep their homes. There is a difference here between those called as leaders and those who are followers in the kingdom of God.

The men Jesus chose as leaders and intimates merit closer examination. They were simple folks, not ecclesiastics or aristocrats, not learned or wealthy. The common ordinary class of people believed Jesus and came to hear Him. Others came to hear but refused to believe. A person should feel less concern over what he is when called than over what Jesus Christ can make him when he obeys.

Second, the men Jesus chose were busy about their day's work—menial yet necessary chores. This was also true of prophets and kings. Amos said, "The LORD took me as I followed the flock, . . . Go, prophesy" (Amos 7:15). Saul was searching for strayed donkeys when Samuel found him, and David had to be called to the anointing from his duties of tending sheep. The call of God comes, not just in the house of God or in the secret chamber, but during the course of a day's labor. To heed that call is the meaning of discipleship.

Third, how they were singled out is noteworthy. Undoubtedly these fishermen had seen or heard Jesus before. Eye contact, a head nod of agreement, or a lingering after the crowd departed indicated an attraction to this man. Jesus made no appeals as other people would, no promise of great rewards of wealth, fame, or power that so easily allures people. His simple "Follow Me" appealed directly to their desire for service to Him and to their fellow man. There was a personal attraction to Him. No leader can function long without the trust and steadfast loyalty of his chosen men. The Galileans responded because of who Jesus was, not merely because of what He said.

Fourth, working men have a task-oriented mentality, and Jesus challenged them with a task. Jesus called them not to a life of ease and inactivity but to a cause for which they would both spend and be spent, burn and be burned, and in the end die ignominiously. They had to give all to Him and to others if they were to win something for themselves.

3. Ministry in Capernaum (1:21-34)
a. Excitement in the synagogue (1:21-28)
(Luke 4:32)

(21) And they went into Capernaum; and straightway on the sabbath day he entered into the synagogue, and taught. (22) And they were astonished at his doctrine: for he taught them as one that had authority, and not as the scribes. (23) And there was in their synagogue

41

*a man with an unclean spirit; and he cried out, (24)
saying, Let us alone; what have we to do with thee, thou
Jesus of Nazareth? art thou come to destroy us? I know
thee who thou art, the Holy One of God. (25) And Jesus
rebuked him, saying, Hold thy peace, and come out of
him. (26) And when the unclean spirit had torn him,
and cried with a loud voice, he came out of him. (27)
And they were all amazed, insomuch that they questioned among themselves, saying, What thing is this?
what new doctrine is this? for with authority comman-
deth he even the unclean spirits, and they do obey him.
(28) And immediately his fame spread abroad throughout all the region round about Galilee.*

Jesus entered His ministry in a logical fashion. First,
He was baptized and equipped for service, then tested for
loyalty. He then chose His method and selected His men.
Now He appealed to the public.

Verse 21. Jesus entered Capernaum (a village of
Nahum) and made His headquarters on the northwest
shore of the Sea of Galilee. Here He began to teach in the
synagogues and perform miracles. Any message from God
would most naturally be exposed in the synagogue where
people gathered to hear the Scriptures.

The Sabbath was the seventh day, the end of the week,
and meant cessation of all work and toil (Exodus 20:10).
Every Jew honored this day above all others of the week.

The synagogue was notable as an institution of instruction and teaching. Sabbath services included prayer and a
reading of the Word followed by explanation. Music,
singing, and sacrifices (worship and offering) were practiced at the Temple. The Jews had only one Temple

(Herod's) but many synagogues throughout the land. A synagogue existed in every colony of ten or more Jewish families; it became the more influential institution because of its ubiquity and the nature of its discourse. Adjoining rooms provided space for education of children and hosting events pertaining to Jewish culture.

As a local center of Jewish religion and culture, the synagogue provided a time and location for launching a new message. The ruler of the synagogue arranged services and administered affairs. A cash collection was made daily and the proceeds distributed as alms to the poor. The duty of the *chazzan*, or minister, was to bring out and replace the sacred scrolls of Scripture, to maintain the sanitation of the building, to sound blasts on the silver trumpet denoting the arrival of the Sabbath, and to ensure education of the elementary-age children of the community. However, there was no permanent preacher or teacher for the exposition of Scripture. The ruler of the synagogue could call on any competent person to read and interpret Scripture. Jesus took advantage of this opportunity, and as a man with a message, He was called upon to teach.

Verse 22. Jesus' teaching or doctrine astonished the hearers, accustomed as they were to the scribes. His method and authority seemed like a new revelation, not the old scribal interpretation of laws. The Jews were bound to the sacred Torah, or law, which had been elaborately constructed about the nucleus of the Decalogue (Ten Commandments). The law included the Pentateuch, or five books of Moses, Genesis through Deuteronomy. The divine writings, holy and binding in religious affairs, necessitated deep and meticulous study. The Torah expressed broad principles subject to interpretation and application to everyday living. Consequently, a system of rules and regulations developed over the years. To study and interpret the law, scribes evolved, a group of scholars who were experts in the law.

The greatest and most coveted title among scribes was rabbi, a designation not unlike the modern rank of professor emeritus. The first duty of scribes was to take the moral principles of the Torah and develop policies (rules) for every situation encountered in life. The scribe had an endless task as rules and regulations proliferated to embrace arising interactions and relationships. Secondly, the scribes served as teachers of their developments, thus transmitting them to the people. Most of these rules were never written down but followed only as the oral law. The Pharisees considered the oral law to be as binding as the written law. Scribes became expert at memorizing and relating their regulations. Thirdly, the scribes acted as judges of specific situations, which gave rise to new laws from each case.

In contrast, Jesus taught with personal authority, not as scribes who continually avoided independent judgment and referred to other teachings as a basis for decisions. Jesus needed no authority beyond Himself. He spoke with independent judgment, cited no authorities, quoted no other masters. He spoke with a positive, definite certitude that was the antithesis of the careful scribes.

Verses 23-24. People possessed of demons, or unclean spirits, were not uncommon in Palestine. In some cases, the possessed individual was mentally ill or demented. At other times, the person was physically ill, often with paralysis. Regardless of the symptom or type of possession, all demonic activity opposed God's will. Demonic possession created for the individual and for society a disharmony of mind and will, spirit and body.

In this passage the demon-possessed individual was in the synagogue and upon seeing Jesus began to cry out. The unclean spirit (or spirits, as indicated by the plural pronoun) cried out an interesting question: "Art thou come to destroy us?" This suggests that the demons knew they would be destroyed. Moreover, they definitely recognized Jesus, calling Him by name and identifying Him as the "Holy One of God" (Luke 4:34), a rare title from Psalm 16:10.

Verses 25-26. In the first century, exorcists claimed to be able to cast out demons using elaborate incantations, spells, and magical rites. By contrast, Jesus caused demons to depart with a simple word of command. The authority lay in Jesus' words, and the people were astonished at His power.

The most striking and extraordinary feature of Jesus' deeds was the successful healing of all manner of illnesses without pharmaceuticals, surgery, drawn-out therapy, or even anointing. All of the Gospels speak of it, Acts 10:38 acclaims it, and Paul, Peter, James, and John noted the exceptional power of Jesus to cure the ill and infirm.

What Jesus did was an act of power, *dunamis*, or according to John, *semeion*, a sign, a marvelous thing. Never were these deeds done to amaze, surprise, or please the crowds. Never were they done for money, gifts, or with a charge for service. At His temptation Jesus rejected once and for all the misuse of God's power by theatrical showmanship.

Still, there was a element of uniformity in all healings greater than mere need. Not all those in need of therapy were cured; not all the blind eyes were opened or lame limbs restored. Two commonalities appear both from the standpoint of the individual in need and of Jesus Christ. First, miracles resulted when Jesus had compassion—more than just great concern, but intense personal identification with the suffering individual, and second, Jesus never operated out of the perfect will of God.

To humans, miracles are acts of power attributed to God as He intervenes in the course of nature or interrupts the normal cause and effect of a pathological syndrome. In Mark 6:5-6, Jesus could do no miracle because the people lacked faith in Him; hence it is necessary that individuals respond to the presence of Jesus in faith, trust in God, and desire or will for themselves to be cured. Absence of faith and obedience arrest the flow of God's power. Where people accepted the will of God, fully trusted Him, fully obeyed, and fully praised, the power of God was demonstrated.

Verses 27-28. The people's amazement prompted questions of the source of this authority. Did a new doctrine make demons obey His command? Jesus' fame as an authoritative teacher and exorcist quickly spread throughout the regions of Galilee.

b. Healing of Peter's mother-in-law (1:29-31)
(Matthew 8:14; Luke 4:38)

(29) And forthwith, when they were come out of the

synagogue, they entered into the house of Simon and Andrew, with James and John. (30) But Simon's wife's mother lay sick of a fever, and anon they tell him of her. (31) And he came and took her by the hand, and lifted her up; and immediately the fever left her, and she ministered unto them.

Verses 29-31. Jesus, accompanied by James, John, Simon, Andrew, and perhaps others, departed the synagogue and entered the private house of Peter and Andrew (Matthew and Luke name only Simon). Jesus had not been in the house long ("anon") until He heard of Simon's mother-in-law lying sick of a fever. The prevalence of marshes in the region led to hordes of biting insects that could readily transmit dangerous parasites to humans, resulting in intense fevers.

No specific mention was made of Simon's wife but it can be inferred that Simon was the head of this house and that his mother-in-law resided there. I Corinthians 9:5 implies that his wife traveled with him on missionary tours. Tradition says she suffered martyrdom, led to her death in the sight of Simon, whose final counsel was, "Remember thou the Lord."[1]

Jesus took the feverish woman's hand and raised her. Luke 4:39 adds that He rebuked the fever. The fever left and she arose at once, strong enough to perform domestic duties. Customarily the main Sabbath meal was eaten at the sixth hour (12:00 noon); perhaps this constituted her service to the assembled guests.

Several things are noteworthy about Jesus and this private miracle. First, unlike psychics, neither audience nor support group was necessary for Him to heal. Second, this urgent need had more importance than His own repose after a dramatic and tiring day at the synagogue. Third, Jesus again dispensed with elaborate incantations, formulas, or spells of the many false healers and simply spoke authoritatively to work the cure. Jesus possessed both unique insight and unique power.

Also noteworthy is that the disciples, even at this first day of unveiling of special power, had already come to depend on Jesus for their needs. The healed woman's action here was exemplary: no sooner had she recovered than she began to serve.

c. Healing ministry at sundown (1:32-34)
(Matthew 8:16; Luke 4:40)

(32) And at even, when the sun did set, they brought unto him all that were diseased, and them that were possessed with devils. (33) And all the city was gathered together at the door. (34) And he healed many that were sick of divers diseases, and cast out many devils; and suffered not the devils to speak, because they knew him.

Verses 32-34. Mark pointedly notes the time "at even, when the sun did set." The appearance of three stars in the evening sky officially ended the Sabbath day. Now the aftermath of a day in Capernaum began to be felt. People now brought their burdens—notably diseased and demon-possessed loved ones—to a new authority. All the city gathered at the outer threshold to Simon's home, where Jesus healed many and cast out demons. As in verse 25, He forbade the demons to speak, because they recognized Him.

The people came because Jesus recognized neither place (synagogue, house, street) nor person. They came because He did more than expound and preach—He got things done. Finally, and sadly, people came not because of their love for Him but because they wanted what He could do for them. Although humanity universally has a claim to Him, far too many religionists today approach Jesus on these same terms.

4. Tour of Galilee (1:35-45)
(Matthew 4:23; Luke 4:42)
a. Departure from Capernaum (1:35-39)

(35) And in the morning, rising up a great while before day, he went out, and departed into a solitary place, and there prayed. (36) And Simon and they that were with him followed after him. (37) And when they had found him, they said unto him, All men seek for thee. (38) And he said unto them, Let us go into the next towns, that I may preach there also: for therefore came I forth. (39) And he preached in their synagogues throughout all Galilee, and cast out devils.

Verses 35-37. This passage provides insight into the personal dedication of Jesus. He must be with the Father, and early morning was the best time and prayer the best way to begin. He would soon embark on a preaching tour of the Galilean towns and must be fortified with power from on high. Crowds and urban centers conflicted with His purpose. Miracles attracted attention to Jesus, often winning the applause of admiring crowds, but here they were counterproductive to the purpose of God. Jesus shunned people's praise that He might be enriched with the power of God.

Simon and the other disciples followed with news that everyone sought Him. Luke 4:42 relates that the multitudes would have stayed Him, or hindered His departure. This entanglement Jesus avoided. The greater purpose of God was uppermost in Jesus' mind, and He must go into other towns and cities to spread the good news of the kingdom. The secret to power with God was communion and obedience to His will. God always empowers those who seek Him early. To meet people one should first meet God.

Verses 38-39. Prayer cannot substitute for action, however, and Jesus expressed His plans to move on to other towns because that is why He came. Verse 39 provides the method—preaching—and strategy—visiting the synagogues. Galilee boasted nearly two hundred villages and towns with several thousands of inhabitants, according to Josephus. To these Jesus was sent (Luke 4:43).

Mark summarized in one sentence what must have been a lengthy tour. As Jesus went, He preached and healed. At this point Jesus was a man of action as well as a man of prayer. To every word He suited an appropriate action; the two are inseparable. Merely stating a problem or exposing a need does not solve it. Exhortation and good preaching alone never suffice; people need action.

Jesus recognized the composite of spirit and body of man. The spirit and body make possible the mind, will, and emotion. If Jesus had been concerned only with the spirit, man's body would waste; if only the body, the spirit would languish. But Jesus aimed to redeem the whole of man, not just a fragment. Even though the body is weak and diseased or starving, there can be a comforting peace and communion of the spirit. On the other hand, distress is not relieved, pain is not diminished, and man's suffering is not abolished by spiritual communion alone. The great appeal of Christianity is that it couples education for the mind, healing and medicine for the body, and the good news of salvation for the soul.

The Old Testament high priest ministered with his head in the shekinah of the Holy Place, but beneath his feet was soil. Jesus never divorced heaven and earth but linked them together in strong bonds. Specializing in heaven and spiritual things often results in neglect of the earthly and practical. The visionary idealist is of little value to a starving man (James 2:15-16). During His ministry Jesus worked to restore relations of words and deeds, spirit and body, heaven and earth.

b. Cleansing of a leper (1:40-45)
(Matthew 8:1; Luke 5:12)

(40) And there came a leper to him, beseeching him, and kneeling down to him, and saying unto him, If thou wilt, thou canst make me clean. (41) And Jesus, moved with compassion, put forth his hand, and touched him, and saith unto him, I will; be thou clean. (42) And as soon as he had spoken, immediately the leprosy departed from him, and he was cleansed. (43) And he straitly charged him, and forthwith sent him away; (44) and saith unto him, See thou say nothing to any man: but go

51

thy way, shew thyself to the priest, and offer for thy cleansing those things which Moses commanded, for a testimony unto them. (45) But he went out, and began to publish it much, and to blaze abroad the matter, insomuch that Jesus could no more openly enter into the city, but was without in desert places: and they came to him from every quarter.

Although all the Synoptic Gospels record this miraculous healing, Mark provides the greatest detail. A "leper" in those days might have had symptoms of any one of several skin diseases. Leviticus 13-15 describes early diagnosis and symptoms of leprosy, how the priest detected it, expulsion procedures for the uncleanness, and cleansing rituals. In some cases leprosy appeared to be hereditary. When fully enveloping the body, this loathsome defilement was altogether revolting and needed both healing and cleansing. God pointed to leprosy as a type to represent the disease of sin.

Two types of leprosy are known: lepromatous and tuberculoid. The former type, more common in Bible times, began with brown spots on the face, ears or limbs, which later thickened to lumps or nodules that lysed the skin covering to become ulcerated sores. In time, deformity from contraction of tissues resulted. Tuberculoid leprosy results in numbness of affected skin and deformity of digits from paralysis and muscle atrophy. All lepers were pronounced as unclean; those in advanced stages were isolated outside the camp.

The disease then known in the Middle East is apparently not the modern-day form of leprosy. Quarantine is unnecessary today because the pathogen *Mycobacterium leprae* is not highly contagious or infectious.

With no medicinal cure, only by the mercy of God did one recover from this hopeless affliction. Under Jewish law, afflicted individuals were to warn others of their condition by loudly crying, "Unclean, unclean!" Jesus demonstrated His power over this disease and in so doing displayed His authority over the greater disease of sin of which leprosy is a type.

Verse 40. A leper approached Jesus, beseeching, kneeling, and declaring in faith that Jesus could make him clean. Luke 5:12 notes that the man was "full of leprosy"; the disease had progressed over his entire body. This man fell in worship, prostrating his body to Jesus as to God. He did not entreat Jesus to appeal to God on his behalf; he instead declared in faith: "If thou wilt, thou canst make me clean." Any reservation the man had did not pertain to Christ's power, but to the will of God. Would Jesus heal and cleanse him, or had God decreed this bodily ailment necessary to his soul's health?

Verse 41 reveals that the purpose of an ever-compassionate Jesus is superior to the purpose of the ceremonial law. The law forbade contact with a leper, but Jesus touched this man, thus defying defilement. His touch was a healing touch, His words both affirmed His willingness and pronounced the work done: "I will; be thou clean."

Verse 42. Divine power was instantaneous, and as soon as Jesus spoke the leprous symptoms began to disappear. It is noteworthy that for most diseases, effecting a cure is all that is necessary to the healing process. Not so with leprosy. As is the case with sin, not only must it be cured but the individual must be cleansed. Simple healing, like simple cessation of sinning, is not enough. Man must also be cleansed of the nature and state of sin inherited from Adam, by receiving power over it. We are not sinners because we commit sin; we commit sin because we are sinners. Likewise, the leper was not a leper because he was unclean; rather, he was unclean because he was a leper. Nothing short of the mercy and favor of God can work repentance of sin and impart a new nature in the individual.

Verse 43-44. Christ sternly charged the former leper and sent him away with instructions to show himself to the priest and to offer for ritual cleansing the things Moses called for in Leviticus 14. These instructions served at least three purposes. First, the man's silence focused attention away from the miracle and toward Christ's teaching. Second, the presiding priest would investigate the case, become aware of Jesus, and know that Jesus recognized his lawful position. Finally, the priest would know that the cleansing was not of the law, but of grace.

Verse 45. The healed leper, far from holding his peace, went everywhere excitedly declaring his cleansing. This resulted in crowds too dense for Christ to enter the city openly and minister effectively. He withdrew into a solitary place; however, the people discovered Him and continued to come from every quarter.

Mark's first division covers about twelve months of public ministry, beginning with John's baptism and terminating with the cleansing of the leper. There was little opposition from the prominent sects at this point; Jesus ministered openly with the only interference coming from anxious and demanding crowds.

5. Conflicts with the Scribes (2:1-3:6)
a. Paralytic forgiven and healed (2:1-12)
(Matthew 9:1-7; Luke 5:18-21)

(1) And again he entered into Capernaum after some days; and it was noised that he was in the house. (2) And straightway many were gathered together, insomuch that there was no room to receive them, no, not so much as about the door: and he preached the word unto them. (3) And they come unto him, bringing one sick of the palsy, which was borne of four. (4) And when they could not come nigh unto him for the press, they uncovered the roof where he was: and when they had broken it up, they let down the bed wherein the sick of the palsy lay. (5) When Jesus saw their faith, he said unto the sick of the palsy, Son, thy sins be forgiven thee. (6) But there were certain of the scribes sitting there, and reasoning in their hearts, (7) Why doth this man thus speak blasphemies? who can forgive sins but God only? (8) And immediately when Jesus perceived in his spirit that they so reasoned within themselves, he said unto them, Why reason ye these things in your hearts? (9) Whether is it easier to say to the sick of the palsy, Thy sins be forgiven thee; or to say, Arise, and take up thy bed, and walk? (10) But that ye may know that the Son of man hath power on earth to forgive sins, (he saith to the sick of the palsy,) (11) I say unto thee, Arise, and take up thy bed, and go thy way into thine house. (12) And immediately he arose, took up the bed, and went forth before them all; insomuch that they were all amazed, and glorified God, saying, We never saw it on this fashion.

Verse 1. Jesus returned to Capernaum. His reputation from His travels and from His previous visit preceded Him, so that news spread of His being in "the house," His usual place of residence, maybe Simon's house.

Verse 2. In biblical times Jews customarily opened the door upon arising in the morning. This open door invited any and all who wished to enter. Soon a crowd gathered until the house and courtyard were filled and the pathways leading to the door thronged. To these people Jesus preached, or spoke the Word. The object of His ministry was to reach lost humanity with the gospel message. Miraculous demonstrations were always subordinate and designed not only to help the needy but also to arrest people's attention so that they would hear the Word.

Verses 3-4. All the Synoptic Gospels record this incident in minute detail.

Palestinian houses were generally constructed with flat roofs made of wood beams spread about three feet apart. The distance between beams was spanned by wood or tile covered with soil or sod. The rooftop was used for repose in the evenings; an outside stairway permitted access.

Four men came bearing on a stretcher a man too infirm to walk. Blocked by the crowd, the four transported their burden to the rooftop. They created an opening by removing tiles between the beams, then lowered the man, undoubtedly by ropes or similar extensions on the four corners of the stretcher. This approach showed ingenuity but was not without risk to the victim of palsy (paralysis) or the house itself. It was this not-to-be-denied faith that Jesus witnessed and commented on.

Verse 5. Jesus observed their faith and then in an

unusual way effected the cure by saying, "Son" (the Greek word means "child"), "thy sins be forgiven thee." The association between suffering and sin was a natural one since most Jews felt that there was cause and effect; that is, sin actually caused suffering. Any who suffered did so because of sin in his life. Job 4:7 and John 9:2-3 deny that this is always the case, however.

Rabbis held that no sick man was healed until his sins were forgiven, for a sick man experienced the anger of God. It is true that many illnesses and diseases are directly due to sin—not necessarily sins of the victim but sometimes inherited or suffered due to others' sins. Ultimately all illnesses can be traced to man's sin in the Fall.

In this man's case consciousness of sin might have produced a psychosomatic reaction causing real paralysis. He was apparently physically bound as a result of sin, for when he was forgiven, the handicap lifted. This represents the first recorded occasion in which Jesus extended the gift of forgiveness.

Verses 6-7. Present in the assembly were scribes, interpreters of the law who understood the import of Christ's words about forgiveness of sin. Immediately they began to reason in their minds: Nobody but God can forgive sin, this man said He forgives sin; therefore, He put Himself up as God. Anyone who assumed the place or power of deity, however, was guilty of blaspheming God. Blasphemy was punishable by stoning under the law (Leviticus 24:16). Their error, of course, was that Jesus was indeed the Son of God—God manifested in flesh (John 1:14)— but in their darkness they could not comprehend this shining ray of light.

Verses 8-9. A contrary spirit in the presence of God

cannot be concealed, and Jesus perceived their negative thoughts. He also perceived the direction of their reasoning and issued a challenge. The scribes reasoned that no one can really know for sure whether or not a man's sins have been forgiven. Jesus avoided a theological debate by asking whether it is easier to say (and bring to pass) something visible or something invisible. Because in this case the paralysis was caused by sin, its remedy had to be the absolution of sin. When the grip of sin on the soul was broken, the grip of paralysis on the body would be loosened; therefore, if the words of Christ can bring about the latter, might not the former also be affirmed?

Verses 10-12. Concluding that even their skeptical reasoning would comprehend the logical association, Jesus said, "That ye may know that the Son of man hath power on earth to forgive sins," and turning to the victim of palsy, continued, "Arise, and take up thy bed." The man arose, took up his bed, and, witnessed by all, went forth. The people's response was amazement and praise of God.

The scribes' response was denial. Jesus dealt with a mounting wave of opposition among religious leaders over their often erroneous teachings. By their own stated beliefs, only forgiveness of sin would effect a cure. Since the man was obviously cured, according to their doctrine he must also be forgiven by God. Because the Word was spoken by Jesus, Jesus must be who He claimed to be. This they refused to accept. Their exposure and utterly foolish appearance in this exchange ignited an inner rage that could be appeased only by the death of this man.

William Barclay suggested three possible meanings of this incident of forgiveness:[2] (1) Jesus conveyed God's forgiveness to the man, as Nathan was messenger to

David (II Samuel 12:1-14). (2) Jesus acted as God's representative since John 5:22 states that judgment is committed to the Son. (3) Jesus displayed the true attitude of God toward man. The Jews perceived God as a stern, severe God of justice, law, and demand for sacrifice. Jesus extended compassion, mercy, and love to lost creation, eager to forgive and restore.

The more direct way to view the incident is that Jesus was God manifest in the flesh—the visible, incarnate manifestation of the Spirit (I Timothy 3:16). Because He was God, the appeal need go no further. If the Jewish opponents, correct in their reasoning that only God forgives sin, could not accept that a mere carpenter from Nazareth was the Messiah sent from God, how could they ever accept that He was God?

b. Call of Levi and his feast (2:13-17)
(Matthew 9:9; Luke 5:27)

(13) And he went forth again by the sea side; and all the multitude resorted unto him, and he taught them. (14) And as he passed by, he saw Levi the son of Alphaeus sitting at the receipt of custom, and said unto him, Follow me. And he arose and followed him. (15) And it came to pass, that, as Jesus sat at meat in his house, many publicans and sinners sat also together with Jesus and his disciples: for there were many, and they followed him. (16) And when the scribes and Pharisees saw him eat with publicans and sinners, they said unto his disciples, How is it that he eateth and drinketh with publicans and sinners? (17) When Jesus heard it, he saith unto them, They that are whole have no need of

the physician, but they that are sick: I came not to call the righteous, but sinners to repentance.

Verses 13-14. Jesus must have resided for some time in Capernaum teaching the people. He departed again (as before) traveling southward, when He saw Levi the son of Alphaeus at the place of toll. Alphaeus was also the father of James (Mark 3:18). Luke 5:27 uses the name of Levi, while the Gospel of Matthew exchanges the name for Matthew (9:9). We can assume that Matthew and Levi are two names for the same individual, although a direct statement is lacking.

Levi gathered taxes, probably for Herod Antipas and not Rome. Capernaum was the first town inside Herod's territory on the road coming from the provinces ruled by Philip; he could there conveniently receive import and export taxes on shipping. However, like collectors in the service of Rome, Levi was intensely disliked, even hated. The people never knew how much tax was fair or what would be levied, and they generally viewed all tax gatherers as extortionists who fleeced the public to line their own pockets. In spite of the public view of the man, Jesus wanted him as a disciple. To the man spurned by his fellows, hated by everyone, friendless, with no place to go, Jesus had great appeal. He arose and followed.

Of the disciples we know about, Levi made the most complete surrender of vocation. To boats, lake, and fish one might return, but to walk away from service to Herod was to forfeit forever the chance to take up where he left off. What Jesus expected Levi to do is not clear, unless he was indeed Matthew, one of the Twelve, who traveled with and shared the life of Jesus on earth.

The decision to follow was totally in Matthew's favor. First, he freed himself from Herod, taxes, and extortion and set his mind at rest because his hands were clean. In this life some people are poor, while others are merely "broke"—temporarily without resources. There is often little hope for the poor, but one who is merely broke will find another means of resource. Matthew was perhaps broke, without luxury or comfort because of his choice, but he was not poor. A man with his mind at peace with God is never poor.

Second, he had a job far superior to the one he left. He apparently possessed an orderly mind, systematic work habits, and a penchant for writing. Matthew gave the world a book on the teachings of the One he chose to follow that contains the greatest instruction anyone can receive. Third, the decision brought fame and worldwide acclaim as a disciple of the most famous person who ever lived, whereas refusing the call would have meant a second-rate existence and the continued hatred of his contemporaries.

Verses 15-17. It appears that Levi made a meal at his house (Luke 5:29) and invited old friends, fellow tax collectors and sinners, to join his new friends for food. All sat together at the table. The ever-present scribes and Pharisees, pious scholars and devout keepers of the Mosaic law, observed Jesus with this crowd and criticized His conduct. Separated ones kept themselves from sin and impurity. Speaking to the disciples, they questioned how it was that He ate and drank with sinners. Jesus heard their question and offered a condemnation of His own: The well do not need a physician, but the sick. "I came not to call the righteous, but sinners to repentance."

Jesus implied that a physician's calling and honor is to associate with the sick, whereby without fearing infection himself, he might help them. The physician who heals must converse with the sick; Jesus came to cure and heal for the glory of God and the good of the people. He was the physician of sinners, never their companion. The Pharisees on the other hand were companions to sinners and never truly their physician. It was they who desired to be deemed righteous and whole and thus voluntarily excluded themselves from the Great Physician's help.

Jesus pointedly referred to the two classes of people in Palestine: those who kept the law, including the oral traditions of the scribes, and the common people. The latter did not generally observe all the rules and regulations of the orthodox religious leaders. One rule forbade Pharisees from having anything to do with common folks, whether fellowship, conversation, travel, or even business. Intermarriage was out of the question, and a pious one must never provide or accept their hospitality. In accepting Levi's offer, Jesus threw the gauntlet of defiance in the face of the religious law keepers.

To the Pharisees the word used here for sinner, *hamartolos*, meant more than one who broke the moral law; it also referred to one who ignored ceremonial law and oral scribal law. Thus adultery and eating pork were both considered sinful; the man who stole and the man who failed to wash in correct fashion were both held to be sinners. Among Levi's guests, no doubt, were those of both types.

The Pharisees' attitude toward sinners was one of contempt and fear of defilement. Ignorant, unlearned people could never be pious. The more one knew of the law, the holier one became in their view. They shunned the common people. Jesus came to common people, sat with them, and loved them.

c. Question about fasting (2:18-22)
(Matthew 9:14; Luke 5:33)

(18) And the disciples of John and of the Pharisees used to fast: and they come and say unto him, Why do the disciples of John and of the Pharisees fast, but thy disciples fast not? (19) And Jesus said unto them, Can the children of the bridechamber fast, while the bridegroom is with them? as long as they have the bridegroom with them, they cannot fast. (20) But the days will come, when the bridegroom shall be taken away from them, and then shall they fast in those days. (21) No man also seweth a piece of new cloth on an old garment: else the new piece that filled it up taketh away from the old, and the rent is made worse. (22) And no man putteth new wine into old bottles: else the new wine doth burst the bottles, and the wine is spilled, and the bottles will be marred: but new wine must be put into new bottles.

Verses 18-20. Close on the heels of the question of eating with sinners was the question on fasting. Pious Jews fasted regularly, although only the Day of Atonement was a compulsory fast during which Israel confessed and received forgiveness for national sin. Fasting was practiced on Mondays and Thursdays by the stricter sects and generally extended from sunrise to sunset or from 6:00 A.M. to 6:00 P.M. Jesus was not opposed to fasts; He endured a lengthy fast in the wilderness after His baptism.

Fasting holds benefits and advantages unobtainable in any other manner. Self-denial of pleasure and comfort disciplines the flesh and lets a person know that he is master of such comforts and that they can be surrendered. The period of self-denial is followed by keen thankfulness and appreciation for God's gifts.

The Pharisees, however, had degraded the fast to a self-display, whitening their faces and wearing garments in disarray to call attention to themselves, their acts of devotion, and their own goodness. Their fast was a ritual designed to claim God's attention; in reality, devoid of any expression of contrition or feeling from the heart, their fast was no more than convention.

Jesus' disciples were to fast in a different manner and spirit, without visible signs of their fast. Jesus referred to the Jewish wedding feast as an explanation of why they did not fast at this time. The week following the wedding was often the happiest time of a man's life; in true open-house fashion, he invited friends, or children of the bridechamber, to share a time of feasting and fellowship. According to rabbinic ruling, those attending the bridegroom could be exempt from any religious observances that would curtail their merriment and joy. Jesus compared His disciples to the select guest children of the bridechamber; they were temporarily exempt from fasting.

This incident contains a precedent for the Christian attitude of joy. To be with Christ and to enjoy His fellowship is to have joy. In addition, this is the first occasion when Jesus alluded to His being taken away from them. No doubt the meaning of this remark passed by the disciples, but Jesus saw Calvary ahead. He lived in the shadow of the cross daily, marching closer, and nowhere at no time did He draw back or hesitate. He knew the end, the chosen route, and only courage of the most splendid sort would take Him unflinchingly to the waiting cross.

Verse 21. Jesus adeptly constructed and used illustrations from everyday life. His homely illustrations and parables always pointed to God and His relationship with man. To Him, everything on earth revealed or spoke of heaven, a place with which only He was intimately acquainted. Now He introduced one of two parables showing that the divine work He came to do could not be blended into the old Jewish religious structure and practice.

Jesus said no one would sew new cloth onto an old garment to patch a rip or tear. The piece of new cloth referred to here is "undressed," unshrunk, or in modern terminology, not sanforized. Washing the old garment would cause the new cloth patch to shrink and pull away, resulting in greater damage than before. Patching up the old Jewish religion would not be effective; there must be a new creation. The old covenant with Abraham marked by circumcision was about to be replaced, not repaired, with a new covenant marked by the shedding of Jesus' own blood.

Verse 22. Christ's next parable related to the practice of storing wine in wineskins, bottles made from animal skins, primarily of kids and lambs. A new skin retains a certain elasticity until it ages into hard, stiff leather. New wine continues to ferment as resident yeasts anaerobically reduce the sugars. One product of fermentation is carbon dioxide gas, which exerts mounting pressure on the container. New wine put into old, inflexible, and unyielding wineskins will rupture the container due to the pressure of the gas, resulting in loss of both bottle and wine. For this reason, no rational person would attempt to store new wine in an old wineskin. New wine must be put into new wineskins, which retain sufficient elasticity to resist the pressure of the fermenting fluid.

Jesus by these illustrations called for a renewed flexibility in religious dogma, an acceptance of a new vessel to contain new wine. The new wine of the Holy Spirit could not be put into the old vessels of Jewish religiosity. There had to be a renewing of the mind and a fresh comprehension of God and how He would save lost humanity through grace. It was time to repent and begin anew. In John 3:5-8 Jesus revealed that a person must be born again, of water and of the Spirit. In II Corinthians 5:17 Paul stated that old things are passed away, all things are made new.

d. Controversies about Sabbath observance (2:23-3:6)

(1) Plucking of grain on the Sabbath (2:23-28)
(Matthew 12:1; Luke 6:1)

(23) And it came to pass, that he went through the corn fields on the sabbath day; and his disciples began, as they went, to pluck the ears of corn. (24) And the Pharisees said unto him, Behold, why do they on the sabbath day that which is not lawful? (25) And he said unto them, Have ye never read what David did, when he had need, and was an hungred, he, and they that were

66

*with him? (26) How he went into the house of God in
the days of Abiathar the high priest, and did eat the
shewbread, which is not lawful to eat but for the priests,
and gave also to them which were with him? (27) And
he said unto them, The sabbath was made for man, and
not man for the sabbath: (28) therefore the Son of man is
Lord also of the sabbath.*

Verses 23-24. Concerning the Sabbath, scribal rules
and regulations had proliferated to be unbearable, and
Jesus' disciples drew the Pharisees' attention by plucking
heads of grain. (American corn, or maize, was unknown
in Bible lands before the discovery of the New World.)
Their crime was not the action itself but that they did it on
the Sabbath. Grain was freely accessible (Deuteronomy
23:25); however, no work was permitted on the Sabbath,
and the scribes had defined and categorized work under
thirty-nine different headings. Among these were reaping,
winnowing, threshing, and preparing a meal. The disciples had plucked the grain, rubbed it between their palms,
separated the husk from the kernel, and eaten the kernel
(Luke 6:1), which according to the Pharisees' petty rules,
constituted reaping, winnowing, threshing, and preparing
a meal. They deemed this to be unlawful work, and they
expected Jesus to deal with these lawbreakers at once.

Verses 25-26. In response, Jesus referred to an incident in I Samuel 21:1-6 when the fugitive David visited the
Tabernacle in Nob seeking food. David made his request
to Ahimelech, the high priest at the time; Jesus referred to
his more famous son, Abiathar, who was also there at the
time and became high priest under David.

There was no food at the Tabernacle except showbread.

The twelve loaves of bread rested on a table of acacia (shittim) wood overlaid with gold (Exodus 25:23-30) that stood before the Holy of Holies in the Tabernacle. Each Sabbath the priests replaced the old loaves and ate them within the Holy Place (Leviticus 24:9). David and his men in their hunger appropriated five loaves of showbread and ate it contrary to the provisions of the law. Showbread was literally the bread "of Thy face" or "of the divine presence" or "of the being who is our Bread of Life." David, with rare insight into the nature and mercy of God, judged that the ceremonial law forbidding people other than priests to eat this bread would be subordinate to the natural law of human need. Jesus here cited the incident relating to what His disciples did, vindicating David's action.

Verses 27-28. Jesus stated that the Sabbath was instituted for the benefit of humans, to refresh and renew the physical body after six days of labor. In this interval, people could think on eternal values and less on temporal, day-to-day actions. Meditation and remembrance of God's mercy and benevolence would lead one to repentance, thanksgiving, and expressions of gratitude on the Sabbath, thus restoring body and spirit.

The Sabbath then was established to serve man, not man to serve the Sabbath. To God, man is more important than the day that was set aside to make his life more meaningful. Further, if the Sabbath was to serve man, there was one sovereign over even the Sabbath: Jesus Himself. In this exchange, Jesus justified the disciples in their "labor" on the Sabbath.

Jesus revealed several powerful and essential truths that help us understand God and His gospel. First, true religion is more than rules. Church attendance, saying prayers, or abstaining from work on a certain day does not make one a Christian. While to a Christian all of these may be important, he must never forget that love, mercy, and forgiveness are more important. Too often the heart of religion is lost in observance of rules and regulations. In Matthew 23:23, Jesus rebuked the Pharisees for neglecting the "weightier matters of the law, judgment, mercy, and faith" while emphasizing the tithe (ten percent) on even minute amounts of spices.

Second, the passage suggests that the claim of human need comes first. When a person is cold, diseased, and hungry it is merciful and kind to meet those demands before appealing to the spiritual need. Missionary work appears most successful when physical and mental needs are met along with the preaching of the gospel. Christianity is to lift the whole man to a higher plane, not just a part. True love for God is expressed in service to those God loves. (See John 21:15-17.)

Third, sacred things should be expended to help people. Bread is to feed the hungry; the Sabbath is sacred indeed when used to meet needs. Our lives will never be more sacred than when we expend ourselves to help others in the name of Jesus (Matthew 25:31-46).

Finally, the law of love is greater in all ways than love of the law.

In summary, chapter two shows Jesus' authority to forgive sin and in so doing establishes that He is God in flesh. In the case of the paralyzed man, when sins were forgiven healing occurred. Levi, undesirable to society, was offered discipleship. Jesus was questioned about eating with sinners and not fasting; His response showed that He was aware of the impending cross. He gave two parables on renewal and showed Himself Lord of the Sabbath.

(2) Man with the withered hand (3:1-6)
(Matthew 12:9-10; Luke 6:6)

In chapter two Jesus demonstrated power over demons, sickness, and leprosy. He was greater than the law, Lord of the Sabbath, and the forgiver of sin. In chapter three, Mark continued to show Jesus' power to heal and silence spirits. His revealed ideas clashed with those of the religious leaders.

(1) And he entered again into the synagogue; and there was a man there which had a withered hand. (2) And they watched him, whether he would heal him on the sabbath day; that they might accuse him. (3) And he saith unto the man which had the withered hand, Stand forth. (4) And he saith unto them, Is it lawful to do good on the sabbath days, or to do evil? to save life, or to kill? But they held their peace. (5) And when he had looked round about on them with anger, being grieved for the hardness of their hearts, he saith unto the man, Stretch forth thine hand. And he stretched it out: and his hand was restored whole as the other. (6) And the Pharisees went forth, and straightway took counsel with the Herodians against him, how they might destroy him.

Verses 1-2. In spite of the cold reception and the obvious animosity among the orthodox leaders, Jesus bravely returned to the synagogue on the Sabbath. On this day, a man whose hand had withered or dried up came to the synagogue. Also on this day in this synagogue a delegation from the Sanhedrin (Jewish religious council) occupied the front seats of honor, having come to protect orthodoxy and deal with false teachers. Specifically, they came to see that Jesus conducted Himself according to their rules. Apparently He deliberately chose to do many works on the Sabbath in order to reveal the errors of the scribes and Pharisees about observing the Sabbath.

They classified every act not absolutely necessary as work, and therefore, if it were done on the Sabbath, it carried the death penalty (Exodus 31:14-16). In particular, they said medical needs could be administered on the Sabbath only if life were in immediate danger. Childbirth, respiratory or pharyngeal illnesses, and accident victims, if alive, could be helped without violating the Sabbath. Military opponents frequently took advantage of this strict observance of the law.

The man with a withered hand needed no immediate medical attention; his life was not in danger. It appears that the religious leaders planted a test case before Jesus that they might accuse Him.

Verse 3. Jesus asked the man to "rise up" that he might be visible and receive the people's compassion at his handicapped condition. Jesus must have wanted no one to miss the callousness of the religious leaders.

Verses 4-5. Luke 6:7 reveals that the scribes and Pharisees watched Him to see if He would heal on the Sabbath. Jesus, knowing their thoughts, asked a question: "Is it lawful to do good on the sabbath days, or to do evil? to save life, or to destroy it?" His implication was that having power to do good but refraining from doing it is wrong. Acts of mercy done on the Sabbath were in agreement

71

with the greater law of love and should be done.

This first question created a dilemma—if it is lawful to do good on the Sabbath, then it is not lawful to do evil, and it is evil to leave one in the condition of this poor man. The second question, "Is it lawful to save life, or to kill it?" caused the crowd to see the sharp contrast between the religious leaders and Jesus. They were bent on taking His life while He was genuinely concerned with the state of this wretched man. They held their peace and spoke no rejoiner.

Their hardness of heart grieved the Master, who looked around at them with anger, indignant at their unbelief, their blindness, their unfeeling consciences. His anger was not for Himself or His defense, as it is with ordinary people.

Verse 6. This marks the first attempt to devise a plan to destroy Jesus. If politics makes strange bedfellows, so does hatred of a common foe. Pharisees kept themselves from Gentiles and considered those who had no regard for the law as being unclean. The Herodians were partisans of Herod, the Jewish prince serving under the Roman procurator or viceroy. The Herodians were unclean because of their intimate dealing, dining, and even living with Romans. In spite of this, the Pharisees counseled with them as their intense hatred for Jesus caused them to sacrifice their own ideals to deal with the present crisis. Accept Jesus they could not, yet no legitimate charge could be levied against Him. It was difficult to see on what common point the pious Pharisees and the worldly, secular Herodians might have agreed to stand together against Jesus.

Jesus and the Pharisees clashed regarding fundamental religious philosophy and values. To the Pharisees, religion was a matter of ritualistic observances. One had to follow the rules, obeying the law and its ramifications to be considered religious. Since Jesus did not go by their rules, He could not be religious; therefore, He was a bad person. But how could a bad rule breaker work miracles and persuade people?

The pharisaic view is today represented by much of Christianity: they attend church, read the Bible, return thanks at mealtime, perform external acts and duties, but acknowledge no supremacy of God in their lives. The religious Jews were without compassion, sacrifice, or concern for the lost or those less fortunate than they. On the other hand, to Jesus religion translated into service, not servitude to works. Fallen man needed to hear about the love of God reaching to him. Relationship was preferred to ritual; anyone in need was sure to attract the Lord's attention.

6. Ministry to the Multitudes (3:7-12)
(Matthew 12:15; Luke 6:17)

(7) But Jesus withdrew himself with his disciples to the sea: and a great multitude from Galilee followed him, and from Judaea, (8) and from Jersusalem, and from Idumaea, and from beyond Jordan; and they about Tyre and Sidon, a great multitude, when they had heard what great things he did, came unto him. (9) And he spake to his disciples, that a small ship should wait on him because of the multitude, lest they should throng him. (10) For he had healed many; insomuch that they pressed upon him for to touch him, as many as had

73

plagues. (11) And unclean spirits, when they saw him, fell down before him, and cried, saying, Thou art the Son of God. (12) And he straitly charged them that they should not make him known.

Verses 7-8. The statement "withdrew . . . to the sea" suggests that the foregoing interchange (verses 1-6) was in an interior city. Herod Antipas occupied Sepphoris as his chief city and capital, and there both Herodians and Pharisees would be numerous. This city was one of the five places where the Sanhedrin convened. Undoubtedly, with these two groups plotting against Him, Jesus felt it expedient to withdraw to more neutral ground where He could minister unencumbered. As He withdrew, people from Galilee, Judea, Jerusalem, Idumaea, and even from the foreign cities of Phoenicia, Tyre and Sidon, followed Him.

Verses 9-10. The diseased, infirm, sick, and those with plagues (literally "scourges" or painful disorders) pressed or fell upon Him, clinging to Him. He was so successful in healing "many" that they no longer waited to be touched but sought to touch Him.

The press and insistent demands of the heterogeneous multitude caused Jesus to prepare a safety escape route should it be necessary. A small boat ("ship") was made ready and kept close by.

Verse 11. People with unclean spirits apparently fell down before Him and not on Him as did the afflicted. This response was mediated by fear and acknowledgment of His supremacy and power over them, even though they were of different kingdoms. Their cry was one of recognition when they saw Him: "Thou art the Son of God."

Jesus had been proclaimed Son of God at His baptism by a heavenly voice, which those of the fallen spirit world might have heard. Surely the unclean spirits observed miracles, the previous casting out of one of their fellows, and the people's response to Jesus. The Old Testament uses "son of God" to designate angels (Job 1:6), while "son" designates the nation of Israel (Exodus 4:22), the king of Israel (II Samuel 7:14), and in intertestamental times, a good man. In the New Testament the term "son" is one of close intimacy and fellowship. Timothy was called Paul's son (I Timothy 1:2, 18) and Mark was called Peter's son (I Peter 5:13) because they could interpret the great apostles' minds. No other word could be used to describe Jesus' relationship with God!

Verse 12. Jesus charged the unclean spirits to remain silent about His identity. It would not do at this time for the people to know He was the Messiah, for He was not what they longed for and expected. The people's idea of the Messiah was a king with mighty armies who would lead the Jews in a victorious uprising against Rome, giving them world supremacy. If the people knew that the Messiah had come, they might irrationally defy and revolt against their captors, only to be crushed. Jesus needed time to instruct the people about the Messiah and His work, love, service, and peacefulness, and to replace the popular ideal with the true Messiah.

7. Appointment of the Twelve (3:13-19a)
(Matthew 10:1; Luke 6:13; 9:1; cf. Acts 1:26)

(13) And he goeth up into a mountain, and calleth unto him whom he would: and they came unto him. (14)

And he ordained twelve, that they should be with him, and that he might send them forth to preach, (15) and to have power to heal sicknesses, and to cast out devils: (16) and Simon he surnamed Peter; (17) and James the son of Zebedee, and John the brother of James; and he surnamed them Boanerges, which is, The sons of thunder: (18) and Andrew, and Philip, and Bartholomew, and Matthew, and Thomas, and James the son of Alphaeus, and Thaddaeus, and Simon the Canaanite, (19a) and Judas Iscariot, which also betrayed him.

Verses 13-15. After a night in prayer (Luke 6:12), at daybreak Jesus, exercising His own will, called unto Himself "whom he would." They "came unto him," implying that they forsook further vocation of their own and now devoted themselves to Him. Of those who came, He "ordained" or appointed twelve. Formal or ceremonial consecration to the office of apostles and empowerment was to transpire later (cf. John 20:22; Mark 6:7); for now Jesus asked only that each one dedicate himself and become His apostle. With this call they would henceforth "be with him" as disciples and attendants to preach, cast out demons, and heal sicknesses. Through these select men Jesus multiplied His own ministry.

"The Twelve" denotes the apostles; there were many other disciples (Luke 6:13; Mark 6:30). Twelve, selected as representative of true Israel, symbolized universality or perfection. One was a traitor and was later replaced.

By these actions Jesus fulfilled very practical needs. First, if His impact and message was to endure, it would have to be transmitted to faithful, trained men who would carry on in His physical absence. Second, with none of the modern conventions of printing or audiovisual recording, masses could be reached only by men on whose hearts He had imprinted His message. They would be like sowers, spreading the precious seed of the gospel everywhere they went, dedicated to the dissemination of the message of Christ.

Verse 16. This passage names the men Jesus selected. Beginning with Simon, Mark dutifully provided the names of those in fraternity with the Lord. Mark's arrangement of the names seems to imply a listing, probably relative to prominence of personality. Other lists in Matthew 10, Luke 6, and Acts vary the positions.

The disciples were a mixed group. Simon, surnamed Peter, although named here, had been called previously. Mark's scanty reference to Peter lent credence to the theory held by early church writers that Mark wrote this Gospel for the fisherman. "Simon" is from a Hebrew word meaning "to hear."

Verse 17. With Peter stood James and John. They were sons of Zebedee and are here surnamed "Boanerges," the Aramaic pronunciation of the Hebrew "sons of thunder." The description referred to their natural disposition: zeal and sudden, decisive character. (These two desired to call down fire on a Samaritan village and coveted seats of honor next to Jesus.) These men transformed by the grace and power of God were indeed thunderous in their apostleship. No doubt James's vehement preaching led to his early martyrdom at the hands of Herod (Acts 12:1-2). John began his Gospel with literary explosiveness equal to a thunderbolt—"In the beginning was the Word, and the Word was with God, and the Word was God" (John 1:1). Peter, James, and John were the "inner circle" apostles of Jesus.

Verse 18. Then follow the names of Andrew (Peter's brother and the first disciple, whose name means "manly"), Philip, and Bartholomew. Bar-Tolmai, the son of Tolmay, appears to be a patronymic name, "bar" meaning "son of." It has been supposed that Bartholomew's real name was Nathanael of Cana in Galilee. His close association with Philip in all the Synoptic Gospels and the fact that Philip introduced him to the Lord (John 1:46-51) points to the conclusion that Bartholomew's name was Nathanael, meaning "gift of God."

Next named was Matthew, who in his own writings assigns himself the label "publican," or tax collector, and a position in the list after Thomas (Matthew 10:3). Mattathias means "gift of Jehovah," translated as "Theodore" in Greek. Thomas had a surname meaning "twin" (John 11:16).

There follows the name of James son of Alphaeus (possibly the same as Cleopas). He was called "the less," probably in distinction to the other James, "the great," son of Zebedee. The Bible also identifies one of the Lord's brothers as James. This man became leader of the church in Jerusalem and wrote the New Testament epistle bearing his name. Some suppose he is the same as James the Less, but this is unlikely. It is possible that James the Less was a cousin (brother in an expanded sense) of Jesus. (See Mark 15:40; John 19:25.)

The next apostle was referred to under three names: Thaddaeus, Lebbaeus, and Judas. The last was most likely his proper name, the others distinguishing him from the traitor bearing the same name. This Judas was the brother of James the Less (cf. Luke 6:16; Acts 1:13).

Then comes Simon the Canaanite, more appropriately rendered the Cananean, since he was likely born in Cana of Galilee. Luke calls him Simon the Zealot, or Zelotes, a member of the fiercely nationalistic party who, armed with hidden daggers, practiced underground revolutionary tactics against Rome.

Verse 19a. Mark names Judas Iscariot last with the note: "which also betrayed him." The name Iscariot was no doubt derived from the Hebrew words *ish kerioth*, meaning "a man of Kerioth." Jesus chose him to be a disciple, knowing that he would not be true. Several reasons lay behind this unlikely choice. First, his being chosen in spite of his future black intent demonstrates the superiority of love and grace and God's response to a person's present faith. Second, the betrayal was prophesied to be by a friend, one who dined with Him. Third, it introduces the caution that even elect people might fall from a position of grace.

We can make a number of interesting observations about Christ's selection of the Twelve.

1. There were no priests or theologians in the Twelve.

2. None were wealthy, of special social position, or educated beyond elementary level.

3. All were mature, adult men; at least some were married.

4. Extremes of philosophy, views, and values are evident in the contrast between a traitorous tax collector and an intensely patriotic Zealot.

5. Three pairs of brothers—Andrew and Peter, James

and John, and James the Less and Judas—demonstrated the power of brotherly love and also the power of family values in those of similar upbringing. (For instance, the same qualities that made Peter stick with Jesus were also inculcated from childhood in his brother Andrew.)

6. Two were possibly kinsmen of Jesus.

These men appear to be twelve ordinary individuals who had been deeply moved and attracted to Jesus. They were at times slow of comprehension but never fools. It required great courage to become a follower of a man who had no official recognition, who disregarded man-imposed rules and regulations, who cleverly sidestepped the orthodox leaders, and who was already openly accused of sin, blasphemy, and heresy.

The disciples chose to identify with a man who demonstrated no regard for the cardinal laws of human survival.[3] First, to Jesus His own personal safety was less important than His stand for right. When others read the words of opposition and played it safe, Jesus boldly defended moral quality regarding only what was right, not who was right. Second, people desire to be secure in their role and jobs and to live materially and financially risk-free. Not so Jesus. His security was to do the will of the Father regardless of the risk. Finally, Jesus was insensitive to the "verdict of society." His character was unimpeachable before God, and what His peers thought and said about Him was second to God's view. Too often "What will people say?" governs human actions more than "What will God say?" Jesus came to introduce a kingdom where security is freedom from materialism, where safety is moral righteousness, where pleasing God supersedes pleasing society, and where to die is to live.

8. Mounting Opposition to Jesus (3:19b-35)
a. Anxiety of His friends (3:19b-21)
(John 10:20)

(19b) And they went into an house. (20) And the multitude cometh together again, so that they could not so much as eat bread. (21) And when his friends heard of it, they went out to lay hold on him: for they said, He is beside himself.

Verses 19b-21. The latter phrase of verse 19 more correctly prefaces verse 20; once in the house, a multitude quickly gathered. The pressure of the insatiable crowd precluded even taking normal meals. Mark gives no account of the Sermon on the Mount, which followed the calling of the disciples, or of additional miracles wrought by the Lord, as does Matthew.

Mark's purpose seems to be to reveal the total lack of familial support. A contrast was seen in the multitude desiring to be near, to hear, and to experience this man, and His own family, who concluded that He was mad (Greek *existemi*), insane, or "beside Himself" (verse 21; John 10:20). John 7:5 indicates that His brethren did not believe on Him. His mother and brothers, out of personal concern but lacking understanding, nonetheless attempted to rescue Jesus and restrain His activities (Mark 3:31-32).

b. Charge of collusion with Beelzebub (3:22-30)
(Matthew 9:34; 12:24; Luke 11:15)

(22) And the scribes which came down from

81

Jerusalem said, He hath Beelzebub, and by the prince of the devils casteth he out devils. (23) And he called them unto him, and said unto them in parables, How can Satan cast out Satan? (24) And if a kingdom be divided against itself, that kingdom cannot stand. (25) And if a house be divided against itself, that house cannot stand. (26) And if Satan rise up against himself, and be divided, he cannot stand, but hath an end. (27) No man can enter into a strong man's house, and spoil his goods, except he will first bind the strong man; and then he will spoil his house. (28) Verily I say unto you, All sins shall be forgiven unto the sons of men, and blasphemies wherewith soever they shall blaspheme: (29) but he that shall blaspheme against the Holy Ghost hath never forgiveness, but is in danger of eternal damnation: (30) because they said, He hath an unclean spirit.

Verse 22. Scribes sent by the Sanhedrin to keep an eye on Jesus here rendered their expert opinion. Never was His ability to exorcise demons questioned; the evidence was too great and the practice not uncommon to religious leaders. Rather, their question was how was it done—by what authority or power did He cast out demons? It apparently never penetrated their prejudiced and malice-filled minds that what they witnessed was indeed the power of God. The prominence of complete cures and testimonials could not be hidden, denied, or overlooked. They concluded that Jesus was Himself possessed by Beelzebub,[4] who gave supernatural powers. By the chief of demons Jesus could cast out demons of lesser power.

Verses 23-27. Jesus appealed to common sense by asking how Satan could cast out Satan. Any kingdom rifted by internal schism could not long stand. Jesus' parable here seems to follow the simple logic of the syllogism and proceeds deductively from a general condition to a specific one. Verse 27 is unique in that Jesus made a pointed reference to Himself and His own work on earth. He again used deductive reasoning:

Major Premise: To spoil a strong man's goods, one must first bind the strong man.

Minor Premise: By casting out Satan I have bound the strong man.

Conclusion: Now I will spoil his house.

Jesus came to seek and save the lost. Through their sin in the Garden of Eden humans fell under the dominion of Satan. Against this strong man ordinary humans were and are quite helpless. Being subject to him, they are captives. In order for Jesus to accomplish the feats He quoted in Luke 4:18-19 (cf. Isaiah 61:1-2), the strong man had to be bound. When Jesus cast out demons it vividly demonstrated that Satan had met a greater power and was forced to free his captives.

This passage does not show that Satan is bound and no longer has power over sinful people; rather, it shows that his defenses have been breached and his house plundered because One more powerful than he has begun the conquest. All Christians filled with the Spirit of God and acting in the authority of the name of Jesus have greater power than Satan. Indeed, "greater is he that is in you, than he that is in the world" (I John 4:4).

Clearly Jesus regarded the conquest of demon spirits, insanity, diseases, sickness, infirmities, and all maladies of humanity as part of the total campaign to utterly defeat Satan on earth. Salvation of the body and its ultimate redemption is part of the good news that Jesus came to reveal.

Verses 28-30. Jesus next turned to the more serious offense that the religious leaders had committed: they were close to blasphemy against the Holy Ghost. Mark adds verse 30 as an explanation to bridge the space between verse 27 and 28. Jesus provided hope in the forgiveness of sins: all sins can be forgiven, even blasphemies against other people. However, the one sin more grievous, more horrid than all others is the sin of blasphemy against the Holy Ghost. Jesus issued a warning because of a verbal accusation against the divine power of God in Christ, for the religious leaders attributed the incarnate love and power of God to Satan.

How opposite is the function of the Holy Spirit to their accusation! First, the Holy Ghost reveals God's truth to humanity; this they refused to believe. Second, the Spirit endows a believer to recognize truth when confronted with it; this they denied. When someone denies the works done by the Spirit of God for human benefit, he rejects grace and truth. By this rejection, he spurns and turns aside the Spirit. When this becomes a permanent attitude, he cuts himself off from the possibility of accepting forgiveness. When religious leaders in their prejudice and malice hinder the work and influence of God by claiming it is Satan's doing, they put themselves in peril of entering this state. To be "in danger of eternal damnation" may be read as "is guilty of an eternal sin," from which there is no turning and the sin remains. (See John 9:41.)

Whenever a person refuses to accept revealed truth or

denies the Spirit of God access to his life, he soon loses all semblance of spirituality. Unused muscles atrophy and he soon cannot walk; denial of truth soon results in the inability to discern truth from error (II Thessalonians 2:10-12). The goodness of God and the evil of Satan are to a blasphemer indistinguishable.

Barclay quoted Rawlinson, who called blasphemy the "essential wickedness," the epitome of all evil.[5] Henry Swete said, "To identify the source of good with the impersonation of evil implies a moral wreck for which the Incarnation itself provides no remedy."[6]

Of the sin of blasphemy, religious leaders are more in danger than sinners.

c. Identity of His true kindred (3:31-35)
(Matthew 12:46; Luke 8:19)

(31) There came then his brethren and his mother, and, standing without, sent unto him, calling him. (32) And the multitude sat about him, and they said unto him, Behold, thy mother and thy brethren without seek for thee. (33) And he answered them, saying, Who is my mother, or my brethren? (34) And he looked round about on them which sat about him, and said, Behold my mother and my brethren! (35) For whosoever shall do the will of God, the same is my brother, and my sister, and mother.

Verses 31-32. Flesh-and-blood relatives of Jesus (His brothers and mother) came to the house but were unable to reach Him (Luke 8:19). They sent Him a message through the crowd, which He in turn used to teach a

85

kingdom relation.

Verses 33-35. Who is the mother or brother of the Lord? Those who have a common spiritual purpose (verse 35). People often have more in common with those of similar tastes, values, vocations, or locale than with blood relatives, and this is certainly true of those who have common spiritual values.

For the Christian, kinship with Jesus lies first in the new-birth experience, which grants sonship to the believer (Romans 8:8-9, 14-17). We are now the sons of God by the bond of His Spirit. Second, kinship with Jesus means that His interest and our interest are the same. Jesus went to the lost, wept over His city, fasted, prayed, preached, and taught. If His interest so motivated Him, Christians too must be motivated by that interest. Third, kinship means obedience. Just as Jesus was totally obedient to God, the Christian desiring kinship with Jesus must be equally obedient. Finally, kinship means a willingness to sacrifice, suffer persecution, endure pain, and even die that God might be glorified.

9. Parabolic Teaching to the Crowd (4:1-34)

Jesus began using parables as a means of instruction. Up to this point He tried by direct approach to teach principles of the kingdom (Matthew 5-6; Luke 6:20-49) and met unbelief, skepticism, and lack of comprehension. The parable (Greek *parabole*, likeness) provided a means of setting one thing beside another for comparison.

The Hebrew word for parable *(mashal)* may also be translated as proverb or byword, but the two differ in intent and content. The parable presents truth in simili-

tude and is figurative, a method of illustration, an earthly
story with a heavenly application. Bernard Ramm used
Dodd's definition: "At its simplest . . . [a parable] is a
metaphor or simile drawn from nature or common life
arresting the hearer by its vividness or strangeness and
leaving the mind in sufficient doubt about its precise
application to rouse it into active thought."[7]

A parable is not a fable, neither trivial nor fantastic,
nor a myth from popular folklore. The parable is not an
allegory that seeks to draw meaning in all its points. It differs from figures of speech such as metaphor and simile,
although elements of these various forms of communication may be present in the parable. A parable may be an
expanded proverb, but a proverb is a commonly accepted
bit of experiential wisdom condensed into a single pithy
statement.

The word *parable* has several meanings but its Greek
root is *para*, meaning "beside of." Theologically it is a
story from the natural world that has a counterpart in the
spiritual world. A parable typically has four components.
First, there is an everyday earthly thing, event, or wisdom.
Nature, farming, animals, kings, princes, dining, fishing,
cultural mores, and the like form pictorial and concrete
instruments for grasping abstract ideas. Second, a parable
has theological truth, a spiritual intent. Third, the relationship between the spiritual lesson and the earthly component is analogical, giving illustrated argument by its
analogy.

Finally, every parable must have the component of
interpretation. Its two levels of meaning, its elements and
actions, call for proper identification. To attempt to find a
lesson or message for every detail of a parable would

make it into an allegory, which seeks deeper spiritual interpretation of every part. Parables call for interpretation that should be limited to the major points.

To summarize, Jesus began to teach in parables which, unlike allegories, do not carry a meaning or message in every detail. Using analogies with living organisms and their care, Christ described the character of human relationships: man to God, man to man, husband to wife, father to children. Although parabolic teaching techniques have been popular since Old Testament times because of ease of application and effectiveness (II Samuel 12:1-7a), Jesus' mastery of the parable and its penetrating depth remains unequaled.

a. Setting for the teaching (4:1-2)

(1) And he began again to teach by the sea side: and there was gathered unto him a great multitude, so that he entered into a ship, and sat in the sea; and the whole multitude was by the sea on the land. (2) And he taught them many things by parables, and said unto them in his doctrine,

Verses 1-2. Chapter and verse divisions are subjective and at times disrupt the intent of the evangelist. Chapter four continues the preceding instruction on relationship with Jesus; only Mark mentions that Jesus moved to the seaside. Jesus increasingly made use of the outdoors for public sermons, for the multitude had long since outgrown houses and courtyards. Once again a ship became His pulpit as He gained breathing room by sitting in the boat afloat on the sea (Mark 3:9). From here the Master instructed the multitude on the shore.

Jesus was flexible in His methods of teaching, and as He moved outdoors He began using less direct methods of instruction. The formality of a designated room, a stalwart pulpit, and a cushioned pew appeals to most churches and preachers, but if the gospel is to reach people we must be ready to adopt less conventional approaches. The challenge confronting the church today is to reach a technological and highly urban world population of apartment dwellers.

b. Content of the teaching (4:3-32)
(1) Parable of the sower (4:3-20)
(Matthew 13:3, 18; Luke 8:4, 11)

(3) Hearken; Behold, there went out a sower to sow: (4) and it came to pass, as he sowed, some fell by the way side, and the fowls of the air came and devoured it up. (5) And some fell on stony ground, where it had not much earth; and immediately it sprang up, because it had no depth of earth: (6) but when the sun was up, it was scorched; and because it had no root, it withered away. (7) And some fell among thorns, and the thorns grew up, and choked it, and it yielded no fruit. (8) And other fell on good ground, and did yield fruit that sprang up and increased; and brought forth, some thirty, and some sixty, and some an hundred. (9) And he said unto them, He that hath ears to hear, let him hear. (10) And when he was alone, they that were about him with the twelve asked of him the parable. (11) And he said unto them, Unto you it is given to know the mystery of the

kingdom of God: but unto them that are without, all these things are done in parables: (12) that seeing they may see, and not perceive; and hearing they may hear, and not understand; lest at any time they should be converted, and their sins should be forgiven them. (13) And he said unto them, Know ye not this parable? and how then will ye know all parables? (14) The sower soweth the word. (15) And these are they by the way side, where the word is sown; but when they have heard, Satan cometh immediately, and taketh away the word that was sown in their hearts. (16) And these are they likewise which are sown on stony ground; who, when they have heard the word, immediately receive it with gladness; (17) and have no root in themselves, and so endure but for a time: afterward, when affliction or persecution ariseth for the word's sake, immediately they are offended. (18) And these are they which are sown among thorns; such as hear the word, (19) and the cares of this world, and the deceitfulness of riches, and the lusts of other things entering in, choke the word, and it becometh unfruitful. (20) And these are they which are sown on good ground; such as hear the word, and receive it, and bring forth fruit, some thirtyfold, some sixty, and some an hundred.

Verses 3-8. Jesus put into practice His adopted mode of instruction by relating the parable of the sower. The first component of a parable is given, i.e. the common reality of everyday life. It is not unlikely that Jesus drew His parable from an observation on the spot, noting a lone sower in the fields bordering the lake.

Sowing of seed was done by hand. From a bag container of seed often strapped onto the shoulder, the sower indiscriminately scattered handfuls of seed as he walked across the fields. Modern farm operations place seed directly into a prepared bed so that there is little loss of seed. In Palestine, seedbeds were minimally prepared and there remained areas of rocky soil and areas infested with weeds. Because fields were open, passersby traversed the land and the soil became hard packed on the footpath. All this was common to the understanding of the people.

Seed that fell onto the footpath became food for birds. Seed that fell into shallow, stony soil germinated but found no means of sending down deep a root system to nourish the plant in time of drought stress. These plants grew slowly, became stunted, and eventually withered. Some seed fell into soil infested with weeds, thorns, or thistles, which grew more vigorously and competitively stole the resources of moisture, nutrients, and light. Although the plant survived, it was choked and produced no fruit. Other seed fell onto good ground.

There are four primary requirements for plant productivity. First, there must be the proper kind and amount of nutrient and mineral resources in the soil to sustain the plant. If one major nutrient (nitrogen, potassium, phosphorus) or minor element (calcium, iron, sulfur) is lacking, plant growth will be slow. Growth proceeds according to the law of the minimum; that is, the element in short supply dictates the growth rate of the plant. In some cases the soil might hold enough moisture for small plants, but as they grow so does the demand for water until water becomes the limited resource.

Second, growth in plants requires light. Sunlight is the ultimate source of all energy. Plants trap the light energy in chlorophyll (green pigments) and use it to drive complex biochemical synthesis of sugars. Without light or in shaded areas, plant growth is restricted.

A third essential for plants is water. Soil moisture dissolves the nutrients necessary for plant growth and is absorbed by the roots. The nutrients travel through stem and leaf vessels to where new growth, expansion, and division occur. Moisture provides turgor in leaves and helps maintain a lower temperature by transpiration. No plant will survive long without a source of moisture.

Finally, a plant must have space, both for its roots to penetrate the soil and for its canopy to be displayed to the atmosphere where it can absorb and exchange gases and intercept light.

A plant grown under conditions of limited nutrients, light, water, or space (density of plants) does not reach its potential for fruitfulness. Two additional factors further influence yield. First, even though the plant may set its fruit, that fruit can become the target of plant pathogens (blights or wilts) and pests such as insects or mites. Growing plants must be protected from the ravages of insects and plant diseases. Second, there is the intrinsic or genetic potential of the plant. Some varieties of the same crop plant produce much more than others. Through plant breeding, fields of many agricultural crops steadily increase to produce thirty or sixtyfold.

Verse 8 indicates that seed falling on good ground yielded fruit "that sprang up" in turn and increased. The final result was that seeds falling in good ground produced thirty, sixty, or even a hundredfold. The gospel was meant to be transgenerational, and in successive generations it should become increasingly effective.

Verse 9. Jesus appealed to His audience to "listen up" with the words, "He that hath ears to hear, let him hear." Luke 8:8 says, "He cried," but Mark uses, "He said." Jesus often used this statement when the content of the subject matter was obscure or symbolic and there was a chance of being misunderstood. Moreover, hearing implies action; those merely curious to hear new facts or to witness the fame of the speaker would not take these life-enriching words to heart.

Verses 10-13. "When he was alone" is peculiar to Mark's Gospel. Moreover, Mark alone records that Jesus was with the Twelve and others when they questioned the meaning of the parable, indicating a later time. Jesus explained that many people were not ready to receive the teachings because of unbelief or ignorant skepticism.

Jesus instructed the disciples to search out His words in order to become able ministers of the gospel. Those having no desire for this truth, "them that are without"—without knowledge or desire for knowledge—will eventually lose what knowledge they have of truth. The quotation from Isaiah 6:9-10 describes folks who hear and see but do not respond, nullifying the hearing and seeing. Proper hearing and seeing will evoke a behavioral response.

Jesus did not intend for parables to be cryptic or obscure, but He went to great effort to be clearly understood. He also knew the principle of teaching which says that a person must discover for himself in order to fully comprehend. Not all soil was good soil, and not all good soil would produce at maximum potential.

The parable is a valuable test of character. It arrests the mind. Truth in parable is veiled and yields its secrets only to the active seeker. Here lies the intent of parabolic teaching as an analogy of natural things to spiritual things. Its spiritual intent can be "heard" and learned by the responsive individual but remains "hidden" to the unresponsive individual due to the hardening of his heart.

Verses 14-20. Jesus' manner of explanation turned the parable into an allegory. (Because parables were to be heard, creating their impact verbally, they would normally not be allegorized.) First, the sower sows the Word, or as Matthew wrote, "the word of the kingdom." The wayside refers to those who hear but their hearts are hard, callous, and unresponsive so that the evil one comes immediately and easily takes the unappropriated Word from their hearts.

Stony ground represents some who hear the truth and receive it with gladness. The seed quickly germinates and utilizes the store of endosperm within the seed; however, the plant is not able to put down adequate roots. As a result, there is no self-sustaining growth. Though the purity, justice, and mercy of the Word brings a flush of gladness, the subsequent affliction or persecution offends and aborts further growth.

The third class of soil describes other people into which the Word falls, germinates, and flourishes. Thorns compete for the nutrients of the soil but do not prohibit growth as do the wayside and rocky soils. Instead, "deceitfulness of riches," "lusts of other things entering in," and secular, temporal, and even religious cares choke and strangle the plant into unfruitfulness. Riches are comparable to thorns, for they pierce the soul through with many sorrows (I Timothy 6:10). How difficult it is for a rich person to enter the kingdom of God! (Matthew 19:23).

Finally comes good ground, representing the hearts of people who receive the Word with joy, who cherish, retain, and nourish it above all else. As there are three grades of bad soil so there are three grades of good soil, yielding thirty, sixty, and one hundredfold.

Each soil type represents a spiritual nature of people. The Word (seed) is a living entity that becomes fruitful only in response to the recipient's nature. Thus it is the learner's responsibility—not the sower's—to make the Word fruitful. The harvest is sure. Regardless of the lost seed, there will be a harvest!

(2) Responsibility of the hearers (4:21-25)
(Matthew 5:15; Luke 8:16; 11:33)

(21) And he said unto them, Is a candle brought to be put under a bushel, or under a bed? and not to be set on a candlestick? (22) For there is nothing hid, which shall not be manifested; neither was any thing kept secret, but that it should come abroad. (23) If any man have ears to hear, let him hear. (24) And he said unto them, Take heed what ye hear: with what measure ye mete, it shall be measured to you: and unto you that hear shall more be given. (25) For he that hath, to him shall be given: and he that hath not, from him shall be taken even that which he hath.

Here recorded are distinct sayings of Christ: the candle's secrets revealed, return of what is given, and the giving of more to the one who has already. Whereas Mark puts these verses together, Matthew repeats them throughout several verses: 5:15, 10:26, 7:2, 13:12, and 25:29

for verses 21, 22, 24, and 25 respectively. This leads us to conclude that Jesus spoke these sayings on more than a single instance to different audiences in different places, and although Mark places them together, they should be considered singly.

Verse 21. The modern translation of the Greek word rendered "candle" is "lamp" (Matthew 5:15), inferring the lamp of divine truth shining in the works and words of Christ. Light transmitted to the human soul has a divine origin and is to be manifested for the glory of God. Christian light bearers are not so much to be seen as they are to enable others to see. Truth is intended to be displayed unconcealed and highly visible.

Jesus could no more accomplish His purpose by hiding in a closet than could a concealed or covered lamp. First-century Christians who refused to worship the Roman emperor risked death, but Christianity was a light to be witnessed, for which many converts accepted the risk as had Jesus before them.

Verse 22 reveals that a truth which might now be hidden will be manifest in proper time and order. Here again Christ's saying appears to apply to truth that people had attempted to suppress. Jesus, as Truth, could not be hidden indefinitely. Because truth is indestructible, it will withstand all attempts to suppress, eradicate, or obfuscate it.

Our Lord was well aware that the secrets of nature, the universe, and physical science would increasingly yield to the unrelenting persistence of human inquiry. He also knew that people could not forever hide from themselves as their guilt instinctively demanded. Deception is only temporary; truth will always be revealed in the presence of God. Jesus desired that His life, and ours, be such that everyone can openly look upon it and marvel at the mercy, grace, and justice of a loving God.

Verses 23-24. Verse 23 instructs us to hear, while verse 24 tells us to heed—attend to, obey, or follow—what we hear. To hear is to listen and internalize the message. Internalized messages are not forgotten and can be conveyed to others.

Verse 24 further states that a law of proportions is at work. What we give in life determines what we get. The person who freely gives himself to the gospel of Christ and to others will in turn freely receive of God. "He which soweth bountifully shall reap also bountifully" (II Corinthians 9:6).

This law operates in many areas of life. The more someone devotes study to a given topic, the more he receives from it. Even difficult and relatively uninteresting parts of the Bible hold a rich harvest for the persistent inquirer. Likewise, the worship of God requires more than superficial praise. To approach the house of God merely to receive for our needs is selfish and unrewarding. To approach church without expectation is to respond merely to routine fulfillment of duty; to approach it without preparation of mind or heart is to leave disappointed. How different the church is to the worshiper who has prepared his heart and mind through sacrifice and prayer, who fully expects to meet God, and who approaches humbly and uncritically to bless God because He is God.

Finally, our personal relationships reflect what we are. Critics attract critics; irritable and capricious fault finders gravitate to those of like qualities. A person must show friendliness to have friends (Proverbs 18:24). And when one is truly convinced and believes on Jesus, he will himself be convincing and believable.

Verse 25. This verse describes a law similar to the law of giving and receiving: the law of increase. To him who has, more will be given. When a person uses his talents, they increase. This law is true in all areas of life, whether mental, physical, or spiritual. The more learning one has, the more he can attain. Knowledge builds readily and easily on existing knowledge. Use of physical skills enables one to supplement and embellish them with even greater skills. To keep ourselves physically fit is to avoid losing the fitness we have. The reward for good works is the opportunity to do more works (e.g., II Peter 1:5-7). Because of faithfulness in shepherding, David was given a bear, then a lion, then Goliath, then a kingdom—each challenge met brought even greater challenge.

The opposite is also true: he who fails to use his gifts will lose the ability to do so. Someone who evades responsibility, fails to study and acquire knowledge, and is negligent in financial affairs proves himself to be untrustworthy. Gradually the privileges of responsibility, stewardship, and independence will be taken from him.

(3) Parable of the seed growing (4:26-29)

(26) And he said, So is the kingdom of God, as if a man should cast seed into the ground; (27) and should sleep, and rise night and day, and the seed should spring and grow up, he knoweth not how. (28) For the earth bringeth forth fruit of herself; first the blade, then the ear, after that the full corn in the ear. (29) But when

*the fruit is brought forth, immediately he putteth in the
sickle, because the harvest is come.*

Verses 26-29. The parable of the seed is the one parable that only Mark gives. As in the parable of the sower,
the seed is the gospel, the field is hearers, and the harvest
is the culmination of the age. Here the likeness ends
because this parable apparently depicts the kingdom of
God, actually the reign of God. When the reign of God is
come, people will accept on earth the will of God as it is in
heaven.

The parable embodies several lessons. First, humans
are helpless in the agricultural enterprise. They can prepare the soil and sow the seed, but they must wait for the
miracle of growth. The secret of life is withheld from
man; he cannot create as God creates. Man can discover,
rearrange, and develop, but only God can make life.

Second, the parable describes features of the kingdom
of God. Much like the growing seed, the kingdom mysteriously contains within itself the life that makes it grow
constantly and almost imperceptibly day by day. God's
work is unceasing, quiet, and inevitable as He works out
His purpose (verse 28).

Third, the harvest will come (verse 29). Once man's
work is done, the seed will do its work, assisted by earth
and sun and independent of the sower's labor. The earth
bears fruit of itself. Full maturity is coming, and we are to
wait in patience and hope, never despairing, but confident
that the full grain will be in the ear. When the fruit is
ready, when the work of the gospel is done, individuals
and eventually the entire church will be taken as a harvest
(I Thessalonians 4:13-18).

To desire to terminate or conclude the process of preparation for the harvest suggests that a person wishes to escape part of the work of the kingdom in the ripening process. A despairing world seeks by suicide, euthanasia, and abortion to alter the process when in reality God may use suffering, hardship, disappointments, and heartbreak to show in a more glorious way His own grace and to perfect the "full corn in the ear."

(4) Parable of the mustard seed (4:30-32)
(Matthew 13:31; Luke 13:18)

(30) And he said, Whereunto shall we liken the kingdom of God? or with what comparison shall we compare it? (31) It is like a grain of mustard seed, which, when it is sown in the earth, is less than all the seeds that be in the earth: (32) but when it is sown, it groweth up, and becometh greater than all herbs, and shooteth out great branches; so that the fowls of the air may lodge under the shadow of it.

Verses 30-32. Jesus likened the kingdom to something every Jew would know. A grain of mustard seed meant the smallest possible measure of an item, for from that tiny bit of life sprang forth a plant with spreading branches that might reach ten feet in height. Kingdoms in Old Testament times were often compared to trees. Small provinces, city-states and nations within an empire were likened to birds accepting the refuge of its strength (Ezekiel 17:22; 31; Daniel 4:10-12, 20-22). Using common Jewish imagery, Jesus related to His hearers what they might expect from the kingdom of God.

We can learn several important lessons. First, we should not despise the day of small beginnings. When our impact on a city or institution is small, let us remember the mustard seed. A small witness here, a hospital visit there, a baptism—all add to the church. No natural organism, plant, or animal ever came into being fully mature; no institution, bank, government, or nation ever began full grown.

Second, the church is like an empire. It will not remain small but will grow, take in new territory, and enlarge its borders until what began with one individual will end with the entire world. Daniel saw the kingdom as a stone, hewn out of the mountain without hands, as it grew until it filled the whole earth (Daniel 2:34-35). Christianity is large enough for varied opinions and ideas to lodge within its branches, but unless they are part of the tree itself they are in the kingdom but not part of the kingdom. Barclay stated, "It is good for a man to have the assurance that he is right, but that is no reason why he should have the conviction that everyone else is wrong."[8] As an empire, the kingdom is a place where all nations meet. God knows no prejudice for humanity.

c. Summary of the parabolic section (4:33-34)
(Matthew 13:34)

(33) And with many such parables spake he the word unto them, as they were able to hear it. (34) But without a parable spake he not unto them: and when they were alone, he expounded all things to his disciples.

Verses 33-34 illustrate the most fundamental principle

101

of the teaching and learning theory: the teacher must never teach above the level of the pupil's ability to learn. Simply, if the pupil fails to learn, the teacher has not taught. The two events are inseparable components of the same thought process in two persons. Many things can be learned without a teacher, but the wise and successful teacher is tied to the pupil's ability to learn from him.

Jesus as a wise teacher exhibited two very important characteristics. First, He drew attention to the topic of instruction, never to Himself as a man. The risk of any teacher, preacher, or leader is to be so in love with himself, especially when people feel his influence, that he jeopardizes the message itself. The display of the teacher can compromise the truth. Pithy phrases, one-liners, witticisms, extraneous anecdotes, and stories are for illustration only.

Second, He avoided emphasizing His vast superiority over the people as much as possible. Teachers, because they possess the facts, often are tempted to talk down to their pupils. The wise teacher realizes that learning is a shared and mutually rewarding experience. In this he facilitates the learning process.

Several Christian qualities mark the good teacher. He has insight into the learners' mind and world; he is patient, unhurried and even tempered. A good teacher strives to uplift and not humiliate the learner. An offended learner becomes preoccupied with defending his bruised ego and balks at further instruction. A kind teacher always has at heart the interests and motives of his students.

As with the teacher, several qualities mark the receptive learner. Those who learned most from Jesus' parables were first able to hear them. They listened intently and worked to comprehend and internalize the information. They sought Him "alone" for further explanation, which suggests that to them remembering superseded forgetting and that they desired to be with the teacher. No Scripture is of one's private interpretation (II Peter 1:20); hence, the wise learner seeks company with the teacher.

Notes

[1]Eusebius III:30.

[2]Barclay, 43.

[3]*Ibid.*, 72.

[4]Sometimes given as Baal-zebub, "lord of flies," the Phoenician idol. Beelzebub is the prince of demons (Matthew 10:25; 12:24; Mark 3:22; Luke 11:15, 18-19). Beelzebub signifies "lord of the dwelling," and Jesus identified him as Satan.

[5]Barclay, p. 76.

[6]Henry Barclay Swete, *The Gospel According to St. Mark*, 3rd ed. (London: Macmillan, 1904), 68.

[7]Bernard Ramm, *Protestant Biblical Interpretation* (Ann Arbor, MI: Baker, 1970), 276.

[8]Barclay, 108.

B.

Withdrawals from Galilee
(4:35-9:50)

B. Withdrawals from Galilee (4:35-9:50)
1. First Withdrawal and Return (4:35-6:29)
a. Stilling of the tempest (4:35-41)
(Matthew 8:23; Luke 8:22)

(35) And the same day, when the even was come, he saith unto them, Let us pass over unto the other side. (36) And when they had sent away the multitude, they took him even as he was in the ship. And there were also with him other little ships. (37) And there arose a great storm of wind, and the waves beat into the ship, so that it was now full. (38) And he was in the hinder part of the ship, asleep on a pillow: and they awake him, and say unto him, Master, carest thou not that we perish? (39) And he arose, and rebuked the wind, and said unto the sea, Peace, be still. And the wind ceased, and there was a great calm. (40) And he said unto them, Why are ye so fearful? how is it that ye have no faith? (41) And they feared exceedingly, and said one to another, What manner of man is this, that even the wind and the sea obey him?

Verses 35-36. This miracle occurred at evening of the same day as the foregoing instruction. At Jesus' command the disciples, without extensive preparation or provisioning of the boat from which He had taught, headed across the Sea of Galilee. Mark notes smaller boats "with them," probably a result of enterprising boatmen to be near Jesus while He taught. Once He departed, the crowd on shore

107

dispersed, leaving those in the boats to witness the miracle.

Verses 37-38. Fierce and sudden storms were common on the Sea of Galilee, initiated as winds sweeping down from the adjacent mountain were channeled through passes opening up on the lake. The lake responded to the great gusts of wind with high waves and much turbulence.

A storm such as this now overtook their boat. Matthew 8:24 says that the waves "covered" the boat; Luke 8:23 shows it filling with water and "in jeopardy." Jesus reclined on a cushion in the stern (hinder) part of the boat in the designated place for passengers. In spite of the pitching and tossing of the boat and the inevitable splashing of water, Jesus slept.

When the boat was apparently uncontrollable and at the mercy of the wind and waves, "they" awoke Him with, "Master, carest thou not that we perish?" The directness of the question, the impatient and even irreverent tone, has been attributed to Peter.

Verse 39. Jesus arose, first rebuked the wind, then said to the sea, whipped into frenzy by the fierce winds, "Peace, be still"—literally, "Be silent, be muzzled." There is no evidence that the winds gradually subsided; they ceased immediately!

Verses 40-41. Jesus turned to the disciples and continued the rebuke: "Why are ye so fearful? how is it that ye have no faith?" Their faith in Him whether awake or asleep should have been like that of the psalmist: "Behold, he that keepeth Israel shall neither slumber nor sleep" (Psalm 121:4). At these words they feared even more, expressing to each other the nature and power of One whom even the wind and sea obey.

This miracle is both literal and representational. The tempest on the sea can be a symbol of trials and temptations that beset the Christian in his journey through life. With Jesus in the ship every storm but challenges our faith to believe that all is well. Though the billows of life toss high, the heart and soul rest secure and safe in the knowledge that at a single command all turbulence ceases. In His presence we can face even the wildest storm with courage and certitude. Storms of fear, doubt, anxiety, and worry that attack at the most inopportune times respond to "Peace, be still." These words calm the storms of sorrow, winds of adversity, and sea of turmoil. The sailors' words can be echoed by all people who have gone through life's storms and have had the Master intercede just in time.

It appears that for the disciples, control of diseases and human maladies was easier to believe in than control of the elements. In some instances people's own will and strength may enable them to shake off disease, but making the very elements obey their command is another matter altogether.

God, who created the atoms, elements, and substances, certainly holds the power to regulate and adjust weather. He has the power to remove danger or to help us meet and safely withstand danger. Only God knows which is best for the individual, and it is His sovereign will to teach by using the test. Later, the apostle Peter wrote, "Casting all your care upon him; for he careth for you" (I Peter 5:7). What tests, trials, temptations, and persecutions Peter must have suffered since the calming of the sea that he could make so definite an assertion!

Jesus continued on the same day to teach by example

and action. After victoriously confronting nature He now confronted a man made insane by demonic (unclean) spirits. The incidents in chapter 5 are instructive as the wise Teacher conditioned and trained His most intimate followers.

b. Cure of the Gadarene demoniac (5:1-20)
(Matthew 8:28; Luke 8:26)

(1) And they came over unto the other side of the sea, into the country of the Gadarenes. (2) And when he was come out of the ship, immediately there met him out of the tombs a man with an unclean spirit, (3) who had his dwelling among the tombs; and no man could bind him, no, not with chains: (4) because that he had been often bound with fetters and chains, and the chains had been plucked asunder by him, and the fetters broken in pieces; neither could any man tame him. (5) And always, night and day, he was in the mountains, and in the tombs, crying, and cutting himself with stones. (6) But when he saw Jesus afar off, he ran and worshipped him, (7) and cried with a loud voice, and said, What have I to do with thee, Jesus, thou Son of the most high God? I adjure thee by God, that thou torment me not. (8) For he said unto him, Come out of the man, thou unclean spirit. (9) And he asked him, What is thy name? And he answered, saying, My name is Legion: for we are many. (10) And he besought him much that he would not send them away out of the country. (11) Now there was there nigh unto the mountains a great herd of swine feeding. (12) And all the devils besought him, saying, Send us into the swine, that we may enter

into them. (13) And forthwith Jesus gave them leave. And the unclean spirits went out, and entered into the swine: and the herd ran violently down a steep place into the sea, (they were about two thousand;) and were choked in the sea. (14) And they that fed the swine fled, and told it in the city, and in the country. And they went out to see what it was that was done. (15) And they come to Jesus, and see him that was possessed with the devil, and had the legion, sitting, and clothed, and in his right mind: and they were afraid. (16) And they that saw it told them how it befell to him that was possessed with the devil, and also concerning the swine. (17) And they began to pray him to depart out of their coasts. (18) And when he was come into the ship, he that had been possessed with the devil prayed him that he might be with him. (19) Howbeit Jesus suffered him not, but saith unto him, Go home to thy friends, and tell them how great things the Lord hath done for thee, and hath had compassion on thee. (20) And he departed, and began to publish in Decapolis how great things Jesus had done for him: and all men did marvel.

Verses 1-2. The lake (Sea of Galilee) is about thirteen miles long and eight miles wide; the distance to the southeast shore is approximately five miles. After the stormy crossing Jesus and the disciples disembarked on the east shore the country of the Gadarenes (probably the town of Gergasa).[1]

Here in Gentile territory Jesus met a Gentile man who had an unclean spirit and made his dwelling (home) in the tombs. Palestinian tombs were hewn from limestone or more often located in natural caverns large enough to be

111

inhabited by a man. The superstitious Jews taught that demons lived in such places, as well as in dirty places, woods, deserts, gardens, and desolate areas. They also believed that demons became especially active at nightfall; thus the time of their peak activity was approaching when Jesus landed on the shore.

Verses 3-5. These verses provide a vivid picture of what today would be termed extreme stages of manic-depressive psychosis: vigorous activity, combativeness, and self-destructiveness. Then, as now, people dealt with such cases by attempting to restrain the violent outbursts of activity. Their methods were useless against the superior strength of the one possessed. Man could neither bind nor tame him. To man, his case was quite hopeless and helpless.

Verses 6-7. When the possessed man saw Jesus afar off, he ran to Him and worshiped, calling Him Jesus, Son of the most high God. As the demons in 1:24 recognized Jesus, so did these. They questioned their relation to Him at this time. The term "most high God" seems to be the term for the God of Israel used by pagans and Gentiles (Daniel 4:2, 17). Sherman Johnson suggested that the demons in the man called the name of Jesus as a sort of exorcism in reverse, using an Old Testament expression to adjure by God's authority. It was a futile attempt to protect themselves by intimidating Jesus while acknowledging the ability of Christ to "torment" them.[2]

Verses 8-9. Jesus spoke authoritatively to the demons to come out, adding "thou unclean spirit." He used no incantation or formula to cast them out. Next, He asked for a name, to which the demons responded, "Legion." This may have been boasting about the large number present or an evasion of a specific name. At any rate, the answer provided more of a description or group designation than a name. Again, one might suspect an effort by the demons to intimidate Jesus by the sheer weight of numbers. A legion (Latin *legio*) was the largest single unit in the Roman army and included cavalry and infantry, consisting of six thousand men.

Verses 10-12. The demons begged not to be sent into the desert (dry places) or Gehenna (lake of fire). The close proximity of a herd of swine suggested an alternative, and they "all" besought Him to "send" them into the swine. The region belonged to a league of ten Gentile city-states, Decapolis, and pork was likely eaten there.

This is a rare instance of destructiveness associated with Christ's ministry. Why would Jesus allow these swine to be destroyed? Perhaps the owners were Jewish, in which case they were breaking their religious law by owning hogs. Or perhaps Jesus allowed this as a graphic object lesson of His superior power and authority. In any case, of what value is a herd of animals compared to a human soul?

Jesus demonstrated His absolute authority in three ways: (1) the demons made their petitions of Him, appealing to His clemency, knowing full well His power over them; (2) the surrendering of a name gave one a certain authority over the demons yet they could not withhold from Him a name; and (3) Jesus granted them permission to enter the swine. This final act ("gave them leave") resulted in complete if reluctant obedience of the demons to Jesus Christ. In three separate steps Jesus cast out the demons (spoke to them to depart, questioned them, and gave them leave to enter swine) and restored sanity to a human being.

Verse 13. The swine herd at once stampeded violently down a slope and into the sea. It has been erroneously suggested that the animals fled from the noisy insane demoniac and those privy to the conversation concluded that the demons had entered into the pigs. The parenthetical expression giving the number of swine (two thousand) agrees with the idea of a large number or "Legion" (cf. Matthew 26:53; Luke 8:30).

Verses 14-15. The Gentile herdsmen quickly fled the area and related the story in the city and country so that a delegation came to check out the story. What they found was nothing short of amazing: the crazed man, now clothed and in his right mind, sat peaceably. Mark previously makes no mention of clothing, but Luke and Matthew indicate his nakedness. The stories of the demoniac and the swine were both confirmed, with the result that the witnessing people became fearful.

Verses 16-17. Frightened and superstitious people destroy what they fear, and here was something they could not understand. Therefore, the inhabitants requested ("prayed") Jesus to depart from their region, thereby missing the opportunity for Him to minister to them.

Verses 18-20. Jesus went to the ship, followed by the delivered man, who desired to stay with Him. Christ's instruction, "Go home to thy friends, and tell them," broke the tradition for secrecy established in Mark (1:44; 3:12; 5:43).

At times it is much harder to stay and testify than to go. This man had to face the villagers as the man bought with a herd of swine. If ever a man had a convincing testimony of deliverance, this man did. Being clothed and sane

114

would convince many, and the memory of two thousand choking swine stood as a personal memorial to his deliverance. Here was definite, unanswerable proof confirmed by an entire community.

When Jesus delivered, He always left a witness. Priests confirmed the lepers, lame men carried their beds, the blind leaped for joy, and feverish women resumed domestic duties. This message differed in that it was a report to Gentiles and focused on the work of "the Lord" rather than the work of the Jewish Messiah, much like the Old Testament story of the Syrian leper (II Kings 5:15-17). It is noteworthy that Jesus instructed Jews to remain silent, while instructing Gentiles to testify. Perhaps He wanted to avoid a premature peak in His ministry based on mistaken Jewish Messianic hopes of an earthly kingdom at that time.

This story teaches powerful lessons. First, demons possess the power to make a person insane or crazy, but their power is limited. They cannot kill a person, nor can they completely prevent him from worshiping God. Second, that humans are superior to demons is implied by the vast number in the individual (at least two thousand). Third, a person in his right mind will be clothed, sitting at the feet of Jesus in gratitude and admiration.

c. Two miracles upon returning (5:21-43)

Mark next relates events that occur after Jesus crossed the lake from Gergasa (verses 21-24). Among the gathered crowd was a ruler of the synagogue desperately burdened and seeking healing for his daughter. Before Jesus could reach the sick child, another unique and

115

beautiful healing occurred. The two stories intertwine with sufficient delay for the girl to be reported dead.

Almost like an artistic drama, Mark in Scene I shows Jairus meeting Jesus with a plea for Him to come. In Scene II the trip is interrupted by an equally desperate woman desiring healing. Scene III resumes and concludes the story of Jairus. It is noteworthy that the stories are mingled because Jesus' healings reflect two motifs. In some healings, the sick person's faith was necessary to receive divine healing (5:25-34; 9:14-29). In others, the sick person's faith was not evident, often not even possible (1:29-31; 7:24-30; 8:22-26), that the focus might rest on Jesus as the healer. The thing that set these apart from pagan or Jewish stories of healing was the presence of Jesus Himself.

(1) Plea of Jarius (5:21-24)
(Matthew 9:18; Luke 8:40)

(21) And when Jesus was passed over again by ship unto the other side, much people gathered unto him: and he was nigh unto the sea. (22) And, behold, there cometh one of the rulers of the synagogue, Jairus by name; and when he saw him, he fell at his feet, (23) and besought him greatly, saying, My little daughter lieth at the point of death: I pray thee, come and lay thy hands on her, that she may be healed; and she shall live. (24) And Jesus went with him; and much people followed him, and thronged him.

The Jewish synagogue arose out of necessity during the Babylonian captivity, and it boasted two chief officers.

There was a sole ruler or president *(rosh kha-keneseth)* and an attendant *(hazzan)* (Luke 4:20) for each synagogue, although larger synagogues might have had several such officers or a governing band, as implied by Mark's use of the plural. Rulers in general and Jairus *(Jair* or *Yair;* Numbers 32:41) in particular owed his appointment to elders of the local Sanhedrin. His was a position of prominence and dignity and he a person of importance. He hosted the synagogue service and was responsible for assigning duties, keeping order, and selecting speakers on occasions.

Verses 22-23. In desperation Jairus pushed his way through the crowd to Jesus, announced his need, and made his request. Although he was a man of worth and dignity, the tragedy of a sick and dying child stripped away all pretense and pride. Prejudice against Jesus and the opinions of his peers mattered little to a desperate father.

The doctrine of laying on of hands for healing is unique to the New Testament (Hebrews 6:2) and characteristic of Mark's Gospel (6:5; 8:25). It apparently was not practiced in Old Testament times.[3]

Verse 24. As Jairus, accompanied by Jesus and no doubt the Twelve, departed for his house, the great crowd of highly excitable people "pressed" upon Him.

(2) Woman with the flow of blood (5:25-34)
(Matthew 9:20; Luke 8:43)

(25) And a certain woman, which had an issue of blood twelve years, (26) and had suffered many things of many physicians and had spent all that she had, and was nothing bettered, but rather grew worse, (27) when

117

she had heard of Jesus, came in the press behind, and touched his garment. (28) For she said, If I may touch but his clothes, I shall be whole. (29) And straightway the fountain of her blood was dried up; and she felt in her body that she was healed of that plague. (30) And Jesus, immediately knowing in himself that virtue had gone out of him, turned him about in the press, and said, Who touched my clothes? (31) And his disciples said unto him, Thou seest the multitude thronging thee, and sayest thou, Who touched me? (32) And he looked round about to see her that had done this thing. (33) But the woman fearing and trembling, knowing what was done in her, came and fell down before him, and told him all the truth. (34) And he said unto her, Daughter, thy faith hath made thee whole; go in peace, and be whole of thy plague.

Verses 25-26. Among the crowd was a woman who for twelve years had borne a hemorrhage. (Jairus's daughter was twelve years old.) She endured much of many doctors because as remedy after remedy failed, techniques became increasingly experimental. This added to her suffering without bettering the condition. No doubt this woman had tried many of the eleven cures for this ailment provided in the Talmud, most of which were superstitious and paganistic (e.g., carrying about a barley corn found in the dung of a white female donkey).

Verses 27-28. Her approach to Jesus from behind provided some protection in anonymity since her issue made her ceremonially unclean (Leviticus 15:25-27). The best she could do was to touch the lower portion of His outer garment, likely the *himation* commonly worn by Jews. Her reasoning was satisfied with this minimum because she had already purposed in her heart that she would be made whole by touching His garment. Besides, she was unclean.

Verse 29. "Straightway" she knew that she was healed and made whole. As her mind accepted the fact, her body responded and the "fountain of her blood" ceased.

Verse 30. She was not the only one to sense a power at work. Jesus immediately knew that "virtue" went from Him and by what means, hence His question.

Verses 31-33. The disciples, not perceiving the significance of what Jesus meant by "touch," countered with a question as if to say, "Who can tell?" As typically noted in Mark, Jesus paused and looked around (3:5, 34; 10:23; 11:11) to see the woman fearful and trembling nearby. Undoubtedly her fear came from awe of Jesus but also that she would be found out as an unclean person. She did the only right thing: she confessed.

Verse 34. Jesus' term "daughter" identified her as a daughter of Abraham (Luke 13:16) and at the same time reassured her with acceptance and warm affection. "Thy faith"—not the touch on clothing or contact with the great Healer—"hath made thee whole." (Luke 8:46-48 places more emphasis on the virtue and power of Jesus than on the woman's faith.) Then came the Hebrew blessing, "Go in peace."

(3) Raising of Jairus's daughter (5:35-43)
(Matthew 9:23; Luke 8:49)

(35) While he yet spake, there came from the ruler of the synagogue's house certain which said, Thy daughter is dead: why troublest thou the Master any further? (36)

119

As soon as Jesus heard the word that was spoken, he saith unto the ruler of the synagogue, Be not afraid, only believe. (37) And he suffered no man to follow him, save Peter, and James, and John the brother of James. (38) And he cometh to the house of the ruler of the synagogue, and seeth the tumult, and them that wept and wailed greatly. (39) And when he was come in, he saith unto them, Why make ye this ado, and weep? the damsel is not dead, but sleepeth. (40) And they laughed him to scorn. But when he had put them all out, he taketh the father and the mother of the damsel, and them that were with him, and entereth in where the damsel was lying. (41) And he took the damsel by the hand, and said unto her, Talitha cumi; which is, being interpreted, Damsel, I say unto thee, arise. (42) And straightway the damsel arose, and walked; for she was of the age of twelve years. And they were astonished with a great astonishment. (43) And he charged them straitly that no man should know it; and commanded that something should be given her to eat.

Verse 35. As Jesus concluded his conversation with the woman healed of the flow of blood (verse 34), a messenger reached Jairus with news that his child was dead. Death was the end of the matter to the faithless; their remarks exposed a lack of understanding of Jesus' deep compassion and His power to restore life even to the dead.

Verse 36. The New Testament uses the phrase "Be not afraid" relative to divine revelation (Matthew 1:20; Mark 6:50; John 14:1) and links it to the command to believe, as is the case here. Being afraid handicaps a person's faith.

Fear and faith cannot coexist, being mutually exclusive within a person.

Verses 37-38. It was customary in the Near East to wail, weep, and lament the loss of a loved one in many detailed and elaborate ceremonies. A girl at age twelve (verse 42) on the eve of Jewish womanhood added impetus to the sense of sorrow and loss. Often professional mourners, flutists, and wailers were employed to add to the general tumult expressing grief. These mournings stressed the final separation of death and served to let everyone within hearing know the anguish of hopelessness. Mourners were to avoid work, wearing shoes, and any form of anointing of the body for three days.[4] No means of personal comfort could be sought and no travel was allowed. The mourner bound up his head, his face was unshaven, and he could not read the Law or Prophets, but he could read Job, Jeremiah, or Lamentations.

Verse 39. Jesus asked why the ado over a sleeping damsel in order to point out the deficiency in their faith. He referred to death as sleeping (cf. Psalm 13:3), reflecting the Christian belief in the resurrection of the dead. (See I Thessalonians 4:13; John 11:11-13.) He was misunderstood by those in attendance; the mourners laughed Him to scorn.

Verses 40-43. Outsiders witnessed the miracle, but only the most intimate and concerned individuals. Jesus took the child by the hand and spoke in Aramaic, "Talitha cumi" (cf. 7:34). Mark provides the interpretation as an authoritative command: "Damsel, I say unto thee, arise." His command to give her something to eat, which followed her resurrection, confirmed the complete restoration of spirit

121

and body. It also reflected in a unique way the personality of Jesus, His concern for the good news, His call for faith in God, and His endearing human compassion.

d. Rejection of Jesus at Nazareth (6:1-6)
(Matthew 13:54; Luke 4:22;
Matthew 4:23; 9:35; 11:1; Mark 1:38)

(1) And he went out from thence, and came into his own country; and his disciples follow him. (2) And when the sabbath day was come, he began to teach in the synagogue: and many hearing him were astonished, saying, From whence hath this man these things? and what wisdom is this which is given unto him, that even such mighty works are wrought by his hands? (3) Is not this the carpenter, the son of Mary, the brother of James, and Joses, and of Juda, and Simon? and are not his sisters here with us? And they were offended at him. (4) But Jesus said unto them, A prophet is not without honour, but in his own country, and among his own kin, and in his own house. (5) And he could there do no mighty work, save that he laid his hands upon a few sick folk, and healed them. (6) And he marvelled because of their unbelief. And he went round about the villages, teaching.

Verse 1. It has been stated that Jesus honored Bethlehem by His birth, Nazareth by His upbringing, Capernaum by His ministry, and Jerusalem by His death. From Capernaum (near the sea) Jesus traveled to Nazareth. His first trip to Nazareth was to announce the beginning of His ministry (Luke 4:16), an effort that met with rejection and near disaster. Now with His disciples and considerable fame as a miracle-working prophet and rabbi, He again turned homeward.

Verses 2-3. The community place of exposure to the public was the synagogue on the Sabbath. There He went to teach. The hearers were astonished that this local boy had such ability and wisdom, perfect holiness and beauty in teaching, and worked signs and wonders before their eyes. Isaiah 11:2 uses wisdom and might as corresponding to word and deed for Israel's coming King. In Job 12:13 these terms refer to God. I Corinthians 1:24 calls Christ the power and wisdom of God. Before Nazareth that day stood the King of kings, Israel's Messiah, God Himself in the person of Jesus Christ. And they refused to acknowledge Him.

Not a few people were envious, and their words implied skepticism and contempt meant to put Him in a place equal to them. The word used for carpenter is *tekton*, one who joins or fastens wood as a craftsman. The *tekton* was skilled with his hands so that with few tools he could build a fence, repair a wall, or construct a house.

Jewish law required a father to do certain things for, with, and to every firstborn son. Joseph met the customary requirements by circumcision (Genesis 17:10-14; Luke 2:27), redemption (Exodus 13:2, 12; Numbers 3:42-51; Luke 2:27), teaching of the law (Deuteronomy 6:6-9; 11:19-20), and teaching a trade by which Jesus could make a living. To fail to meet the vocational need was in the Jews' eyes to teach robbery.

At this time Joseph, Mary's husband, was presumably dead, else he would no doubt have been mentioned here (cf. Mark 3:32). James, Joses, Judas, and Simon were undoubtedly sons of Joseph and Mary and therefore the Lord's half brothers.

Verses 4-5. Jesus' works and words transcended those of a mere carpenter, and the people of Nazareth were offended. In the same way that we view someone an expert when he is a stranger from another city, to these people, one born and raised among them of so humble an origin could not be doing and saying these things. True, Jesus was a carpenter, but He was more than a carpenter. True, He was the son of Mary, but He was also the Son of God.

Jesus responded to their disbelief and did no mighty works there except healing a few sick folks, because their doubt restricted the manifestation of His power. Does this mean that the amount of faith or power required to heal the sick is less than to work "greater" miracles? Any miracle by any measure, great or small, requires the principle of intervention and suspension of natural laws of cause and effect. Thus, any miracle is equally convincing, but skeptical people always find a way to disbelieve.

The absence of miracles shows the need for compliance of man's will and trust for perfect unity with God. Jesus was hampered by lack of faith, jealousy, envy, and skepticism. How many church assemblies fail to realize the miraculous due to these same spiritual and mental attitudes? Doubt and disbelief hinder ministry. Congregations "preach" well over half the sermon by creating an atmosphere of faith and expectancy and by worship.

Verse 6. This verse contains sharp contrast in its two statements. Surrounded by abundant evidence, the people of Nazareth caused the Lord to marvel at their hardness of heart and stubbornness of mind. Perhaps as a consequence of their refusal to accept Him, He went throughout Galilee, from village to village, teaching those who would accept. The second part of this verse introduces the mission discourse (verses 7-13).

e. Mission of the Twelve (6:7-13)
(Matthew 10:1: Mark 3:13; Luke 6:12-13; 9:1)

(7) And he called unto him the twelve, and began to send them forth by two and two; and gave them power over unclean spirits; (8) and commanded them that they should take nothing for their journey, save a staff only; no scrip, no bread, no money in their purse: (9) but be shod with sandals; and not put on two coats. (10) And he said unto them, In what place soever ye enter into an house, there abide till ye depart from that place. (11) And whosoever shall not receive you, nor hear you, when ye depart thence, shake off the dust under your feet for a testimony against them. Verily I say unto you, It shall be more tolerable for Sodom and Gomorrha in the day of judgment, than for that city. (12) And they went out, and preached that men should repent. (13) And they cast out many devils, and anointed with oil many that were sick, and healed them.

Verse 7. The two parallel versions of the disciples' mission differ in several important respects, including provision, equipment, and purpose. Mark's version shows the Twelve, selected in chapter 3 and there named, being commissioned with power over unclean spirits, paired, and sent out. The pairing of ministers for the work of the gospel was a common mode: Peter and John (Acts 3:1-10;

8:14-25), Barnabas and Saul (Acts 9:27-30; 11:25-26; 12:25; 14:20-28), and Paul and Silas (Acts 15:40-17:14).

Verse 8. They were to go without making special provisions, depending on God to provide simple needs; thus they would need no "money." Luke writing to the Greeks used the metal "silver"; Matthew 10:9 says gold, silver, and brass. They were to take with them only a staff for personal protection against animals. (The parallel passages in Matthew 10:10 and Luke 9:3 forbid acquiring extra staffs, but apparently they could use their personal walking staff.) Their authority extended to heal sickness and disease (Matthew 10:1), but Mark focuses on wresting from Satan's grip the hearts and minds of people.

Verse 9. The customary Jewish dress consisted of an inner garment, *chiton* or tunic, and an outer *himation*, or cloak. The girdle formed a band about these two garments and could be doubled over to make a pouch or pocket for valuables. A headdress of blue, black, or white cotton or linen was folded to encircle the head and it protected the back of the neck. Finally, there were sandals made of leather, wood, or woven grass. The scrip was a wallet or bag used for food.

Sandals and two undergarments implied a long journey to the Jews; here, sandals were allowed, change of raiment was not. Matthew 10:10 forbids the taking of shoes. Sandals protected only the soles of the feet from the hard, rocky surface of Palestinian roads, while shoes covered the top of the feet also. Shoes were more protective, but less cool and inappropriate for a long journey.

Verse 10. The pairs of ministers were to depend entirely on local hospitality. They were instructed to find and remain in a lodging throughout their stay in a village. This command served several purposes. First, the disciples accepted what was offered and were content not to seek better accommodations. Second, to change lodging would make them appear restless and unstable and risk offending their host. They were to go village to village and not burden any by remaining in residence too long.

Verse 11. People who refused to hear or accept their words were to evoke a testimony against themselves. To shake off the dust from the feet symbolized that the messengers had done their duty in toil and labor to reach the people with the gospel and also witnessed that the disciples were free of further responsibility of the fate of those who would not obey.

Most scholars today attribute the clause "it shall be more tolerable for Sodom" to Matthew, for it does not appear in the oldest existing manuscripts of Mark's Gospel.

Verse 12. The disciples went and preached that people should repent. The purpose of the gospel is repentance and restoration; to this cause all miracles and confrontations with the devil are subordinate. The disciples did not have to create a message, only proclaim what they had heard from Jesus. They preached no opinions, personal convictions, or human philosophies, but the King's message: repentance and mercy.

Verse 13. The use of olive oil as a medicine having remedial or therapeutic powers is well documented in antiquity. People employed oil for anointing local areas of the body to a full immersion bath. The apostles used it more for an outward visible sign that healing was done by the name of Jesus than for its curative power. It is the oil of gladness symbolic of God's mercy and joy. James 5:14

advocates the use of oil for faith healing in the New Testament church.

f. Reaction of Antipas to the reports about Jesus (6:14-29)
(Matthew 14:1; Luke 9:7)
(1) Excited reaction of Herod Antipas (6:14-16)

(14) And king Herod heard of him; (for his name was spread abroad:) and he said, that John the Baptist was risen from the dead, and therefore mighty works do shew forth themselves in him. (15) Others said, That it is Elias. And others said, That it is a prophet, or as one of the prophets. (16) But when Herod heard thereof, he said, It is John, whom I beheaded: he is risen from the dead.

Mark inserts another incident between verses 13 and 30, where the mission story resumes—the same literary device used in 5:25-34. The interlude relates the story of Herod's anguish, fear, and capricious treatment of John the Baptist. It begins with a question of identity: Just who was this miracle-working itinerant preacher?

Verses 14, 16. Mark says "king" Herod, as does Matthew 14:9, but the latter also calls Herod "the tetrarch" (14:1). The meaning of *tetrartos* is fourth; hence, a tetrarch (e.g., Herod) was sovereign of the fourth part of a territory. The Herod here was Herod Antipas, son of Herod the Great and his wife Malthace. He was born c. 20 B.C., became tetrarch of Galilee and Perea at the passing of Herod the Great about 4 B.C., and ruled until A.D. 39.

Hearing of Jesus, Herod Antipas was perplexed (Luke 9:7), thinking that John the Baptist had risen from the dead. It is interesting to speculate why Herod had never heard of Jesus before this time. It could be that he officially resided in Tiberias of Galilee. There is no evidence that Jesus or the disciples ever visited Tiberias, and it being a Gentile city, there was little cause to do so.

Herod's conclusion might have been based on fear or superstition over the reports of powerful ministry reminiscent of John. He might have subscribed to the common Pythagorean view of transmigration of souls. Regardless, the knowledge that he had killed an innocent and holy man tormented his mind and conscience.

Verse 15. Others thought Jesus was Elias. Elijah was expected to return to Israel at the Messianic era (Malachi 4:5-6), so Jews and even Samaritans could readily believe that the miracle worker was Elijah.

Some thought Jesus was a prophet or like a prophet. This office had associated with it various acts of power, healings, and teachings. The common people as well as Jesus' own disciples recognized a prophet's status (Luke 7:16; 24:19). Only the Messiah merited higher rank than a prophet among the Jews.

The three conclusions drawn about the identity of Jesus reflect the inner nature and feelings of Herod and the Israelite nation.[5] First, haunted by John the Baptist's execution, Herod concluded that John had returned to reckon with him over his cowardly deed. Second, there was the conclusion of the nationalists, who expected Elijah as forerunner to the Messiah. Finally, there was the verdict of those waiting patiently for the voice of God to speak after nearly four hundred years of silence. They listened intently to every teacher, questioning: "Could this be the voice of God?" In Jesus they received an affirmative answer. The voice of God was again heard in the land.

(2) Explanatory account of John's death (6:17-29)
(Matthew 14:3)

(17) For Herod himself had sent forth and laid hold upon John, and bound him in prison for Herodias' sake, his brother Philip's wife: for he had married her. (18) For John had said unto Herod, It is not lawful for thee to have thy brother's wife. (19) Therefore Herodias had a quarrel against him, and would have killed him; but she could not: (20) for Herod feared John, knowing that he was a just man and an holy, and observed him; and when he heard him, he did many things, and heard him gladly. (21) And when a convenient day was come, that Herod on his birthday made a supper to his lords, high captains, and chief estates of Galilee; (22) and when the daughter of the said Herodias came in, and danced, and pleased Herod and them that sat with him, the king said unto the damsel, Ask of me whatsoever thou wilt, and I will give it thee. (23) And he sware unto her, Whatsoever thou shalt ask of me, I will give it thee, unto the half of my kingdom. (24) And she went forth, and said unto her mother, What shall I ask? And she said, The head of John the Baptist. (25) And she came in straightway with haste unto the king, and asked, saying, I will that thou give me by and by in a charger the head of John the Baptist. (26) And the king was exceeding sorry; yet for his oath's sake, and for their sakes which sat with him, he

would not reject her. (27) And immediately the king sent an executioner, and commanded his head to be brought: and he went and beheaded him in the prison, (28) and brought his head in a charger, and gave it to the damsel: and the damsel gave it to her mother. (29) And when his disciples heard of it, they came and took up his corpse, and laid it in a tomb.

Mark's narrative of the execution of John the Baptist provides drama of the most intense human kind. The scene, the characters, their positions in society, the holy man of God, intertwining personal relations—all work to make a gripping real-life story surpassing even the most entangled web of the fiction writer. The story is told objectively without religious overtones and with no judgment passed on participants.

Verses 17-20. Philip married his niece Herodias (his half-brother's daughter) and resided in Rome as a wealthy private citizen. On a visit Herod Antipas seduced Herodias and took her away from Philip.

The marriage entanglements of the Herod family were incredible. Herod the Great married several women. Toward the end of his life his jealous and suspicious nature led him to murder several family members. (See Figure 1.)

According to the Jewish historian Josephus, John the Baptist was imprisoned at Machaerus, a fortress east of the Dead Sea where Herod the Great had built a splendid fortress palace.[6] Herod and the chief men of Galilee celebrated there (verse 21), else John would not have been so close at hand (verses 27-28).

John repeatedly condemned Herod's unlawful, adulterous, and incestuous relationship (Leviticus 18:16; 20:21).

Matthew 14:5 says that Herod would have killed him but for the people; Mark says that Herodias would have killed John but could not because Herod feared him (verse 19). The apparent conflict in the two Gospels is cleared up in verse 20, which shows that Herod gradually came under John's powerful influence and his malice dissipated, being replaced by awe and respect, although Herod did not repent and dissolve the marriage.

Herodias was the daughter of Aristobulus, son of Herod the Great and Mariamne the Hasmonean. She married Herod Philip, her half-uncle, son of Mariamne the Boethusian. They had one daughter, Salome. Herodias was niece and sister-in-law to Herod Antipas (son of Herod the Great and wife Malthace). For him to marry Herodias he first had to divorce his wife, daughter of the Nabataean King Aretas IV. Aretas defeated the tetrarch in A.D. 36, an act regarded by the Jews as divine retribution for what he did to John.

Verse 21. Herod's birthday was either the actual day of his birth or the day he began to reign. The planned celebration included a banquet or dinner attended by courtiers, tribunes, military or police officers (Herod was not allowed an army, only a police force), and the aristocracy of the province.

Verse 22. For entertainment, Salome (born c. A.D. 20 as the daughter of Herodias and her first husband) danced. It is consistent with the lewd, sensual nature of the Herodians that the princess herself came and performed as the customary dancing woman, displaying herself before drunken men. Ordinarily professional prostitutes performed solo dances of licentious pantomimes as entertainment. Salome's act was also consistent with her depraved character and that of her mother, who allowed, even encouraged, the dance. In a similar situation Queen Vashti refused to dance for the king, and it cost her position (Esther 1:10-19).

Verse 23. Herod and his guests were so pleased that in a generous and rash gesture the tetrarch swore to give Salome anything, up to half the kingdom. Oriental despots often granted requests under oath when pleased by entertainers (Esther 5:3; 7:3).

Verses 24-25. Salome went immediately to her mother with the oath of Herod, and Herodias instructed her to ask for the head of John the Baptist. The girl came at once with her petition, adding the gruesome touch of "in a charger," or wooden platter.

Verse 26. Mark again refers to the tetrarch as king and depicts him in a quandary over the request. For the sake of his repeated oaths, his position, and the fragile credibility of his word, he did not have the will to refuse her.

Verses 27-28. The executioner, a soldier of the guard, went immediately, beheaded John, and brought his head on a platter to the girl, who in turn presented it to her mother. Jerome related the tradition that in her triumph, Herodias barbarously drew out and thrust the tongue through with a needle.[7] Her behavior undoubtedly represented a vain attempt to appease a conscience tormented by John's indictment.

Verse 29. Josephus indicated that the headless remains of John were cast out of the prison and neglected. When his faithful disciples heard the tragic news, they claimed the corpse and gave it proper burial.

Herod was most human in this story. He was at one and the same time haunted by sin and right. His sensitive

133

conscience resulted in acceptance and rejection of John's preaching. A double-minded man will vacillate and fall prey to those of stronger will. Herod feared what people might say more than he feared what God would do. His action was one of a coward doing the wrong thing, his thoughts were of a sinner desiring to do a righteous thing.

What options were before him? He could have denied the request as unrelated to "half the kingdom" promised, as irrational for a princess, as sinful, or as unreasonable. Right alone is sufficient justification to the person who desires to do right; any justification is sufficient for the person who desires to do wrong.

The shape of evil in Herodias was much blacker than in Herod. Nothing in life is quite so bad as a bad woman, perhaps because so much is expected of womanhood. Herodias wished to silence the one individual courageous enough to point out her sins, and schemed to kill John so that she would be free of moral reprimands and thus sin in peace. While she no longer had to face John, she still had to face God.

From this point the saga of Antipas and Herodias is one of overshadowing judgment. As noted, Antipas was defeated in A.D. 36 by his former father-in-law, Aretas, and put to flight. The couple was exiled by Roman decree to Lyons because Antipas's ambition led him to seek the title of king, an act viewed with suspicion by the emperor. From Lyons they never returned. Nicephorus recorded that in a winter accident Salome fell into water through ice that snared her neck and nearly severed the head from her body.[8]

Figure 1
Partial Family Tree of Herod the Great

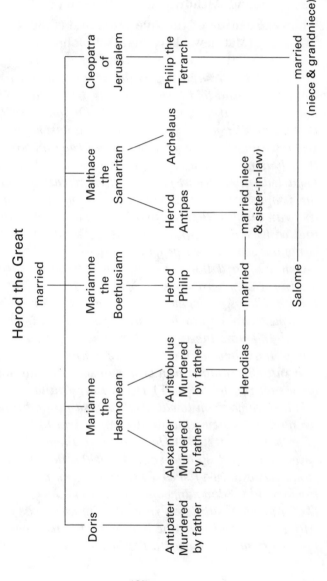

2. Second Withdrawal and Return (6:30-7:23)
a. Feeding of the five thousand (6:30-44)
(Matthew 14:15; Luke 9:10; John 6:1)

(30) And the apostles gathered themselves together unto Jesus, and told him all things, both what they had done, and what they had taught. (31) And he said unto them, Come ye yourselves apart into a desert place, and rest a while: for there were many coming and going, and they had no leisure so much as to eat. (32) And they departed into a desert place by ship privately. (33) And the people saw them departing, and many knew him, and ran afoot thither out of all cities, and outwent them, and came together unto him. (34) And Jesus, when he came out, saw much people, and was moved with compassion toward them, because they were as sheep not having a shepherd: and he began to teach them many things. (35) And when the day was now far spent, his disciples came unto him, and said, This is a desert place, and now the time is far passed: (36) send them away, that they may go into the country round about, and into the villages, and buy themselves bread: for they have nothing to eat. (37) He answered and said unto them, Give ye them to eat. And they say unto him, Shall we go and buy two hundred pennyworth of bread, and give them to eat? (38) He saith unto them, How many loaves have ye? go and see. And when they knew, they say, Five, and two fishes. (39) And he commanded them to make all sit down by companies upon the green grass. (40) And they sat down in ranks, by hundreds, and by fifties. (41) And when he had taken the five loaves and the two fishes, he looked up to heaven, and blessed, and

brake the loaves, and gave them to his disciples to set before them; and the two fishes divided he among them all. (42) And they did all eat, and were filled. (43) And they took up twelve baskets full of the fragments, and of the fishes. (44) And they that did eat of the loaves were about five thousand men.

Verses 30-31. The "apostles" (this is Mark's only use of the word) returned from their mission and came to Jesus to report all that transpired on their journey. (See Luke 10:17.) Jesus drew them aside in a "desert place" to rest, suggestive of a Sabbath rest. Because of the many people, their traveling contained no leisure, no time even for necessities, and the disciples were weary. Matthew 14:12-13 suggests that Jesus, expecting a public uprising over the murder of John, withdrew to avoid false accusations.

Verse 32. The desert place Jesus had in mind was across the lake, near Bethsaida on the northeast shore of the Sea of Galilee (Luke 9:10). Their route was from west-northwest to the east.

Verse 33. The people saw them depart, noted their direction, and surmising their destination, walked the twenty or so miles around the lake. They were waiting when Jesus and the disciples reached shore.

Verse 34. In spite of His need for rest, when Jesus saw the multitude and recognized the effort expended to reach Him, He was moved with compassion and taught them, for they were as sheep having no shepherd. (See Numbers 27:17; I Kings 22:17; Ezekiel 34:5.) The nature of sheep is one of dependence and helplessness. No animal is more at the mercy of the elements or wolves than sheep.

Verses 35-36. Jesus initially fed the people with teaching. When the day drew to a close, the people, being far from home with no food after having expended much energy in reaching Jesus, were hungry. His disciples advised Jesus to "send them away" to go into villages and buy bread.

Verse 37. Jesus instead instructed the disciples to feed them. The man of God must show hospitality. Elisha also made a similar command (II Kings 4:42).

John 6:5-6 adds details not in the Synoptics: "Whence shall we buy bread? . . . This he said to prove him: for he himself knew what he would do." Philip was chosen as spokesman because in the past he had been simple and teachable, asking straightforward yet sincere questions the others would not. Even two hundred pennyworth—a penny was the *denarion*, a Roman silver coin representing a workingman's daily wage—was far from enough to feed such a crowd.

Verse 38. Jesus asked how many loaves of bread were available. The answer was, "Five, and two fishes." John 6:9 adds the detail of "barley" loaves and "small" fishes of a boy's lunch. Barley made a poor quality bread, about a third the value of wheat bread (Revelation 6:6), the latter being the finest (Psalm 81:16). The fish served as condiment for the flat barley loaves and were probably pickled, smoked, or salted. The numbers (five and two) appear to have no special meaning.

Verse 39. "Much" green grass (John 6:10) marks the time as about April because it was a desert area and only briefly after spring rains would the grass flourish. Moreover, it was near the time for the Passover feast (John 6:4).

Verse 40. The people sat down (reclined) in ranks of fifties and hundreds, probably for order, ease of counting, and accessibility in distributing the food. Men might have been seated separately from women and children as implied by Matthew 14:21.

Verses 41-44. The Lord took the five loaves and two fishes in His hands, looked to heaven, and blessed the food in a formal return or offering of thanks for the meal. This pattern for prayer, "saying grace" as a table blessing, continues in Christian use. The usual Jewish prayer at the beginning of a meal is, "Blessed art thou, O Lord our God, King of the world, who hast brought forth bread from the earth." When Jesus broke and divided the loaves and fishes, in His hands a miracle took place.

The *modus operandi* of Christ here might have been to bless and break the bread and then fill each disciple's basket, from which he distributed to the companies. The Jews' custom was to carry with them a basket of food so they would not have to eat Gentile food and disobey the dietary laws. As each disciple gave of his store, it multiplied; at the end there still remained a full basket for each disciple.

John 6:30-34 connects this miracle with another wilderness miracle (the manna, Exodus 16) and with Christ's identity as the Bread of Life (verses 48-51). The New Testament uses feeding as a metaphor for receiving spiritual truth (John 10:9; I Corinthians 3:2; I Peter 2:2). Mark 6:34 connects Jesus' teaching with feeding: "teach them many things." Jesus is like a father who blesses the bread and distributes it to his family (His disciples, 3:34-35), who in turn give to the hungry. Jesus as the Bread of Life is the source of all spiritual gifts to satisfy those longing for spiritual bread.

Doubters of God's miraculous power have offered several flimsy explanations for this miracle. (1) The crowd, seeing the few loaves and fishes, produced their own selfishly concealed lunches. (2) The account is purely symbolic and spiritual as Christ by His own sacrifice feeds souls as a sort of Eucharist. However, this is the only miracle story recorded in all four Gospels, which marks without question its authenticity. Anything short of the truth would not be so accurately reported.

b. Walking on the water (6:45-52)
(Matthew 14:22; John 6:16)

Three Gospels include this story. Jesus left His disciples, sending them across the lake while He Himself dismissed the crowd and sought solitude for prayer. Mark 6:51-52 and John 6:25-27 imply that Jesus selected the location and timing of this miracle to connect it with the feeding of the multitude, but He was disappointed when His disciples failed to see the connection. The feeding depicts Jesus as Bread of Life, while the walking on water depicts Him as overcomer of death (Matthew 14:20-32). Both miracles reveal Him as Creator and Lord of all.

(45) And straightway he constrained his disciples to get into the ship, and to go to the other side before unto Bethsaida, while he sent away the people. (46) And when he had sent them away, he departed into a mountain to pray. (47) And when even was come, the ship was in the midst of the sea, and he alone on the land. (48) And he saw them toiling in rowing; for the wind

was contrary unto them: and about the fourth watch of the night he cometh unto them, walking upon the sea, and would have passed by them. (49) But when they saw him walking upon the sea, they supposed it had been a spirit, and cried out: (50) for they all saw him, and were troubled. And immediately he talked with them, and saith unto them, Be of good cheer: it is I; be not afraid. (51) And he went up unto them into the ship; and the wind ceased: and they were sore amazed in themselves beyond measure, and wondered. (52) For they considered not the miracle of the loaves: for their heart was hardened.

Verse 45. The exact place of this miracle cannot be confirmed. Mark places the feeding on the east shore, with the disciples departing toward Bethsaida. Two villages bore the name, one being Bethsaida Julias, east of the Jordan River and just north of where the river entered the lake. Julias was rebuilt by Philip and named in honor of Augustus's daughter. The other Bethsaida might have been a village on the lake, Khis-beh el-Araj.

Verse 46. Northeast of the Sea of Galilee the land rises abruptly into a high tableland. Into this solitude our Lord retreated to pray independently of the disciples and the crowd. Here in secret He poured out His heart in communion with God. It is noteworthy that this prayer came after ministering to the multitude by instruction and feeding. Our prayer after a message should be that what has been planted and watered will fall in fertile ground. We must realize that the demands of ministry require constant spiritual renewal.

Verses 47-51. Evening came and the winds on the sea

arose. Jesus saw the disciples "toiling" at the oars, straining to propel the ship against contrary winds from the west. This was probably no ordinary squall or storm on the sea because storms usually appeared from the north.

The fourth watch of the night means the fourth three-hour shift that began the previous evening, about three A.M. to six A.M. The Jews divided the night into three watches (Judges 7:19), the Romans, four. During longer nights the Jews adopted the Roman time division, retaining their three watches for short nights. This means that for about nine hours the disciples had rowed steadily. Since they were in the "midst of the sea," they had traversed approximately three miles.

At this point the Lord approached the weary disciples by calmly walking on the sea in spite of fierce wind and pitching waves. Skeptics comment that in the shallows filled with alluvium, Jesus could have appeared to be walking on water. Mark destroys this argument by fixing their location as the "midst of the sea." He was divinely buoyed so that any other suggestion is contrary to sound reasoning and honesty. To walk on the shore or in the shallows would generate little fear or troubling of mature men. Neither would they be "amazed . . . beyond measure" and filled with wonder.

The duration of the trial served to test their faith in God, to harden them to struggles, and to provide a greater appreciation for divine intervention when it did come. So often Christians struggle to the last watch, amid dangers and fears, against superior and uncontrollable forces, to learn patience, perseverance, and unrelenting confidence in Him.

c. Ministry of healing among the people (6:53-56)
(Matthew 14:34)

*(53) And when they had passed over, they came into
the land of Gennesaret, and drew to the shore. (54) And
when they were come out of the ship, straightway they
knew him, (55) and ran through that whole region
round about, and began to carry about in beds those that
were sick, where they heard he was. (56) And whither-
soever he entered, into villages, or cities, or country,
they laid the sick in the streets, and besought him that
they might touch if it were but the border of his garment:
and as many as touched him were made whole.*

Verse 53. The regions of Gennesaret were apparently
the object of crossing the Sea of Galilee. Gennesaret lay
on the north shore of Galilee west of Jordan, an agricul-
turally fertile plain about four miles long where tropical
as well as temperate fruit grew.

Verses 54-56. As the disciples and Jesus disembarked
from the ship the people of the region recognized Him
("had knowledge of Him," Matthew 14:35). At once they
began to run through the region gathering up the sick,
even those confined to beds, and brought them to Jesus.
In every village, city, or rural area the sick lay in the street
and path before Him, desiring at least to touch the border
of His garment. All that did so were made whole of their
sickness.

It appears that Jesus healed in two ways: by touching
the sick (Matthew 8:3, 15; 9:29; 17:7; 20:34; Mark 1:41; 7:33;
Luke 5:13; 7:14; 22:51), and also by allowing the sick to
touch Him or His clothing (Matthew 9:21; 14:36; Mark

3:10; 5:28; 6:56; Luke 6:19). The two techniques appear about an equal number of times in the Synoptics. The fame of Jesus is evident in this incident since He was immediately recognized. The faith of the people is also evident in that they took advantage of His presence to heal their sick.

The hem (Greek *kraspedon*, Matthew 9:20, 14:36, 23:5; Luke 8:44), a woolen tassel or fringe was required at each corner of the outermost garment (Numbers 15:38-41; Deuteronomy 22:12). At least one thread of the twisted tassels was to be blue as a reminder to keep the holy commandments. Religious leaders of that day believed these tassels conferred special sanctity and were rebuked for efforts to enlarge them (Matthew 23:5).

In no instance did Jesus ever deny Himself to those whom He came to seek and save. This contact, initiated by physical need for healing, demonstrated that regardless of the nature of sickness, who brought them, how many came, or any other characteristic, the power of Christ to heal was unlimited. This incident stands in sharp contrast to Matthew 13:58 when "he did not many mighty works there because of their unbelief." Whenever people responded in faith by bringing the sick, diseased, and infirm, Christ met the need and healed them.

d. Controversy concerning defilement (7:1-23)

Chapter 7 of Mark's Gospel opens with an interaction between hypocritical Pharisees and scribes and Jesus. The dispute centered around the washing of hands practiced by the Pharisees according to a well-developed tradition. Jesus showed that their religious practices were vain, they denied Moses, they refused to support their parents, and they allowed tradition to render the Word ineffective.

In verses 14-23 Jesus explained the true source of defilement as inward, naming thirteen specific defilements. There followed a withdrawal in which a Syrophoenician woman appealed to Jesus for healing and persisted until she received "out of due season." The chapter closes with the healing of a deaf and dumb man and the testimony of Christ: "He hath done all things well."

(1) Condemnation of human tradition (7:1-13)
(Matthew 15:1)

(1) Then came together unto him the Pharisees, and certain of the scribes, which came from Jerusalem. (2) And when they saw some of his disciples eat bread with defiled, that is to say, with unwashen, hands, they found fault. (3) For the Pharisees, and all the Jews, except they wash their hands oft, eat not, holding the tradition of the elders. (4) And when they come from the market, except they wash, they eat not. And many other things there be, which they have received to hold, as the washing of cups, and pots, brasen vessels, and of tables. (5) Then the Pharisees and scribes asked him, Why walk not thy disciples according to the tradition of the elders, but eat bread with unwashen hands? (6) He answered and said unto them, Well hath Esaias prophesied of you hypocrites, as it is written, This people honoureth me with their lips, but their heart is far from me. (7) Howbeit in vain do they worship me, teaching for doctrines

the commandments of men. (8) For laying aside the commandment of God, ye hold the tradition of men, as the washing of pots and cups: and many other such like things ye do. (9) And he said unto them, Full well ye reject the commandment of God, that ye may keep your own tradition. (10) For Moses said, Honour thy father and thy mother; and, Whoso curseth father or mother, let him die the death. (11) But ye say, If a man shall say to his father or mother, It is Corban, that is to say, a gift, by whatsoever thou mightest be profited by me; he shall be free. (12) And ye suffer him no more to do ought for his father or his mother; (13) making the word of God of none effect through your tradition, which ye have delivered: and many such like things do ye.

Verses 1-2. Certain Pharisees and scribes came to Jesus from Jerusalem, perhaps seeking occasion against Him even at the peak of His popularity. They soon found reason to criticize: violation of their outward ceremonial washings of the hands before and during courses of eating a meal. It is probable that the disciples did initially wash their hands before eating but not according to the tradition of the elders and certainly not in the manner approved by the religious leaders.

Verses 3-4. The term rendered "oft" meant to wash with the fist closed, vigorously rubbing the closed hand in the palm of the other while dipping in water continuously, then pouring clean water over the hands while holding the fingers pointed downward to allow the water to run off the fingertips. This was done to avoid the attacks of a demon called *shibta*. To eat with unwashed hands was to be unclean in the sight of God and did not necessarily infer rudeness or unsanitary practice.

These elaborate rules and detailed instructions came not from the Decalogue or even the Pentateuch with its many regulations, but from the scribes, that class of legal experts who arose in the fifth and fourth centuries before Christ. They amplified, expanded, and made into numerous injunctions the moral principles of the law. Their interpretations became known as oral law, or the tradition of the elders (ancients such as Hillel and Shammai). The oral law was later summarized in writing as the Mishnah.

The Jews practiced ablution (washing) before eating, after a market visit, and when washing cups, bowls, pots, and vessels. They even cleansed the couches or beds on which they reclined while dining (verse 4).

In these verses Mark lets the Gentiles know something of the extent of Jewish religion concerning uncleanness. Vessels could be clean from a hygienic standpoint, yet be ceremonially unclean. Uncleanness resulted from contact with an unclean person, a Gentile, or unclean food or water. Also, a hollow pottery vessel could become unclean inside but not outside. A flat rimless plate could not become unclean; however, a plate with a rim could. Hollow vessels of leather or glass could become unclean inside and outside. Unclean earthen vessels were destroyed by breaking; other vessels could be immersed, boiled, purged with fire, and if metal, polished.[9] To the Pharisees and scribes such regulations were the essence of religion and necessary to please God. Not so with Jesus; hence, the conflict.

Verses 5-9. The question asked of Jesus here was why did the disciples not follow the tradition of the elders but ate bread with unwashed hands. Jesus, taking advantage of the teachable moment, placed two charges before these legalists. He pointed out that Isaiah 29:13 prophesied their hypocritical behavior of substituting insincere honor with the lips for cleanness of the heart or inner person. Jesus accused them of hypocrisy in religion because they obeyed external legalities of traditional rituals and professed to be holy while completely disregarding the condition of the heart and conscience.

Why wash cups when the heart was filled with envy, hate, bitterness, or pride? Such hypocrisy and legalism never failed to adhere meticulously to human traditions but always disregarded God in the inward parts. Goodness, purity, and sanctity were often identified with religious acts to the exclusion of heart change, true repentance, and faith toward God. No amount of church attendance, careful stewardship, Bible study, prayer, or fasting can make holy an unpenitent legalist who harbors pride, grudges, or envy in the heart.

Verses 10-13. Jesus next used an example from Moses (whose written word is called the Word of God in verse 13) to expose their rationalization about not obeying the voice of God. It appears that they equated true religion not with obedience to the Word of God but with clever arguments, twisting of meanings, and splitting of hairs to avoid doing what the Word commanded, thereby nullifying the command of God in order to follow their own traditions.

The Hebrew term *corban* in the Old Testament meant an offering or gift "brought near." It was a sacrifice, bloody or not, offered to God (Leviticus 1:2-3; 2:1; 3:1; Numbers 7:12-17). By New Testament times the meaning had been extended to refer to money and resources given to God or directed toward a sacred destiny and, therefore, not available for personal use.

The Jews often used *corban* as a rash vow that they had no intent to keep. The Pharisees, many of whom were priests, used the term as license to lay claim on what was offered to God and to keep it for themselves. Christ's example here shows that the Jews used the practice of pronouncing something *corban* to neatly sidestep the requirement of Moses to honor their father and mother according to the Fifth Commandment. Parents in need were ignored and made to suffer because their children had declared their possessions *corban*, that is, dedicated to God, and hence not allowed to be used to help parents. Jesus made it plain that this behavior nullified the intent of the Word of God. The final statement of verse 13 says that the Jews did "many such like things."

(2) Source of true defilement (7:14-23)
(Matthew 15:10; cf. Galatians 5:19)

(14) And when he had called all the people unto him, he said unto them, Hearken unto me every one of you, and understand: (15) There is nothing from without a man, that entering into him can defile him: but the things which come out of him, those are they that defile the man. (16) If any man have ears to hear, let him hear. (17) And when he was entered into the house from the people, his disciples asked him concerning the parable. (18) And he saith unto them, Are ye so without under- standing also? Do ye not perceive, that whatsoever thing from without entereth into the man, it cannot defile

149

him; (19) because it entereth not into his heart, but into the belly, and goeth out into the draught, purging all meats? (20) And he said, That which cometh out of the man, that defileth the man. (21) For from within, out of the heart of men, proceed evil thoughts, adulteries, fornications, murders, (22) thefts, covetousness, wickedness, deceit, lasciviousness, an evil eye, blasphemy, pride, foolishness: (23) all these evil things come from within, and defile the man.

Verse 14. Jesus, sensing the need to clarify His position before the people, called the multitude to Him and explained this most profound teaching. He had just denounced the Jewish tradition of elaborate washings to avoid uncleanness and also the strict adherence to man-made custom as counterproductive to the law of God. Now He proclaimed a most startling and unbelievable truth, which He took pains to make them understand. So He gave a parable.

Verse 15. Jesus spoke a principle of great significance to remove the teaching of the law from traditional changes to which it had been subjected and thus to clarify the difference between external and internal holiness. Impurity sprang from the heart, not from disregard of scribe-imposed rituals. Unless the heart was penitent all washing was without benefit. The things that issued forth from within a person, whether he was washed or unwashed externally, defiled the person.

Verse 16. To emphasize, Christ used the phrase "If any man have ears to hear, let him hear." This phrase occurs fifteen times in the New Testament; here it is a marginal note in the Revised Version.

Verse 17. In spite of His effort to clarify, Christ's statement apparently was too radical to be accepted and believed by the Jews, including His disciples. The laws laid down in Leviticus made strong distinctions between clean and unclean animals, meat, practices, and people. What a person ate, touched, and handled did, under the law, render him ceremonially unclean. Daniel, the Hebrews in Babylon, and all pious Jews avoided defilement by refusing to partake of unclean foods. Privately and inside the house, His disciples (Matthew specifically identifies Peter) called for an explanation of the parable.

Verses 18-20. Jesus explained that things cannot, of themselves, be morally defiled; only people who handled or touched or ate the things. On the matter of eating, He pointed out the difference between the inward nature of a person and the digestive system, which receives food, digests it, extracts and absorbs nourishment, and then eliminates the excess waste in the "draught" (place for body waste; a sewer). The action of the digestive system purges, or makes clean, all foods. The real defilement of a person comes from the vile nature of the heart, which gives rise to evil actions.

Verses 21-23. In Scripture the heart means the mind and will, often equated to the soul. The heart, then, is to be more carefully tended, guarded, instructed, and purged than the hands that the Pharisees so meticulously cleansed. When the heart is pure and clean, the life will be clean and good. Jesus described what can issue forth from the corrupt heart as defilement.

1. *Evil thoughts.* Greek *kakos*; an inherently evil thing; and *dialogismos*; designs of reason, imaginations, or

doubting thoughts that produce mental rebellion and result in evil actions and disputes. (See Luke 9:46; Romans 1:21; I Timothy 2:8; Philippians 2:14.)

2. *Adulteries.* Greek *moicheia*; an unlawful sexual relationship between men and women, whether single or married, that is repeated. In Matthew 5:28 Jesus equated commission of this sin with lust of the eye and lust of the flesh.

3. *Fornications.* Greek *porneia*; a broad term used of adultery (Matthew 5:32), incest (I Corinthians 5:1, 10), idolatry (II Chronicles 21:11; Isaiah 23:17; Acts 15:20, 29), harlotry (I Corinthians 6:13-18), sodomy and male prostitution (I Corinthians 6:9-11; Hebrews 12:16; Jude 6-7; Romans 1:24-29). It can mean all forms of sexual impurity.

4. *Murders.* Greek *phonos*; slaughters; from a verb meaning to kill or destroy. (See Romans 1:29; Acts 9:1; Revelation 9:21.)

5. *Thefts.* Greek *klope*; stealing. Two words are used for a thief or robber: (1) *Hester* is a brigand, outlaw or highwayman who robs by force. Barabbas was such a one (John 18:40). (2) *Kleptes* is a deceitful thief, a sneak, or an embezzler. Judas kept the bag and evidently removed from its contents (John 12:6).

6. *Covetousness.* Greek *pleonexia*; to have more; the love of having, or desiring what is not right to take; literally, having an appetite for what belongs to another. It is a lust for power, luxury, money, or material things. To the covetous, happiness is in things instead of in God.

7. *Wickedness.* Greek *poneria*; malice, referring to a person or thing that is evil in its action; one who desires to do harm to others and to in turn make them bad also.

8. *Deceit.* Greek *dolos*; guile, craftiness, cunning, treachery to deceive.

9. *Lasciviousness.* Greek *aselgeia*; a wanton wickedness with no restraint of shame, disgrace, or discipline. It is sinfulness without qualm or remorse.

10. *An evil eye.* Greek *poneros ophthalmos*; an idiom referring to envy of another's success or happiness and a desire that it would be destroyed.

11. *Blasphemy.* Greek *blasphemia*; when exercised against man, it is slander; when exercised against God, it is blasphemy, insulting God.

12. *Pride.* Greek *huperephania*; an attitude of superiority; to be above others. This may be an inward feeling that is not made public.

13. *Foolishness.* Greek *aphrosune*; moral folly; not a lack of understanding or knowledge but a disregard for consequences that causes one to do a foolish or foolhardy thing.

We are admonished to keep the heart with all diligence, for out of it are the issues of life (Proverbs 4:23). Defilement occurs when we allow the thoughts and innermost secrets of the mind to incubate, fester, and erupt in acts of envy, malice, slander, fraud, indecency, arrogance, or folly.

3. Third Withdrawal and Return (7:24-8:13)
a. Appeal of the Syrophoenician woman (7:24-30)
(Matthew 15:21)

(24) And from thence he arose, and went into the borders of Tyre and Sidon, and entered into an house, and

*would have no man know it: but he could not be hid.
(25) For a certain woman, whose young daughter had
an unclean spirit, heard of him, and came and fell at his
feet: (26) the woman was a Greek, a Syrophenician by
nation; and she besought him that he would cast forth
the devil out of her daughter. (27) But Jesus said unto
her, Let the children first be filled: for it is not meet to
take the children's bread, and to cast it unto the dogs.
(28) And she answered and said unto him, Yes, Lord:
yet the dogs under the table eat of the children's crumbs.
(29) And he said unto her, For this saying go thy way;
the devil is gone out of thy daughter. (30) And when she
was come to her house, she found the devil gone out, and
her daughter laid upon the bed.*

Verses 24-26. Jesus left the house and traveled along
the coastal plain into the Gentile territory of Phoenicia,
north of Carmel. It appears that He sought seclusion but
was unable to find it even in this territory. At Tyre, a
coastal city of Phoenicia about forty miles north of Capernaum, a Greek Syrophoenician woman found Him and
revealed her need. He might escape publicity and crowds
but never the importunity of human need. The woman's
daughter had an unclean spirit; for this cause the woman
flung herself at His feet, pleading for Him to cast out the
demon.

Verse 27. In Jesus' response, "meet" from the Greek
kalos means right, good, or proper. Jews were the children and first recipients of the benefits of salvation, healing, and deliverance from satanic oppression. Jesus
meant that Gentiles could not come before Jews in receiving kingdom benefits.

To call a person a dog was dishonor. To the Greeks "dog" meant a shameless and aggressive woman; to the Hebrews it could mean a contemptuous person, a male prostitute, or a Gentile. What is holy should not be given to dogs (Matthew 7:6; Philippians 3:2; Revelation 22:15). However, the word Jesus used for "dog" was *kunarion,* or little dog, puppy, or lap dog. This word was not meant to be offensive but reflected the common use of the term of that day.

Verses 28-29. The woman acknowledged and accepted her position but responded by noting in repartee that Jesus said "first." She then referred to a custom of wiping the hands not on napkins but on pieces of bread, which were then thrown to the house dogs. Jesus, pleased by her remark, declared her faith to be great (a statement made only twice; see Matthew 8:10-13; 15:28), and that the girl was freed from the demon.

Was it coincidence that Christ, upon completing the discourse with the Pharisees about partaking of clean and unclean, would go out of Jewish territory and give children's bread to an "unclean" Gentile? More probably, He made this excursion and healing a symbol of what would come to Gentiles through the disciples.

Finally, it was significant that the Gentiles seized what the Jews failed to retain and threw away. This Syrophoenician woman with faith so bold laid claim symbolically to what the Jews rejected—unmerited children's bread given to one out of season.

It is of interest to note the contrast between Jesus, who sought solitude and anonymity, and the religious leaders of then—and now—who so often strive for recognition and acclaim.

b. Cure of the deaf stammerer (7:31-37)
(cf. Matthew 15:29)

(31) And again, departing from the coasts of Tyre and Sidon, he came unto the sea of Galilee, through the midst of the coasts of Decapolis. (32) And they bring unto him one that was deaf, and had an impediment in his speech; and they beseech him to put his hand upon him. (33) And he took him aside from the multitude, and put his fingers into his ears, and he spit, and touched his tongue; (34) and looking up to heaven, he sighed, and saith unto him, Ephphatha, that is, Be opened. (35) And straightway his ears were opened, and the string of his tongue was loosed, and he spake plain. (36) And he charged them that they should tell no man: but the more he charged them, so much the more a great deal they published it; (37) and were beyond measure astonished, saying, He hath done all things well: he maketh both the deaf to hear, and the dumb to speak.

Verse 31. Jesus departed from the Phoenician coastal cities of Tyre and Sidon and traveled southward to the Sea of Galilee through Decapolis, the region of ten Gentile cities. Although the action appears to immediately follow the exchange with the Syrophoenician woman, it is more likely that Jesus went north to Sidon before turning south, a journey that might entail as much as eight months. During the journey Jesus had time to instruct His disciples before Jewish opposition mounted. Shortly afterward, Peter declared that Jesus was the Christ (Mark 8:27-29).

Verse 32. As Jesus came into Decapolis He was brought a man who was deaf and had a speech impediment. As is often the case, inability to hear results in inability to speak, there being no reference for proper language utterance without auditory refinement.

Verse 33. Jesus went through an extraordinary sequence of events in healing this individual. First, Jesus took him aside privately, perhaps to better allow the individual to concentrate his attention. A lesson in sign communication followed. When Jesus put His fingers into the man's ears He communicated clearly and without undue embarrassment to the man what He was about to do. Sound traveling as energy waves through the air are transferred via the external auditory meatus (canal) to the eardrum, then through the tiny inner ear bones to the large cranial nerve, where sound is converted to neural impulses to be interpreted by the cortex of the brain. Jesus would repair whatever was wrong with the man's ears so that he could process sound in the normal manner.

Jesus then took saliva from His own mouth and touched it to the dumb man's tongue, another tender action meant to communicate faith and inform the man of what He intended to do. Among the Jews, the spittle of a fasting holy man was reputed to have curative properties.

Verses 34-35. Jesus' upward look told the deaf man the source of blessing he would receive. He spoke an Aramaic word to the man with a sigh or groan. On this command the ears opened and the string (band or chain) of the tongue loosened.

With great concern and dignity Jesus dealt with this individual, not merely as one wanting healing but as a handicapped human being in need of tenderness, consideration, and understanding.

Verses 36-37. Jesus charged the witnesses to refrain from telling the miracle; however, reverse psychology prevailed. The result was astonishment beyond measure as the people declared, "He has done all things well."

c. Feeding of the four thousand (8:1-10)
(Matthew 15:32)

(1) In those days the multitude being very great, and having nothing to eat, Jesus called his disciples unto him, and saith unto them, (2) I have compassion on the multitude, because they have now been with me three days, and have nothing to eat: (3) and if I send them away fasting to their own houses, they will faint by the way: for divers of them came from far. (4) And his disciples answered him, From whence can a man satisfy these men with bread here in the wilderness? (5) And he asked them, How many loaves have ye? And they said, Seven. (6) And he commanded the people to sit down on the ground: and he took the seven loaves, and gave thanks, and brake, and gave to his disciples to set before them; and they did set them before the people. (7) And they had a few small fishes: and he blessed, and commanded to set them also before them. (8) So they did eat, and were filled: and they took up of the broken meat that was left seven baskets. (9) And they that had eaten were about four thousand: and he sent them away. (10) And straightway he entered into a ship with his disciples, and came into the parts of Dalmanutha.

Verses 1-2. "Multitude" implies a large number of persons, given as four thousand (verse 9). For such a large group to assemble, Jesus must have remained on the northeast side of Galilee in Decapolis for some time. A better rendering would be "when there was again a great crowd." The story of the healing the deaf and dumb man (7:31-37) might have drawn many to Christ, as also might have the testimony of the demoniac of Gadara (5:1-20).

The large multitude listened to Jesus with such zealous intensity that His words were greater than food. Undoubtedly, Jesus Himself took little rest or food. After three days the demands of the flesh reasserted themselves, and Jesus looked on His audience with compassion. His first consideration and instinct was to help, to be of service. "Compassion" is used nine times to express the inner feelings of Christ when confronted with distress and misery in human beings (Matthew 9:36; 14:14; 15:32; 20:34; Mark 1:41; 5:19; 6:34; 8:2; Luke 7:13).

Verses 3-4. To send them away fasting and thus avoid involvement and trouble would be the expected human thing to do under these circumstances. The practical difficulty of providing food in a desert place for so many is by human reason insurmountable. In this case it only provided background for the greatness of the miracle that happened. The disciples appeared appalled that Christ would not send them away, although they should have remembered the previous feeding (6:34-44).

Verses 5-7. Jesus asked, "How many loaves do you have?" In other words, "How can you help?" We cannot escape our responsibility to help others by noting the obstacles. Circumstances are never perfect for one to be of service, but every person of a willing mind must help with what he has (II Corinthians 8:12). Seven loaves and a few small fishes were procured, perhaps an unused provision for Christ and His disciples laid by for the frequent excursions into remote places.

Taking charge of the meal, Jesus first commanded the people to sit—actually recline—on the ground in expectation of food. He took the loaves, gave thanks to the Father, and broke the bread for the disciples to distribute. (Customarily, bread baked in hard cakes was broken, rather than cut, to be divided.) He then did the same with the fish. It is always appropriate to give thanks and especially proper at mealtime. Dining together ties fellowship, food, and the flesh to a divine Benefactor and helps people realize the extent of provision of the Father.

Verses 8-9. When the crowd was fed and out of danger of fainting on the way home, Christ sent them away. Of seven loaves there came seven baskets of broken food.

We should not confuse this miracle of feeding with the previous one recorded in Mark 6. The differences are numerous, including the number fed, time of day, locale, season, resources available, and leftovers.

The Lord Himself testified to the two different instances in Mark 8:19-20 by drawing specific details from the memory of the disciples. Thus two separate instances of miraculous feeding occurred. There remains only the question of why two such similar instances.

The evidence here suggests that Jesus continued among the Gentiles what began with the Syrophoenician woman. The miracle occurred in Decapolis, with its Gentile populace. In the feeding of the five thousand, the Greek word *kophinos* translated "basket" refers to a pot-shaped, wide-bottom, narrow-neck basket used by Jews to carry food so they could be sure it was not unclean. Such a basket would hold up to about two gallons. By contrast, the word *sphuris* used for basket in Mark 8:8 denotes a large, open basket used by the Gentiles, similar to a hamper or clothes basket. These baskets were large enough to hold a man. Paul was let down from a window in one (Acts 9:25; II Corinthians 11:33). In sum, Christ's message in this second feeding miracle seems to be that God is God of Gentiles as well as Jews.

Matthew, writing to Jews, recorded both; Mark also recorded both, but Luke and John record only the feeding of the five thousand. In the instance of the five thousand, twelve Jewish baskets were left over, enough for each disciple. In the feeding of four thousand, seven Gentile baskets (much larger and more voluminous) remained, as many baskets as there were loaves. That far more food remained after all had eaten than the original supply would not escape the disciples' notice. God is never limited, even with meager resources provided for His use.

Verse 10. Jesus entered the ship (boat) and crossed the sea to the midwestern shore at Dalmanutha, or Magdala (Matthew 15:39). This was another of several frequent crossings of the Sea of Galilee made by Jesus (verse 13) to provide access to the Jews of Naphtali and Zebulun on the other side (Isaiah 9:1-2).

d. Request for a sign from heaven (8:11-13)
(Matthew 16:1)

(11) And the Pharisees came forth, and began to question with him, seeking of him a sign from heaven, tempting him. (12) And he sighed deeply in his spirit, and saith, Why doth this generation seek after a sign? verily I say unto you, There shall no sign be given unto

*this generation. (13) And he left them, and entering into
the ship again departed to the other side.*

Verses 11-12. Although the desire for signs in a skeptical age seems reasonable enough, there is more behind this request. The Jews sought a Messiah who would promise and do great and shattering miracles reminiscent of the fall of Jericho or the parting of the Jordan. False Messiahs made bold promises and people flocked to them. Jesus refused to be drawn into cheap claims or displays, especially when to Him the whole world spoke loudly of God. The Pharisees looked for God in the abnormal rather than the normal. The Sadducees, who did not believe in miracles, did not expect to see God anywhere in any sign.

The request of the Pharisees was particularly revolting to Jesus for two reasons. First, it was meant to tempt Him. Temptations arise from Satan (Matthew 4:3), self-lusts (James 1:13-15), and people, as in this case. Second, the question and request to see a sign "from heaven" insinuated that all miracles and signs worked by Jesus previously were not "from heaven" but from the devil.

In the face of such unbelief and challenge Jesus was visibly grieved. He sighed deeply, expressing grief and pity and indignation at such gross blindness. In response He used a Jewish idiom to state that the questioners ("this generation") would receive no signs.

The demand was for demonstrative proof of divine authority. Jesus had already resisted theatrical showmanship (Matthew 4:7; Luke 4:12). His previous miracles carried sufficient power and presence of God to convince all but the most hardened unbelievers.

Jesus' response was not in opposition to signs accompanying the work of His gospel; rather, He opposed signs for the sake of signs and human display. Disciples believe and signs follow (Mark 16:16-17). Moreover, signs in themselves never guarantee God's presence. The desire for external proof of God without submission of the heart by faith marked these religious leaders. Jesus, knowing what was in them, refused to commit Himself to them. (See John 2:24-25.)

4. Fourth Withdrawal and Return (8:14-9:50)
a. Warning concerning leaven (8:14-21)
(Matthew 16:6)

(14) Now the disciples had forgotten to take bread, neither had they in the ship with them more than one loaf. (15) And he charged them, saying, Take heed, beware of the leaven of the Pharisees, and of the leaven of Herod. (16) And they reasoned among themselves, saying, It is because we have no bread. (17) And when Jesus knew it, he saith unto them, Why reason ye, because ye have no bread? perceive ye not yet, neither understand? have ye your heart yet hardened? (18) Having eyes, see ye not? and having ears, hear ye not? and do ye not remember? (19) When I brake the five loaves among five thousand, how many baskets full of fragments took ye up? They say unto him, Twelve. (20) And when the seven among four thousand, how many baskets full of fragments took ye up? And they said, Seven. (21) And he said unto them, How is it that ye do not understand?

163

Verses 14-15. This section begins the fourth withdrawal of Jesus from among the Jews, and again it takes Him across the lake to the Galileans in Naphtali and Zebulun. While crossing the lake (an estimated six-hour journey), the disciples discovered they had forgotten to bring bread or to eat before departing, and had only one loaf. Their thoughts were thus preoccupied, but Jesus still mused on the conflict with the Pharisees and the impact His signs had on Herod. To this end He voiced a warning using the term "leaven" in the proverbial sense of doctrine.

Leaven means yeast or yeast-bearing dough placed in bread to make it rise. Yeast is a unicellular microorganism that respires anaerobically to metabolize sugars in a fermentation process. The byproducts of fermentation are ethanol and carbon dioxide gas, which bubbles, causing the dough to rise. Baking the bread vaporizes both the gas and ethanol. Only a few yeast cells are necessary to begin the process, and because cell reproduction is rapid, the entire lump of dough is quickly affected.

To a Jew leaven denoted something tiny that produced spectacular results. It could represent good—for example, the kingdom of God as it penetrates the earth from a small beginning (Matthew 13:33; Luke 13:20-21). A second meaning was symbolic of evil influence. Leavening meant decay, putrefaction, the original sin of human nature. Spiritually, leaven meant doctrine, and Jesus' words conveyed this meaning.

Leaven of the Pharisees could mean their legalistic and unrealistic demands of ceremonialism that obscured true inner sanctification. Leaven of Herod might mean Jewish nationalism (Mark 3:6; 12:13). A third meaning of Jesus' words is more likely. Both Herod and the Pharisees sought to establish an earthly kingdom over which the Jews and their Messiah would rule. Their hypocrisy and ambition Jesus classified as leaven, an influence that easily spread to the detriment of the mass.

Verses 16-18. The disciples misunderstood the comment and among themselves sought to fix the responsibility for not having bread. Jesus in turn appealed to their reason and senses, from which they had yet gained no understanding. With eyes to see and ears to hear and a mind to remember, how could they draw such a conclusion?

Verses 19-21. Jesus reminded them of the miraculous feeding of two great multitudes and questioned them about the leftover fragments. Surely now their dull minds could comprehend that bread or lack thereof was of little concern to Jesus. Matthew 16:12 states that then they understood that He told them to beware not of leaven in bread but of the doctrine of the Pharisees and Sadducees.

b. Blind man at Bethsaida (8:22-26)

(22) And he cometh to Bethsaida; and they bring a blind man unto him, and besought him to touch him. (23) And he took the blind man by the hand, and led him out of the town; and when he had spit on his eyes, and put his hands upon him, he asked him if he saw ought. (24) And he looked up, and said, I see men as trees, walking. (25) After that he put his hands again upon his eyes, and made him look up: and he was restored, and saw every man clearly. (26) And he sent him away to his house, saying, Neither go into the town, nor tell it to any in the town.

165

Verse 22. The disciples and Jesus came to Bethsaida. Again as in Mark 6:45, two choices are possible: Bethsaida Julias in the tetrarchy of Philip or the Galilean Bethsaida cursed by Jesus (Matthew 11:21). Verse 27 suggests the former since Bethsaida Julias was near Caesarea Philippi. Evidence for the Galilean Bethsaida may be inferred from the behavior and instructions of Jesus in taking the blind man from the cursed town before healing him and forbidding him to reenter the town or tell the townsfolk (verses 23, 26). However, the more direct evidence suggests Bethsaida Julias, and other reasons can be provided for Jesus' behavior.

Only Mark relates this incident. Blindness was common in the Middle East due to ophthalmia (eye inflammation) from bright glaring sun and generally poor eye care and hygiene. Conjunctivitis and matter-encrusted eyes were not uncommon as insects transmitted pathogens from person to person. Such an individual was brought to Jesus to be touched, apparently having faith that contact with the divine healer would effect a cure.

Verses 23-26. With tender kindness Jesus led the man out of town away from the crowds where they might concentrate intensely, pray earnestly, and avoid human praise and vain glory. He may have also taken the man aside to avoid embarrassment. Regardless of the reason, Jesus, using methods and techniques the man could understand, gently allowed him to enter the world of the visible.

This is the only recorded miracle performed in two steps or by degrees. All other miracles of Jesus were sudden and complete with no need for a second touch. The reason is not obvious. It is reminiscent of gradual growth in life—children are instructed by degrees, sinners are led to God in gradual steps, sanctification proceeds in orderly fashion to perfection. Any other way would overwhelm individuals. Jesus was certainly not limited to a particular method or technique but dealt with each person as unique and as he was ready to receive. No one receives full vision of God at once.

c. Confession of Peter (8:27-30)
(Matthew 16:13; Luke 9:18; cf. John 6:67)

(27) And Jesus went out, and his disciples, into the towns of Caesarea Philippi: and by the way he asked his disciples, saying unto them, Whom do men say that I am? (28) And they answered, John the Baptist: but some say Elias; and others, One of the prophets. (29) And he saith unto them, But whom say ye that I am? And Peter answereth and saith unto him, Thou art the Christ. (30) And he charged them that they should tell no man of him.

This short passage is laden with meaning and intense, poignant prophecy. Who was Jesus? Proper identity must be established in the minds and hearts of the disciples once and for all if His work was to be accomplished. The time was about halfway through Jesus' ministry, the opposition was gathering momentum, Calvary was looming, but did the disciples truly understand who He was and the intent of His mission?

Verses 27-28. Jesus chose a peculiar site to seek their knowledge of His identity. Caesarea Philippi, in the shadow of idolatrous relationships, became the site of the revelation of the one true God in flesh. Originally called Dan

167

(Genesis 14:14), or Laish (Judges 18:7), Caesarea Philippi marked the place where two streams (Jeor and Dan) flowed together to form the Jordan River. Named Paneas by Gentiles after Pan, the god of shepherds and Greek god of nature, the city was also known as Balinas, where Baal was worshiped and more recently where Herod had built a temple to Caesar, an emperor regarded as a god. Here it would be safe to discuss His Messiahship free of Judean opponents' accusation of usurping Roman authority.

In order to realize the full import of the question of His identity one must know something about the myriad of ideas held by the Jews about Messiah. Many of these ideas arose during the period between Malachi and Mark, the intertestamental period.

Many of the Jews believed that their Messiah would be a king of the house of David. As a divine king, He would usher in a reign of righteousness and power (Isaiah 9:7; 11:1-2; Jeremiah 22:4; 23:5; 30:9). These hopes had taken a severe beating by the cruelties of reality: ten tribes of Israel had been swallowed by the Assyrians; Jerusalem was destroyed by Babylon, who overran Judah; and the captive Judeans had fallen in succession to the Persians, Greeks, and Romans. Instead of ruling, the Jews for centuries had been subjects, and there appeared little hope of breaking Rome's iron yoke. The Jews began to look for a God-sent leader to perform supernatural feats impossible by natural means. Writings of the period preceding the birth of Christ reflect longing for a new age of divine intervention.

Their Messiah would be preceded by a time of terrible tribulation, terror, moral chaos, and political confusion. A forerunner or herald thought to be Elijah would first appear to bring order, heal disputes, and prepare men's hearts to receive Messiah. Because of this belief, many unsettled disputes awaited Elijah. Messiah, Hebrew for "the Anointed One" (Christ is the Greek equivalent), would come in supernatural power, anointed by God, and would deliver God's true followers, the Jews.

Hostile nations would arise against Him but to no avail since their armies would be shattered by the Messiah. Jerusalem would be rebuilt and the dispersion from around the world welcomed to a New Jerusalem. Palestine would reign as the center of the world kingdom from which all enemy Gentiles would be punished. A renovated world would then enjoy endless ages of peace and tranquility because of His reign "there shall be no end" (Isaiah 9:7; Luke 1:33).

These ideas called for violent, nationalistic, vengeful, and bloody conquest, and Jesus had to eradicate such a notion from the minds of the disciples. He had the massive task of reeducating hard, fierce men to accept a conquest of gentleness, kindness, love, and peace. To the Jews of His day, Jesus was most unlike what they desired and hoped for in a Messiah.

How did the multitude view His identity? The common people knew that prophecy had ceased, and therefore many viewed Jesus as one of the old prophets such as Elijah or Jeremiah (Matthew 16:14). Herod himself entertained the idea that Jesus was John the Baptist returned, perhaps following the false notion of transmigration of souls proposed by Pythagoreas. Few if any believed Jesus was the Messiah since He lived in poverty, humility, and not at all regally. The characteristics of the ancients rested upon Him—the tender compassion of Jeremiah and the forceful power of the Elijah that Malachi predicted would return (Malachi 4:5).

It is clear that the Jews confused the first and second advent of Christ: His first coming to seek and save, then after the age of the church, coming to reign in power.

Verse 29. By asking the same question of the disciples, Jesus forced them to think beyond and search for a better answer than the masses had given. Since they had beheld His miracles and authority, partaken of His lifestyle, and heard His doctrine, their witness of His identity was far more critical than others. These who would carry His message after the Ascension must come to an unshakable conclusion about Him.

Peter was the spokesman: "Thou are the Christ." Matthew 16:16-19 adds more detail, but Mark, a record of Peter's own experiences, modestly omits any mention of the great blessing received for this confession. Matthew notes a fourfold blessing associated with knowing Christ: (1) revelation from the Father; (2) name changed from Simon to Petros (Peter), a fragment of rock; (3) a prophetic statement of a prevailing church to be built on the revelation of Christ, and (4) receipt of the "keys of the kingdom," a symbol of authority to loose and bind on earth as God's representative. Matthew also notes that Peter called Jesus "the Son of the living God," which in the fullest sense means that Jesus was actually God manifested in the flesh.

Verse 30. Jesus undoubtedly was pleased at the expression of Peter and the disciples but charged them to tell no one. Reasons for continued secrecy seem to stem from the general political relationship with the Palestinian sects who, if they knew, would want to make Him a king by force, or would use His proclamation to destroy Him before His time.

d. Announcement concerning the cross (8:31-9:1)

Jesus' announcement concerning His passion marks the third phase of His ministry: suffering, rejection, and death.

(1) Coming passion foretold (8:31-32a)
(Matthew 16:21)

(31) And he began to teach them, that the Son of man must suffer many things, and be rejected of the elders, and of the chief priests, and scribes, and be killed, and after three days rise again. (32a) And he spake that saying openly.

Verses 31-32a. With the Messiahship and deity of Christ established, He began to instruct the disciples of the coming passion, death, and resurrection. Faith demands a firm conviction of both the deity and humanity of Christ for the work of salvation through death, burial, and resurrection. Jesus' instruction included coming suffering, rejection, death, and after three days, resurrection. Thus He unveiled for them "openly" what was about to transpire.

(2) Rebuke to Peter (8:32b-33)
(Matthew 16:22)

(32b) And Peter took him, and began to rebuke him.

(33) But when he had turned about and looked on his disciples, he rebuked Peter, saying, Get thee behind me, Satan: for thou savourest not the things that be of God, but the things that be of men.

Verse 32b. Peter, who shortly before declared Him to be Messiah, now took Jesus aside and privately rebuked Him. The fisherman could not grasp how a Messiah could prevail and yet be so maligned and killed; his recourse was to deny and disallow any such happening.

Verse 33. Jesus turned about to the disciples and in turn rebuked Peter. "Get thee behind me, Satan" has a double reference. Jesus spoke the words to Peter but addressed them to Satan since He recognized the true origin of the suggestion that He should not go to Calvary as coming from Satan. Satan had previously tempted Jesus to disobey the will of the Father (Matthew 4:1). Peter spoke the words but Satan instigated the thought; hence the rebuke applied to both.

Further, Peter was accused of not savoring—having interest in, regard for, or feelings about—the things of God. Apparently Peter still retained ideas prevalent among the Jews of an earthly kingdom ruled by the Messiah.

Discouragement from doing the will of God sometimes comes to us from well-meaning friends with the best of intentions. They would dissuade us from accepting our rightful calling of God, whether on a foreign mission field, in a school, a pastorate, or any other place God bids. Jesus' stern resolve always to do the will of God, regardless of the person, cost, or advice of those closest to Him, provides the model.

(3) Teaching about cross bearing (8:34-9:1)
(Matthew 10:38; 16:24; Luke 9:23)

(34) And when he had called the people unto him with his disciples also, he said unto them, Whosoever will come after me, let him deny himself, and take up his cross, and follow me. (35) For whosoever will save his life shall lose it; but whosoever shall lose his life for my sake and the gospel's, the same shall save it. (36) For what shall it profit a man, if he shall gain the whole world, and lose his own soul? (37) or what shall a man give in exchange for his soul? (38) Whosoever therefore shall be ashamed of me and of my words in this adulterous and sinful generation; of him also shall the Son of man be ashamed, when he cometh in the glory of his Father with the holy angels. (9:1) And he said unto them, Verily I say unto you, That there be some of them that stand here, which shall not taste of death, till they have seen the kingdom of God come with power.

Verses 34-35. Verse 34 begins an interval of private discourse between Jesus and His disciples during which a multitude gathered. The lesson was universal. It concerned discipleship and the cost of cross bearing, namely, voluntary self-denial that extended even to life itself.

Because the benefits of the gospel are personal, the costs of the gospel are also personal. Taking up the cross—one's own personal route to follow—implies a daily, hourly, continual, patient walk with God throughout life. Certainly none can say that Jesus was not honest with him. He offered no lure by false pretense, bribes, or an easy route to victory. He offered glory, not peace, and no way could be harder or higher.

To take up one's cross meant to suffer and die as a Roman criminal. The disciples had to understand His message. Jesus never called for His people to face what He would not first face Himself; He never demanded of them to endure what He refused to first endure Himself. To take up the cross is to be crucified to the world, and he who is crucified to the world follows a crucified Christ.

"Let a man deny himself" means to say no to self, to say no to ease and comfort, to say no to self-seeking and self-will, to say no to instincts and desires to touch the forbidden thing, and to say yes to Christ. The cross may require enduring persecution, affliction, sorrows, or martyrdom. Or it may require daily living, being buffeted by Satan but being counted worthy of God to suffer trials. Jesus noted that by escaping the cross one might save his life here but lose it in the hereafter.

Verse 36. Some things are lost by being kept and saved by being used. If one loses his own soul he forfeits his life. "Soul" comes from the word "breath" or the Greek word *psuche*, the life, meaning the mind, the will, and the immortal part of man.

In the second and third centuries, ascetics sought to save their lives by losing it in prayer, fasting, meditation, and cruel, self-inflicted punishment. But such a regimen displays a selfish love for God, not a selfless love of God. To serve God means to serve God's people. Life is to spend, not to keep. When a talent possessed is not used, it is lost; whereas when the talent is used, then other talents are gained (Matthew 25:14-30).

Verse 37. What is an equivalent exchange for a soul? Life defies all compensation, surpasses all values. One soul bought, redeemed by the sinless blood of Christ, far exceeds the value of even the whole world. Some people sacrifice values or honor to show a profit through cheating and dishonest dealings. Some sacrifice principle for popularity in politics or social position. Some people sacrifice the eternal for the temporal, as in the materialist's quest for success. Some sacrifice to buy little temporal things and ignore big eternal things.

Verse 38. Any who deny faith, regardless of position, will be rejected by Christ when He comes in His glory and His power. This verse contrasts shame manifested in the presence of an adulterous and sinful generation of debased people with the glorious company in the hereafter. The cross to the Jews was a stumbling block and to the Greeks foolishness (I Corinthians 1:23). One cannot help but notice the superb confidence of Christ when He speaks of His death on the cross and yet a triumph at the end. A king will be faithful to those who are faithful to him; there will be no honor of victory to those who will not fight.

Chapter 9, Verse 1. Mark 8:38 and 9:1 are part of the same thought, and the chapter probably should have been divided after verse 1. There were those who stood before Jesus who would not taste of death until they saw the kingdom of God come with power.

The superb confidence of Christ is again revealed. Did Christ have a future world conquest? He was born in a small country no more than 150 miles long by 50 miles wide with a relatively small population. He had few true followers; in a short lifetime He managed to anger the powerful leaders so that He was bound for death as a heretic. Who would conclude that this Man had any future

175

or that His doctrine would survive?

Yet, He was confident, never in despair. When faced with the dull minds of His associates, His shrewd opponents, and His powerful executioners, even then He offered a place in His kingdom to any who would take up the cross and follow His lead. Could even the disciples who knew Him to be the Messiah have faith in what this Man now said? It looked hopeless, but Jesus had complete faith in God that what humans would never do, God could and would do. "But be of good cheer," He said, "I have overcome the world" (John 16:33).

This verse has two possible explanations. (1) It alludes to the transfiguration that occurred six days later and that marked the previewing of the kingdom with power. (2) It alludes to the coming of the indwelling Spirit and power at Pentecost. Doubtless, many present were alive at the time of Pentecost, a few months later. There is also a veiled ironic expression in that Christ could have been comparing those present to Himself since He was destined to face death before the kingdom could come with power.

e. Transfiguration on the mountain (9:2-8)
(Matthew 17:1; Luke 9:28)

(2) And after six days Jesus taketh with him Peter, and James, and John, and leadeth them up into an high mountain apart by themselves; and he was transfigured before them. (3) And his raiment became shining, exceeding white as snow; so as no fuller on earth can white them. (4) And there appeared unto them Elias with Moses: and they were talking with Jesus. (5) And

Peter answered and said to Jesus, Master, it is good for us to be here: and let us make three tabernacles; one for thee, and one for Moses, and one for Elias. (6) For he wist not what to say; for they were sore afraid. (7) And there was a cloud that overshadowed them: and a voice came out of the cloud, saying, This is my beloved Son: hear him. (8) And suddenly, when they had looked round about, they saw no man any more, save Jesus only with themselves.

Verse 2. Mark says that after six days, Peter, James, and John, recognized leaders of the disciples chosen to share the garden experience (Matthew 26:37) and the raising of Jarius's daughter (Mark 5:37), were also favored to witness the mysterious incident of the transfiguration.

Although the exact time of day is unknown, it was undoubtedly at night. The exact location is also speculative. Mount Hermon with its 9,200 foot altitude and deep snows located about twelve miles from Caesarea Philippi seems probable as the high mountain "apart."

Jesus separated the three and Himself from the other disciples for a transfiguration. The fact is clear; the meaning is less precise.

Verse 3. Transfiguration (Greek *metamorphoo*; to change form, fashion of appearance, and countenance) resulted in His clothing becoming a shining, glistening white. Mark drew two comparisons: white as snow, and whiter than a fuller (launderer) on earth could make them. A fuller cleansed garments by washing them in a solution of lye, usually accomplished by stamping the clothing with the feet.

Verse 4. Moses and Elijah, Old Testament lawgiver and

prophet, stood talking with Jesus. These representations of the law and prophets meet in Jesus Christ, bearing witness to the Messiah Savior. Moses—who died—could represent the dead saints themselves to be transfigured at Christ's coming (I Thessalonians 4:13-16), and Elijah—who escaped physical death—could represent those who are alive and remain. Their conversation with Christ was about His death to be accomplished on Calvary at Jerusalem (Luke 9:31), which would signal the ultimate end of both law and prophets as forerunners of the Christ.

Verse 5. Simon Peter, confused, startled, fearful, excited, and heavy with sleep (Luke 9:32), blurted out, "It is good for us to be here," then suggested building a tabernacle (Greek *skene*; booth or shade) for each of the three men.

Verse 6. This verse indicates that they were fully awake, precluding a dream or vision, because of overshadowing awe and terror.

Verse 7. A dense cloud—symbolic of God's excellence, presence, and glory since the Exodus, Sinai, and the Temple of Solomon—enveloped, overshadowed, and hid them. (Matthew 17:5 records a bright cloud.) From the cloud a voice stated: "This is my beloved Son: hear him."

The latter "hear him" was not stated at Jesus' baptism announcing Him to the world. Now, in the light of the earlier question of "Whom do men say that I am?", one greater than Moses and greater than Elijah had come. He came to make a new covenant with God; therefore, "hear him."

Verse 8. In awe and bewilderment the disciples were aroused from their face-down position (Matthew 17:6) to discover that they were once more alone with Jesus.

f. Discussion concerning Elijah (9:9-13)
(Matthew 17:10)

(9) And as they came down from the mountain, he charged them that they should tell no man what things they had seen, till the Son of man were risen from the dead. (10) And they kept that saying with themselves, questioning one with another what the rising from the dead should mean. (11) And they asked him, saying, Why say the scribes that Elias must first come? (12) And he answered and told them, Elias verily cometh first, and restoreth all things; and how it is written of the Son of man, that he must suffer many things, and be set at nought. (13) But I say unto you, That Elias is indeed come, and they have done unto him whatsoever they listed, as it is written of him.

Verse 9. Coming down from the mountain, once again (as in 8:27-31), Jesus charged the disciples not to disclose His identity or what they had witnessed in private until the Son of man had risen from the dead, when it would all make sense as the mystery became revealed. Their silence would also prevent envy among the other disciples.

Furthermore, a declaration now of His transfiguration, with the disciples' concept of a king, earthly kingdom, and power, might have initiated a move to forcefully crown Him as king. "Son of man" was a martyr title with expectation of suffering and death. The conversation between Jesus, Elijah, and Moses was of toil, suffering, and death.

The Greek word for "transfigured" here applied to Jesus is also applied to Christians in Romans 12:1-2. As

179

we suffer, we are transformed into His likeness.

The transfiguring incident carries deep meaning, focusing on Jesus Christ. The transfiguration undoubtedly served to encourage Jesus and to confirm His avowed choice of going on to Calvary though the disciples appeared to oppose Him, not understanding the things of God. God voiced His approval.

It also provided a glorious mental image for the apostles to hold in contrast to what they would soon see as an abused, beaten, inglorious, stripped body writhed out its last gasp on the cross. This majestic metamorphosis certainly provided testimony to the glory of Christ, which these witnesses could forever relate as what they saw and heard. (See Luke 1:2; John 1:14; II Peter 1:16.)

Several explanations for the transfiguration are possible. First, the sight of power and dazzling white splendor of a transfigured Christ was indescribable and overwhelming to the disciples. Through this Jesus appeared in a light the disciples had never witnessed. His position was one of majestic splendor and character. He was associated with two of the very greatest men of Israel, Moses as lawgiver and deliverer, Elijah as commanding prophet. (With no written work in the Bible, Elijah is not the most obvious choice of a figure to denote prophetic writings.) Then there was the cloud, a climaxing symbol of the presence of Almighty God. A voice spoke, then Jesus stood alone, fulfilling the law and the prophets, summing them up and surpassing them. He alone was the completion and crown of the Old Testament revelation.

A second explanation is that these figures appear to pronounce the end, being forerunners of the fulfillment of God's purpose in Jesus Christ. Such a role might be in keeping with Jewish belief according to Malachi 4:5. Then too, both figures terminated life on earth mysteriously (Deuteronomy 34:6; II Kings 2:11), making it appropriate for their reappearance in a glorious new ministry.

The sound of a voice, as at the baptism of Jesus, brings to bear a third possible explanation for the transfiguration. The declaration of the Lamb of God by John the Baptist could have its equivalent in the law of the sacrifice. It was customary to hold the paschal lamb for three days to determine if it was indeed free of disease, injury, and infirmity before being declared fit for sacrifice. Jesus was the Lamb, chosen and proclaimed by John and verified by a voice at baptism. Here on the mount again is verification by a heavenly voice that the Lamb has been tested, tried, and tempted, and is without blemish or infirmity. In Deuteronomy 18:18 God declared that a prophet with words in his mouth like Moses would come. "Hear him"—the voice declared Him to be worth listening to.

Verse 10. No sooner was one query resolved than another arose. The disciples now began to question what "rising from the dead" meant. In spite of Jesus' clear instruction, their minds had not accepted death. Only the actual cross and resurrection itself could teach what Christ meant.

Verse 11. After seeing Elijah on the mount with Jesus, the disciples puzzled over why he should disappear. Evidently the scribes taught that Elijah must first appear three days before the Messiah (Malachi 4:5-6). Rabbinic tradition held that on the first day Elijah would proclaim peace to the world. On the second day he would proclaim good comes to the world, and on the third day Jeshua (Salvation) would come to the world. It was Elijah who would settle their long-standing disputes and heal breaches so evident among the Jewish sects and families.

If Jesus was Messiah, why did not Elijah stay to fulfill tradition? This was the intent behind the question of verse 11. Evidently the scribes erred in their concepts of the time of Elijah and Messiah, not distinguishing the first advent (birth, Calvary) with the Second Advent (judgment, glorious reign). Many today feel that Elijah is destined to play a role in the end-time events of Revelation 11:3-12. However, the disciples fully expected the kingdom to come at this time.

Verse 12. Jesus admitted that Elijah was to appear first and restore all things. Matthew 17:13 indicates that the disciples understood Jesus to refer to Elijah as John the Baptist in the role of forerunner. The next verse implies that it was of John that Jesus spoke.

Verse 13. Elias had indeed come and they treated him as they will, as it was written of him. If they did so to the forerunner, what would they do to the Anointed One? This passage clearly indicates that the disciples were blind to the things of God. Their error hid from them the revelation of God.

g. Cure of the demoniac boy (9:14-29)
(Matthew 17:14; Luke 9:37)

(14) And when he came to his disciples, he saw a great multitude about them, and the scribes questioning with them. (15) And straightway all the people, when they beheld him, were greatly amazed, and running to him saluted him. (16) And he asked the scribes, What question ye with them? (17) And one of the multitude

answered and said, Master, I have brought unto thee my son, which hath a dumb spirit; (18) and wheresoever he taketh him, he teareth him: and he foameth, and gnasheth with his teeth, and pineth away: and I spake to thy disciples that they should cast him out; and they could not. (19) He answereth him, and saith, O faithless generation, how long shall I be with you? how long shall I suffer you? bring him unto me. (20) And they brought him unto him: and when he saw him, straightway the spirit tare him; and he fell on the ground, and wallowed foaming. (21) And he asked his father, How long is it ago since this came unto him? And he said, Of a child. (22) And ofttimes it hath cast him into the fire, and into the waters, to destroy him: but if thou canst do any thing, have compassion on us, and help us. (23) Jesus said unto him, If thou canst believe, all things are possible to him that believeth. (24) And straightway the father of the child cried out, and said with tears, Lord, I believe; help thou mine unbelief. (25) When Jesus saw that the people came running together, he rebuked the foul spirit, saying unto him, Thou dumb and deaf spirit, I charge thee, come out of him, and enter no more into him. (26) And the spirit cried, and rent him sore, and came out of him: and he was as one dead; insomuch that many said, He is dead. (27) But Jesus took him by the hand, and lifted him up; and he arose. (28) And when he was come into the house, his disciples asked him privately, Why could not we cast him out? (29) And he said unto them, This kind can come forth by nothing, but by prayer and fasting.

Verse 14. After the night of transfiguration, Jesus and

the three returned to find the disciples among a multitude, confronted by scribes.

Verse 15. Suddenly ("straightway") the crowd, realizing that Jesus had come, ran to greet Him. They were surprised and amazed to see Him and not, as has been suggested, some residual afterglow on His countenance like Moses (Exodus 34:29). His careful charge of silence to the disciples would have been meaningless if others could have beheld for themselves.

Verse 16. Jesus addressed a question to the scribes, perhaps in defense of the disciples. It was He whom the scribes really desired to question anyway.

Verses 17-18. Someone spoke from the crowd to explain the reason for the questions and discussion. "I brought" (Matthew 17:16) indicates that the man came kneeling, pleading for mercy for his son "which hath a dumb spirit" and whom he had brought to Christ. Jesus' being away eight days on the mountain and unavailable prompted the man to speak to the disciples to cast the spirit out. They could not. The disciples apparently had attempted to cast out the spirit but a lack of faith prevented success (Matthew 17:20). The father described the spirit in action: "taketh him . . . teareth him," to which Luke the physician added "bruising him" (Luke 9:39).

Verse 19. Jesus spoke to everyone nearby—scribes, Jews, disciples—and called them "O faithless generation." After all that Christ had wrought to kindle and build faith in the disciples, they still remained skeptical and unbelieving. Quite natural, then, was the concern over "How long shall I suffer you," how many times must I demonstrate before you have faith? Then, out of compassion for this father, Christ said: "Bring him unto me."

Verses 21-22. How long has he been this way? Jesus wanted to know. The answer was, since childhood, and at times it was so severe as to imperil his life. The dad began to recount the fierceness of the attacks that cast the boy into fire or water to destroy him. He ended with the plea, "If thou canst do any thing, have compassion on us, and help us." After days, his hope for a cure had undoubtedly waned because of the failure of Jesus' close disciples. He evidently questioned Jesus' power to help ("if thou canst"), but trusted the compassion!

Verses 23-24. Jesus replied, "If thou canst believe." The question was not one of Christ's power or His compassion but of the man's faith. The exchange, a Hebrew idiom, is lost in the translation, but Herschel Hobbs gives it as "you question my power—I challenge your faith."[10] The cure depended on the man's faith and not Christ's power. The effect on the dad was startling. He cried, "Lord, I believe; help thou mine unbelief," essentially saying, "My faith is weak; do whatever is necessary to heal my faith, then heal my son." His prayer was one to dispel doubts that coexist with faith in the heart.

Verses 25-27. The dispute with the scribes (verse 14) momentarily on hold, now people ran to Jesus and the son. Perhaps to avoid undue crowd involvement Jesus spoke to the foul spirit: "I charge [command] thee, come out of him, and enter no more into him." The wording seems to imply that the spirit would obey and leave now, but might later return but for the second part of the command. A spirit so powerful as to defy the disciples and resist even Christ now resorted to its last mischief: it cried out, convulsed the victim greatly, and left him so spent and exhausted that the onlookers thought him to be dead. In this violent departure the malicious spirit attempted to destroy what it could no longer retain. Jesus took the boy by the hand and lifted him to his feet.

Verses 28-29. Entering into a house, the disciples sought an explanation from Jesus as to why they could not cast out the deaf and dumb spirit. Jesus' reply—"this kind"—may imply spirits of different orders of power with degrees of malice, evil energy, or resistance. Matthew 17:20 states the reason as unbelief; here Jesus called them a "faithless generation" (verse 19). The cure of unbelief and the stimulus for faith is prayer. Fasting is added in certain manuscripts. To be prayerless is to be powerless; genuine prayer is faith activity.

From the Mount of Transfiguration Jesus reentered the valley of unbelief—that of a faithless generation. Their faithlessness stemmed from different causes and perspectives, but it was unbelief nonetheless. Campbell Morgan describes the disciples as having unconscious unbelief; the son, irresponsible unbelief; the father, unwilling unbelief; and the scribes, willful and persistent unbelief.[11] In a few moments Jesus healed the demon-possessed son, comforted the distraught father, instructed the defeated disciples, and silenced the critical scribes.

If the secret of failure is unbelief (Matthew 17:20), then the secret of success is faith. Faith comes through praying. Jesus' answer was not merely that prayer and fasting cast out demons, but in essence, "Have you disciples, alone for eight days, been prayerless?"

h. Renewed teaching about the cross (9:30-32)

(30) And they departed thence, and passed through

*Galilee; and he would not that any man should know it.
(31) For he taught his disciples, and said unto them,
The Son of man is delivered into the hands of men, and
they shall kill him; and after that he is killed, he shall
rise the third day. (32) But they understood not that
saying, and were afraid to ask him.*

Verse 30 is transitional. Leaving Caesarea Philippi,
Jesus and the disciples passed, apparently secretly to
avoid drawing attention, the cities of Galilee en route to
Capernaum. Since Jesus needed more time in private to
instruct His disciples, Capernaum was the logical choice.
Keenly aware that this move southward would ultimately
lead to Calvary, Jesus again announced His intention.
Although commonly called the second pronouncement, it
is actually the third if we count verse 12.

Verses 31-32. The words of the Son of man, "delivered
. . . kill . . . rise up," appeared to be too much for the disciples to comprehend. That Jesus would be delivered
("turned over"), betrayed to men who were His enemies,
and killed but afterward rise again the third day, they did
not understand. The idea Jesus attempted to convey gen-
erated sorrow (Matthew 17:23), but the mystery
remained. The human mind could accept death (hence
the sorrow), but not resurrection. At this point their fear
prohibited further questioning.

i. Teaching in Capernaum to the disciples (9:33-50)
(Matthew 18:1; 20:24; Luke 9:46)

Jesus expounded to the disciples at Capernaum three
lessons: relationship or position in the kingdom (verses

33-37), sectarian exclusivism (verses 38-41), and the seriousness of sinful offenses to believers (verses 42-50).

(1) Question of greatness (9:33-37)

(33) And he came to Capernaum: and being in the house he asked them, What was it that ye disputed among yourselves by the way? (34) But they held their peace: for by the way they had disputed among themselves, who should be the greatest. (35) And he sat down, and called the twelve, and saith unto them, If any man desire to be first, the same shall be last of all, and servant of all. (36) And he took a child, and set him into the midst of them: and when he had taken him in his arms, he said unto them, (37) Whosoever shall receive one of such children in my name, receiveth me: and whosoever shall receive me, receiveth not me, but him that sent me.

Verses 33-34. Safely in their house in Capernaum, Jesus addressed an issue that had arisen during the journey. As the disciples walked along behind their rabbi in Oriental fashion, they began to bicker among themselves up and down the line as to who should be the greatest. (Matthew does not record this question at all, and "among yourselves" is absent from some manuscripts.) Now, ashamed of their expression of childish jealousy, the disciples refused to answer. It is possible that the disciples believed the kingdom was about to come and they were to be selected as chief ministers of state, and each laid claim to the most desirable position. This chastisement of His men came in private, and before Jesus all selfish arguments became petty and meaningless.

Verse 35. Jesus sat down and called for the Twelve. Rabbis exercised their greatest authority from a seated position, and Jesus' words here were most authoritative and critically important: If anyone desires to be first in My kingdom, he shall be last of all and servant (Greek *diakones*, minister or servant). A servant is one who does the command of another. Real greatness is revealed in service.

Jesus faced this issue quite seriously and specified that to rank in His kingdom a person must serve dutifully and without position. Faithful and uncomplaining selflessness is rare in people, whether rich or poor, regal or servile. Jesus made it clear that the disciples should not care for position but cherish the chance to serve. Those in office have the even greater burden of serving God's church. A desire for fame, recognition, and credit nullifies true servanthood.

Verses 36-37. Jesus drove home His lesson by a practical application concerning innocence. Jesus sat a child on His lap (in His arms), and said, essentially, "Whoever receives (shows kindness, love to) a child, simple and trusting, in My name, receives Me. Then, whoever receives Me, receives the One who sent Me." "Receiveth not me" means a person receives not only Christ but focuses on the One who sent Him, namely God.

The Christian experience is practical in its servanthood: to accept even simple children is to accept God Himself; to be accepted with God one must receive all people in love and kindness. All are like little children in that they are victims of the sinful nature. Furthermore, all that is beautiful in Christian service is linked to His name.

The disciples had estimated greatness based on

grandeur—what was bigger was more powerful, more influential, and therefore, greater. Jesus taught that we measure true greatness by caring for people. In a world faced with a caring crisis, where are the compassionate Christians? People care about those in rank of importance, those regarded as leaders, powerful, and wealthy. To God, their worth is no greater than that of a little child. To be a person is all that is required to be significant to God.

Social concern for children goes back to the teaching of Christ. There is no limit to what a child may become, given right training, opportunity, and encouragement. What mother can look her baby in the face and foresee its adult accomplishments, whether professional, mayor, legislator, judge, president, king, saint, teacher, or clergyman? Disciples are to be pliable, trainable as a little child.

(2) Mistaken zeal of John (9:38-41)
(Luke 9:49; cf. Acts 10:15, 35)

(38) And John answered him, saying, Master, we saw one casting out devils in thy name, and he followeth not us: and we forbad him, because he followeth not us. (39) But Jesus said, Forbid him not: for there is no man which shall do a miracle in my name, that can lightly speak evil of me. (40) For he that is not against us is on our part. (41) For whosoever shall give you a cup of water to drink in my name, because ye belong to Christ, verily I say unto you, he shall not lose his reward.

Verse 38. Apparently answering the call of his own conscience and convicted by the words of Jesus about

190

receiving people, John recalled an interaction between a believer and the disciples: "We saw one casting out devils in thy name," and we rebuked him because he did not follow us.

Can anything truly done in the name of Jesus be unacceptable to God? Was John simply moving away from the embarrassing topic of position by noting his own zeal or alluding to the nine disciples' impotence against the spirit at Caesarea Philippi? Spirit has power over spirit; all acts of faith in the name of Jesus bring glory to God regardless of the individual name or affiliation.

Verses 39-40. Jesus warned against acts of zeal for one's own end that lead to exclusivism and not to the honor of God. No one doing a miracle in Jesus' name can speak lightly of Him. If a genuine miracle occurs, then God is in it; therefore we should accept it as being "on our part" and not against us, even if the individual is not of our band. Furthermore, there can be no neutrality in Christ. Matthew 12:30 uses reversed word sequence and also adds that one who does not gather with Christ, scatters abroad.

Many practitioners of Christianity today may be theologically and doctrinally unsound in concept or salvation, but their intent and efforts stem from conviction of the cause of Christ. In their limited understanding they are promoting His cause, as did Apollos (Acts 18:24-25). Without full comprehension of God, their impact does not bring full salvation, but we should not condemn their efforts when accomplished in Jesus' name.

Verse 41. Jesus linked servanthood to reward for even the most simple gestures of Christian kindness. A cup of drinking water offered to a disciple in "my name" merits a reward because "ye belong to Christ." If God acknowledges even a cup of water given in Jesus' name, then to cast out demons should merit even greater reward. Jesus condemned the sectarianism that so often divides people who have the cause of God at heart and much in common. Moses read this behavior as envy and prayed that God would anoint with His Spirit all who desired to work for Him (Numbers 11:26-29).

The disciples should avoid criticizing and discouraging good works. Nothing done in regard for Christ is lost. It is the work of the enemy to put people against each other, dividing their loyalties, expending their energy in petty disputes, and building walls of misunderstanding.

(3) Seriousness of sin (9:42-50)
(Matthew 18:5)

(42) And whosoever shall offend one of these little ones that believe in me, it is better for him that a millstone were hanged about his neck, and he were cast into the sea. (43) And if thy hand offend thee, cut if off: it is better for thee to enter into life maimed, than having two hands to go into hell, into the fire that never shall be quenched: (44) where their worm dieth not, and the fire is not quenched. (45) And if thy foot offend thee, cut it off: it is better for thee to enter halt into life, than having two feet to be cast into hell, into the fire that never shall be quenched: (46) where their worm dieth not, and the fire is not quenched. (47) And if thine eye offend thee, pluck it out: it is better for thee to enter into the kingdom of God with one eye, than having two eyes to be cast into hell fire: (48) where their worm dieth not, and the fire is

not quenched. (49) For every one shall be salted with fire, and every sacrifice shall be salted with salt. (50) Salt is good: but if the salt have lost his saltness, wherewith will ye season it? Have salt in yourselves, and have peace one with another.

Verse 42. This verse contrasts sharply with the preceding one. If a cup of water brings a good reward, then to offend a child ("one of these little ones") merits the severest punishment. Jesus alluded to a form of punishment practiced by Syrians, Egyptians, and Greeks in which a millstone large enough to be turned by a donkey was tied about the neck of a victim and the person was cast into the sea.

Verses 43-48. Still comparing rewards and offenses, Jesus extended the teaching to a personal level. "Offend" carries the same meaning in verses 42, 43, 45, and 47; hence, it refers to any instrument by which sin could be committed: hand, foot, eyes, and by extension perhaps other sense organs such as the tongue or ear. Any instrument in a person, relationship, job, position, or sense that lures one into sin and damnation would be better severed. The hand symbolizes companionship and work; the foot denotes progress and ambition; the eye means vision, which can kindle covetousness and lust. For example, Eve, Achan, and David first were led into sin by its compelling visual attraction.

Because most people protect themselves against accidents and physical injuries, God's treatment of sin does not appear extreme when one compares the temporary with the eternal. It is better to remove anything that hinders and suffer its loss than to keep it as a millstone and perish. It is better to deny oneself sinful pleasures in this life than to be whole here and suffer eternal damnation.

Jesus referred to Isaiah 66:22-24 and compared the end of the obedient servant to the end of transgressor. The Bible uses the Greek word *gehenna* twelve times to denote eternal hell, a place of unending torment and punishment.

The actual word *gehenna* comes from the Valley of Hinnom south of Jerusalem, which had a long history of perpetual incineration. It was a familiar place to the disciples. The site had been used in worship of the idol Molech where people sacrificed their children until the time of Josiah (II Kings 23:10).

It then became a refuse heap, a place of burning the city's garbage, an eternally smoldering fire filled with maggots and other carrion-feeding insects, all vile and unclean. Continual addition of refuse provided fuel for the flames, which were never extinguished. The stench, fire, smoke, vermin, and uncleanness all made Gehenna a vile, repulsive place in the eyes of the Jews. To this Jesus, quoting from Isaiah 66:24, likened hell: an eternal torment where the "worm dieth not, and the fire is not quenched" (verses 43-48). It is a place of an eternal existence forever separated from the presence of God.

Some texts omit verses 44-46, but the symbolism is overwhelming even without these verses. Fire is God's purifier, destroying the perishable, leaving the imperishable. In metaphor it is the holiness of God from which no unclean thing escapes. The worm dying not may mean the memory of the past as one's conscience eternally eats away at him. The Bible speaks of man as a worm (Job 25:6; Psalm 22:6; Isaiah 41:14), and here it may specifically refer to remorse of conscience over failure to obey the gospel.

Jesus' message reveals several truths about hell. First, hell is real, a place of unending punishment. Second, human consciousness is retained, enabling people to feel and know, since body and soul are cast there at judgment (Revelation 20; Matthew 10:28). (See also Matthew 8:12; 13:42, 50; 22:13; 24:51; 25:30, 46; Revelation 14:9-11; 21:8; Isaiah 66:24.) Third, it is better in life to sacrifice whatever leads to sin than to be cast into the place of eternal judgment.

Verses 49-50. The link between the foregoing discourse and these verses appears to be sacrifice. Every one, every offering or sacrifice, shall be salted with fire. Old Testament sacrifices were offered with the preservative of salt (Leviticus 2:13), and in figure here fire is changed for salt. (Some texts omit the latter portion of verse 49.)

The meaning of this passage seems to be twofold. One, the transgressors in hell will be preserved as an eternal example of the justice of God (Isaiah 66:24); sinners are to be salted with the fire of hell. Two, a believer's salt is within himself, preserving all that is useful and beneficial. The Holy Spirit keeps from corruption, and the believer must not lose the Spirit's effect on his qualities and characteristics. Self-exaltation (verse 34), bigotry (verses 38-39), offenses (verse 42), lust and ambition (verses 43-48) can never overwhelm the one with appropriately "salted" sacrifices.

Barclay suggested that these verses represent a compilation by Mark of three sayings of Jesus about salt given on separate occasions:[12]

1. The salt of the covenant required all sacrifice to be salted (Leviticus 2:13; Numbers 18:19; II Chronicles 13:5). Salt rendered the sacrifice acceptable to God.

2. Salt without saltiness in a disciple is useless. It has neither preserving quality to prevent individual corruption nor power to provide the cleansing, purifying antiseptic to a polluted society.

3. Have salt in yourself and live at peace with each other. With the influence of salt, purity is assured and the believer is cleansed of self-seeking, bitterness, and envy, and can live at peace with everyone.

In summary, attention to sin in one's life is not something we should treat lightly or casually ignore. Jesus placed it as top priority in the believer's life. Sins, especially those Jesus singled out in this passage, resist the kingdom of God. He condemned self-serving interests in rank and position by showing the advantage and elevated status of servanthood (verses 33-37).

The sin of intolerance of others hinders the good that people do because they do not "belong" or do it the group way. Jesus made it clear that one cannot be for Christ and oppose those who act sincerely in Christ's interest. When people's doctrines fail to adhere to Scripture, instruction is appropriate (Acts 18:24-26; 19:1-6). Nevertheless, deeds of good people who fear and love God, whatever their conception of the gospel, are a credit to Christ and Christianity. Any effort to administer the things of God that lead people closer to Christ is to be considered gathering. Propagation of false doctrines of non-Christians, cultists, or New Age philosophers who take people away from Christ or the truth is scattering.

Offending or causing offense in others is a sin to be

avoided (verses 42-48). Our life should be one of peace with everyone, and we should make every attempt to avoid recklessly offending any.

Only the salt of the Holy Spirit can preserve and purify the believer from the serious consequences of sin, especially those sins associated with deliberate preference of pleasures.

Notes

[1]Barclay (p. 123) gives their names as Scythopolic (west of the Jordan River), and Pella, Dion, Gergasa, Philadelphia, Gadara, Raphana, Kanatha, Kippos, and Damascus on the east side. The Gospels of Mark and Luke refer to "the country of the Gadarenes"; Bible commentaries place the encounter at Gergasa.

[2]Sherman E. Johnson, *A Commentary on the Gospel According to St. Mark* (London: Adam & Black, 1960), 102.

[3]N. Avigad and Y. Yadin, *A Genesis Apocryphon* (Jerusalem: 1956), col. 20, l. 21f.

[4]Barclay, 134.

[5]*Ibid.*, 147.

[6]Josephus, *Antiquities of the Jews*, 18.5, 2.

[7]*Pulpit Commentary*, 246.

[8]*Ibid.*, 247.

[9]Barclay, 168-69.

[10]Hershel H. Hobbs, *The Gospel of Mark* (Grand Rapids: Baker, 1971), 48.

[11]G. Campbell Morgan, *The Gospel According to Mark* (New York: Revell, 1927), 193.

[12]Barclay, 241.

C.

Journey to Jerusalem
(10:1-52)

C. Journey to Jerusalem (10:1-52)

Verses 1-16 of Mark 10 deal with two moral and spiritual issues—dissolution of marriage and the place of children—and give two stories related to family ideals. In this passage, Jesus explained the moral and spiritual ideals for the human family.

There is obviously a break in time between Mark 9 and 10, the extent of which is evident only from study of the other Gospel records. Mark's setting for chapter 10 is the borders ("coasts") of Judea by the farther side of Jordan. Jesus had departed from Galilee (Capernaum). John indicates that He visited Jerusalem for the Feast of Tabernacles (7:2-10:21) and Feast of Dedication (10:22-39). Between these two visits Luke interjects the ministry of Judea (Luke 9:51-13:22).

Evidently these events advanced Mark's theme little and so were omitted, for he began afterward with characteristic straightforwardness: "And he arose from thence"—which does not matter to him—"and cometh into the coasts of Judaea"—which does matter. The break is a natural one: Mark 1-9 gives the Galilean ministry, Mark 10-15 the Judean ministry. Between these transpire Luke's travel narrative, the sending out the seventy, and the notable parables of Luke 15.

1. Departure from Galilee (10:1)

(1) And he arose from thence, and cometh into the coasts of Judaea by the farther side of Jordan: and the

201

people resort unto him again; and, as he was wont, he taught them again.

Verse 1. In Judea, the people flocked ("resort") to Him and as usual ("wont") He taught them about the kingdom of God.

2. Teaching concerning Divorce (10:2-12)
(Matthew 5:31-32; 19:1; Luke 16:18)

(2) And the Pharisees came to him, and asked him, Is it lawful for a man to put away his wife? tempting him. (3) And he answered and said unto them, What did Moses command you? (4) And they said, Moses suffered to write a bill of divorcement, and to put her away. (5) And Jesus answered and said unto them, For the hardness of your heart he wrote you this precept. (6) But from the beginning of the creation God made them male and female. (7) For this cause shall a man leave his father and mother, and cleave to his wife; (8) and they twain shall be one flesh: so then they are no more twain, but one flesh. (9) What therefore God hath joined together, let not man put asunder. (10) And in the house his disciples asked him again of the same matter. (11) And he saith unto them, Whosoever shall put away his wife, and marry another, committeth adultery against her. (12) And if a woman shall put away her husband, and be married to another, she committeth adultery.

Verse 2. The Pharisees came to Jesus again with a trick question—not to gain instruction but "tempting Him," as with the questions of tribute and resurrection (12:15, 23).

Matthew 19:3 adds "for every cause."

The latter phrase explains the trap laid by these clever men. Regardless of His answer, Jesus would be taking sides in the dispute over divorce that raged among the doctors of the law and religious people of that day. Not all Pharisees were insincere (e.g., Nicodemus) and some might truly have desired a verdict; others desired to test His orthodoxy or obtain an elaboration on the earlier discourse (Matthew 5:31-32).

Mark sensed that their intent was to entangle Jesus in a contradiction, to have Him by His answer cross swords with Herod, who was divorced and had remarried, or to accuse Him of heresy if His answer failed to uphold the law of Moses. Whatever their specific motives, it was not a rhetorical question and their intent was evil.

Verses 3-4. Jesus sidestepped the trap by appealing to the decree of Moses, whom they revered. They rightly responded concerning Moses and the bill of divorce. Matthew 19:7 indicates the question of why Moses allowed divorce, to which Jesus gave the answer in verse 5.

Verse 5. Moses gave the precept because of the hardness (unfeeling, cruelty, unkindness) of people's hearts (i.e., toward rejected women, sanctity of the home, progeny, and institution of marriage). The controversy owed its origin to the intertestamental period a century before Christ when Hillel, a Babylonian Jew, and Shammai, one of his students, held widely divergent views interpreting the laws of divorce.

The law in question was Deuteronomy 24:1, where a man could give his wife a bill of divorce for the cause of "uncleanness." Shammai interpreted uncleanness to mean only moral defilement (adultery); Hillel interpreted this law in favor of the male and grounds for divorce could be trivial: simple displeasure, a poor domestic artisan, a brawler or noisy woman (heard next door), shameful or disrespectful of husband, or simply failure to win the husband's favor. Most Jews, true to human nature, subscribed to the latter view, "for every cause" (Matthew 19:3). Consequently, marriage was a very insecure institution, at least for the woman and children. In Jesus' day many women remained unmarried; others after divorce felt forced to enter into immoral lifestyles (John 4:16-18).

One result of this broad interpretation was that wives were reduced to things owned, a possession of men, without legal rights. They could be put away from a husband with no recourse and disposed of at his will. On the other hand, a wife had no such liberty; at best she could ask her husband for a divorce if he became leprous, engaged in an unclean profession (tanner), ravished a virgin, or falsely accused her of prenuptial sin.[1] A second result of the Hillel/Shammai dispute was that the right to divorce was tantamount to the right to remarry.

Divorce (Greek *apoluo*) means to set at liberty, put away, dismiss, free, undo a bond, release, or cut apart. The Hebrew word *ervah* in Deuteronomy 24:1 is translated uncleanness, shame (Isaiah 20:4), or nakedness. It comes from a term meaning to expose, bare, empty, or discover what was formerly not known or realized (Genesis 9:22-23; 42:9, 12). Uncleanness then could mean something shameful in a wife's background, resulting in a keen disappointment or extreme dislike. In the context of the Old Testament, *ervah* apparently did not refer to moral sin since sexual immorality carried the death penalty.

Moses, in the face of morally lax Israelites, allowed the wife to clear herself by oath (Numbers 5:11-31). The husband was permitted to put the wife away "privily" without trial (Deuteronomy 24:1-4; Matthew 1:19). The practice had become so easy and so common that Moses was compelled to place legal restraints in order to provide a measure of stability for the home and children. At least the bill of divorce required legal steps, recognition of metes and bounds in a degenerate societal order.

Moses was at best trying to control a degenerating institution, and his decree was not to condone the lax interpretation. His precept was permissive and temporary, not imperative and permanent. In other words, divorce was preferred to open adultery in defiance of marriage vows. Moses merely restrained the practice by providing legal steps and a bonafide instrument drawn up to accomplish a divorce. This practice bought time for a man to think it over, but it was at best an imperfect code for an immoral people.

Verses 6-9. Jesus proceeded beyond Moses to the first principle of God. He showed that divine intent was greater than Moses, that God is opposed to divorce, and revealed God's intent for His creation in the institution of marriage, home, and family "from the beginning." In Matthew 5:31-32 and 19:9-12, fornication is the only cause that could disrupt the unity established by God in Genesis 1:26-28.

Genesis reveals that (1) God made the human race male and female, (2) "for this cause" the man leaves parents to cleave to his wife, and (3) the two become one flesh. They are a unit, completing the "image of God" in which they were made. They are dual but not two;

fatherhood is complete and unified only with mother-hood. Divine likeness, God's image in creation, is fulfilled only in the unity of two, male and female.

That two become one flesh (verse 8) is easily seen in the procreation of children. Each child, whether boy or girl, brings to life in the flesh a unification of mother and father. Each child obtains half of its hereditary material, chromosomes, and genes from each parent, thus produc-ing a unique blend, a personality, a soul. Can this individ-ual, the child, be un-unified, "unzipped," or unmade once it is made? Neither should a marriage, in God's order. The unity of two people, male and female, under God's law should never be dissolved by man's law: "What therefore God hath joined together, let not man put asunder" (verse 9). God's law calls for lifelong faithfulness and fidelity, absolute permanency in marriage unity.

Paul used the marriage relationship as a model for the church and Jesus Christ (Ephesians 5:32). Divorce attests to infidelity and broken bonds of unity. Bonding is divine; divorce is human. Marriage represents the closest human bonds, for which a man will leave his nearest kin, mother and father, to cherish, but it is physical and cannot survive death.

Verses 10-12. Matthew 19:10 shows the disciples' own surprise at Jesus' views, and in the house they questioned Him further. They had concluded that it would be better not to marry at all, even though some of them already were married (I Corinthians 9:5). Here in private Jesus explained.

Marriage is not to be avoided but sanctioned. To divorce a wife or husband and then marry another is to commit adultery. Jesus understood the Jews' thinking that divorce was preliminary to remarriage, and thus He equated divorce with adultery. To divorce a wife is to commit adultery against her, to violate her rights and interests. Thus Jesus gave His reasons for opposing divorce while at the same time giving equal rights to women.

Jesus told His disciples "all men cannot receive this saying," then related three exceptions to marriage: a eunuch by birth, a eunuch made so by men, or celibacy by choice (Matthew 19:11-12). He also indicated that in general, marriage is the ideal. "For this cause," because the wife is "bone of my bone and flesh of my flesh," the need is for fundamental completeness and divinely blessed unity.

The church must uphold the teaching of Christ if we are to save our generation. People must understand the seriousness, understand the teaching, teach it, and practice it before a lost world. To forget or set aside divine ordinances invites moral and social disaster. Marriage has a key place in God's order, and in the very next passage, Jesus made marriage and the home a citadel for children and family.

3. Blessing of Little Children (10:13-16)
(Matthew 19:13; Luke 18:15)

(13) And they brought young children to him, that he should touch them: and his disciples rebuked those that brought them. (14) But when Jesus saw it, he was much displeased, and said unto them, Suffer the little children to come unto me, and forbid them not: for of such is the kingdom of God. (15) Verily I say unto you, Whosoever

shall not receive the kingdom of God as a little child, he shall not enter therein. (16) And he took them up in his arms, put his hands upon them, and blessed them.

Verses 13-14. Jewish mothers customarily brought their young children on their first birthday to a great rabbi for blessing. These young children (Matthew 19:13, *paidia*, little children; Luke 18:15, *brephe*, infants) were brought to be touched and blessed in a formal, public laying on of hands. This activity followed the discourse on marriage and might have interrupted the teaching, which could explain the disciples' rebuke of the mothers, often attributed to a desire to protect their Master at this time.

What a contrast in purpose and audience! Whether to argue with hard, calloused self-willed men about divorce and remarriage or to teach and bless unsullied, trusting children gave Jesus no problem. He chose the children, and His response reflects this sentiment. He was indignant, much displeased, and rebuked the disciples. His words, "Suffer the little children . . . forbid them not," spoke joy to the mothers' hearts and much about Himself. He was at this time under the shadow of the cross, moving toward His destiny at Calvary, yet by action He expressed for us the supreme importance of children and their place in the kingdom of God. Jesus cared for children, and because He did, they cared for Him, as did the mothers.

Verses 15-16. "Verily"—the rebuke was strong. One must first receive the kingdom in the heart and affections before entrance. To enter the kingdom of God, which belongs to such children, one must become "as a little child." The kingdom of God is composed of individuals regardless of age who exhibit childlike qualities (Mark

9:37; Matthew 18:4).

We cannot earn, deserve, or make the kingdom of God; we must accept it with childlikeness. Matthew 18:3-4 says we must become as little children; this text says to emulate the child.

Children are marked by trustfulness and faith in the one who loves them and whom they love. Jesus recognized unique potential in every child who came to Him, regardless of name, status, ability, or privilege. Characteristics of both childhood and the kingdom of God include (a) faith, (b) humility, (c) obedience, (d) acceptance of authority, and (e) forgiveness. These are the qualities necessary to receive the kingdom, and Jesus refused to relegate to second place children so admirably adapted from birth.

Alan Cole noted four important lessons from this discourse: (1) the truthfulness of children; (2) the faith and love of parents who entrust their children to Him; (3) the disciples who made their Lord inaccessible to the parents; and (4) the rebuke of disciples for their erroneous assumption (cf. Luke 9:55-56).[2]

In reality a child is God's workshop and the home and parents His tools, so divorce and denial of access are unthinkable. The church of God must stand for the glory of God and the interest of humanity. Does the church make the mistake of the disciples, protecting the Master from people who need Him or relegating to a secondary place those most ready for the kingdom? This Magna Carta of childhood sets precedent for the dedication of babies, for bringing them to God and the church, for laying on of hands, and for prayer and blessing, but not for baptism. Baptism is reserved for those of mature judgment and understanding, faith and repentance.

4. Question concerning Eternal Life (10:17-22)
(Matthew 19:16; Luke 18:18)

(17) And when he was gone forth into the way, there came one running and kneeled to him, and asked him, Good Master, what shall I do that I may inherit eternal life? (18) And Jesus said unto him, Why callest thou me good? there is none good but one, that is, God. (19) Thou knowest the commandments, Do not commit adultery, Do not kill, Do not steal, Do not bear false witness, Defraud not, Honour thy father and mother. (20) And he answered and said unto him, Master, all these have I observed from my youth. (21) Then Jesus beholding him loved him, and said unto him, One thing thou lackest: go thy way, sell whatsoever thou hast, and give to the poor, and thou shalt have treasure in heaven: and come, take up the cross, and follow me. (22) And he was sad at that saying, and went away grieved: for he had great possessions.

All the Synoptics record this story, so its impact on the disciples is evident. The incident concerns the acquisition of eternal life, which to the Jewish mind was surrendered in the Garden of Eden. New Testament doctrines and Gentile thought no doubt led to the question, "How can I get to heaven?" The story is enriched because wealth and opulence confront poverty; position and acclaim face a lowly Nazarene; youth vibrant with life faces a Prophet bound for death; the material faces the immaterial; and temporal values confront eternal values. Here too is the only Gospel record of a person departing from the presence of Jesus with a sad countenance, although many came that way.

Verse 17. Jesus was going forth from the house when one came running to Him, kneeled before Him (*gonupeteo* can be interpreted as literal kneeling or metaphorical) in worship. Matthew 19:20 adds "young man"; Luke 18:18 notes that he was "a ruler." He had evidently waited for such an opportunity, and now with reverence, zeal, and self-interest, sought counsel. "Good Master" (a usual manner of addressing a teacher or rabbi), "what shall I do that I may inherit eternal life?" Evidently this young ruler thought that as an heir to possessions he could also do something to become heir to eternal life.

Verse 18. Jesus' response, best rendered as, "Why ask Me about that which is good?", set the tone immediately that there would be no flattery, that all praise belongs to the only One who is good: God. Some have intimated that Christ either denied that He was good or that He was deity. To the contrary, it would appear that this man was not convinced of the deity of Christ; thus his faith needed to be elevated. Jesus' answer repudiated neither goodness nor deity, but it prompted the man to think about the implications that his own words had concerning the true identity of Jesus. The following syllogism demonstrates the point:

Major Premise: Only one (God) is good.
Minor Premise: You admit that I am good.
Conclusion: Therefore, I am God.

This is the very conclusion the man had not admitted, and with it Jesus thus affirmed His deity.

Verse 19. Jesus told the young man, You know the

commandments given by God; now count the cost of commitment to God. Attachment to a rabbi is not commitment to God. The commands enumerated by Jesus are those of the second table of the Decalogue but not in the sequence of Exodus 20. These six summarize the commands of a person's duty to other people. With the exception of "Honour thy father and mother," all are negative and consist of avoiding doing anyone harm.

Verse 20. The man had observed, kept, guarded all these from youth. Matthew 19:20 adds "What lack I yet?", pointing to the young man's correct idea that there is a higher and more noble call from the Christ.

Verse 21. This verse implies an emotional perception by Mark, correctly observed by his source, that Jesus, looking at one so fresh and sincere, loved Him. Love emanated from the eyes of the Master, but Jesus would not lower the demands of discipleship to gain a convert even of the pious. "One thing thou lackest" answers the question of Matthew. "If thou wilt be perfect," Jesus said, "go . . . sell . . . give . . . come, take . . . follow."

His clear language gives direction for anyone who seeks the challenge. Perhaps we never did anyone any harm, but what good have we done? Respectable Christian character lies not only in avoiding wrong, but in doing right. With simple action statements, Jesus exposed the man's besetting sin of covetousness and the materialistic stumbling block that fed it. The one who never lacked anything was weighed and found wanting.

This man's lack of commitment to keep the commandments of God was exposed. The first table of the Ten Commandments gives God's standard of measurement against which this young man fell short. The four laws are against: (1) polytheism (have no other gods before Him); (2) idolatry (neither make nor bow to any graven image); (3) profanity (the hallowed name is never to be used in vain); and (4) Sabbath breaking (keep a hallowed time).

Jesus' advice and challenge went beyond mechanical law keeping to motive. The youth had never stolen, defrauded, but neither had he been generous. Eternal life should be worth divesting oneself of possessions in order to be like Him, to show the love of God. The man's problem was that his desire for eternal things and his strength of character to achieve them failed to equal the desire for temporal possessions. His great possessions possessed him.

Renunciation of possessions is a potential stumbling block for poor as well as rich. The poor, destitute, and even homeless can also be owned by things deemed great and not to be exchanged.

Verse 22. Jesus watched the mental wheels turn as the man tabulated the cost. "Sell whatsoever"—my goods, land, houses, business, antiques? "Give to the poor"—the wretches on the street, beggars? Return to "take up the cross"—am I to be crucified like a common criminal? "Follow me"—surrender my position of rulership to follow this doomed prophet from Nazareth? This would be a vow of poverty! The man's choice was deliberate: his desire for this life exceeded the desire for eternal life; the price was too high. His countenance registered the decision, action followed, and he turned away sad and grieved, ineligible for a discipleship that demanded a commitment beyond his desires.

In view of the commandments relating to God, Jesus' call to "follow me" works from the conclusion that He is

213

indeed God. If Christ were not deity, then His counsel, when followed, would be a transgression of the second commandment. Not only can possessions imprison and own the owner, they can also produce a false sense of earthly security and obscure possessions that are worth losing life to gain.

5. Discussion about Wealth and Reward (10:23-31)
(Matthew 19:23; Luke 18:24; cf. Matthew 6:19)

(23) And Jesus looked round about, and saith unto his disciples, How hardly shall they that have riches enter into the kingdom of God! (24) And the disciples were astonished at his words. But Jesus answereth again, and saith unto them, Children, how hard is it for them that trust in riches to enter into the kingdom of God! (25) It is easier for a camel to go through the eye of a needle, than for a rich man to enter into the kingdom of God. (26) And they were astonished out of measure, saying among themselves, Who then can be saved? (27) And Jesus looking upon them saith, With men it is impossible, but not with God: for with God all things are possible. (28) Then Peter began to say unto him, Lo, we have left all, and have followed thee. (29) And Jesus answered and said, Verily I say unto you, There is no man that hath left house, or brethren, or sisters, or father, or mother, or wife, or children, or lands, for my sake, and the gospel's, (30) but he shall receive an hundredfold now in this time, houses, and brethren, and sisters, and mothers, and children, and lands, with persecutions; and in the world to come eternal life. (31) But many that are first shall be last; and the last first.

This passage follows the previous teaching and is founded upon the previous incident. The theme (stated three times) is entrance into the kingdom of God; however, it carries a solemn warning about how wealth is valued in a person's life. Then Jesus made a comparison and answered the disciples' question.

Verse 23. Jesus, looking around after watching the rich young ruler depart, sadly exclaimed, "How difficult it is for those who have riches to enter into the kingdom of God!" The difficulty is not in the grace, mercy, or power of God, but with the temptation to amass what anchors the soul to earth, leaving no time or room in the affections for heaven. Too often possessions and their stewardship involve luxury, pride, and ease of life to the detriment of spiritual desire. "Riches," "wealth," and "possessions" include land, houses, appliances, equipment, furniture, and entertainment and leisure technology: television, video, sporting equipment, habits, or gadgets that can be riches, *chremata* (measured by legal tender). How different this reaction to the finding of the pearl of great price, for which the finder joyfully sold all his possessions to purchase (Matthew 13:46).

Verse 24. The disciples were amazed, astonished, and bewildered for two reasons. First, in their experience and mentality, wealth was an advantage, never a hazard, and here was a penniless prophet from Nazareth declaring that the standard of Jews, Romans, and the whole world is reversed.

Second, to the Jews God pronounced favor upon righteous or good people by material blessing. Wealth provided proof of excellent character and favor with God. With the obvious approval of God, how could the affluent have difficulty entering the kingdom? Jesus' remark "for them that trust in riches" (omitted from some texts, including Sinaitic and Vaticanus) implies a reliant confidence in the testimony of goodness and righteousness that possessions supposedly declare. To them riches meant favor.

"The poor have the gospel preached to them" brought rejoicing among the lower classes who lacked man's favor (Matthew 11:5; Luke 7:22; Isaiah 61:1-2). Christianity makes everyone equal. It is often said that the ground is level at the foot of the cross. Entry into the kingdom of God depends not on wealth or poverty, intellect or ignorance, temperament or talent, accounts or debts. It is hard or easy depending on the competing values held by each person.

Verse 25. Some dispute occurs over the hyperbolic expression of just how difficult is "hard" (verse 24), as well as whether the correct word is *kamilos* (rope) or *kamelos* (camel). Some point out that the small postern gate in the city wall was called the eye of the needle, but this is explanation rather than exegesis. Jesus used a metaphor to speak of a spiritual impossibility—not just something rare, but impossible (verse 27).

Verse 26. Again the disciples were astonished and amazed. According to their way of thinking, if the favored rich could not be saved, then who could? Jesus did not answer their question directly because the stage was not yet set for the gospel teaching of absolute dependence upon the grace and mercy of God through faith in Jesus Christ.

Verse 27. Mark underscores the importance of Jesus' next statement by noting that He looked on them with an earnest, intense gaze. He said, "With men it is impossible."

People cannot be saved without the enabling grace of God. Only God makes salvation possible; it is a gift from God and therefore impossible for a person to attain by birth, position, or possessions. However, "with God" a person can receive the impossible.

Materialism fixes a person's heart to this present world, obscuring the world beyond so that he does not readily wish to leave the advantages of opulence for the uncertainty of a life of faith. The prosperity gospel often preached in our generation is a human creation and without scriptural foundation. God does bless His people, but the blessings are not always material, and we are not exempt from the trials of life. Often the unrighteous enjoy great material benefits, and sometimes God may use prosperity to test our attitude because conceit, pride, and self-satisfaction often follow and reveal the character of the wealthy. The law of stewardship makes each person accountable to God for the way he obtains and uses possessions.

Verse 28. Peter's ever active mind drew a comparison between the disciples' own position and that of the rich young ruler. If the rich got nothing, did the poor disciples even stand a chance? It is doubtful that Peter was jealous of another social group, but his question was sincere. Nets and boats or tax receipts were small sacrifices compared to what this man had. Nets, receipt books, and carpenter tools represent livelihood, profession, skill, expertise—what one has and desires to have. Everyone has a "possession" to hang on to, to weigh against eternal life. The extent of sacrifice is the same: all.

Verses 29-30. Jesus pronounced a dual and manifold blessing, both here and hereafter on the person who lost

217

security, family, home, possessions, or career "for my sake, and the gospel's." The Lord pointed to the cause. Some have to sacrifice such things when they accept Christ, and some sacrifice such things in order to further the gospel. Although one cannot serve both God and mammon, one can serve God with mammon.

The quantification of blessing here in this life, one hundredfold, is figurative, for a wife or a mother is unique and cannot literally be replaced one hundredfold. Joining the elect provides brothers and sisters, homes and family members not only numerically greater but with sentiments and affections much deeper than those of the natural family. Heavenly love exceeds earthly affections, and Jesus becomes "all in all." His family is our family: we are "sons" of God, "heirs and joint heirs" with Christ. Whoever does the will of God is brother, sister, mother (Matthew 12:50).

Although the Lord rewards us in this life, we still face persecution from the world. Nevertheless, for every person who is happy in prosperity, hundreds can happily endure adversity (I Peter 4:14). This teaching removes the idea of material loss for material gain. It does not represent a personal investment for an expected return but a changed system of values. (See Ephesians 3:14-16.)

Verse 31. This epigram results from the reversal of values from the temporal to the eternal. The future belongs to the person who renounces wealth for the cause of Christ. To be favored highly in this world because of possessions is a reward for the blessings of God. In the world to come the line is reversed because God values and justly judges a person's motive.

6. Third Announcement of the Passion (10:32-34)
(Matthew 16:21)

(32) And they were in the way going up to Jerusalem; and Jesus went before them: and they were amazed; and as they followed, they were afraid. And he took again the twelve, and began to tell them what things should happen unto him, (33) saying, Behold, we go up to Jerusalem; and the Son of man shall be delivered unto the chief priests, and unto the scribes; and they shall condemn him to death, and shall deliver him to the Gentiles. (34) And they shall mock him, and shall scourge him, and shall spit upon him, and shall kill him: and the third day he shall rise again.

This was the clearest announcement of pending events, and it came on the road from Jericho to Jerusalem. It marks the beginning of the final scene on the road to Calvary. Jesus had withdrawn to the northern area, Caesarea Philippi, then moved south to halt in Galilee. Now by way of the hill country beyond Jordan, He and the disciples were en route to Judea, the seat of His greatest enemies.

Verse 32. Something about Jesus had undoubtedly changed, and the disciples sensed this in the set of His countenance (Luke 9:51), the look on His face (Isaiah 50:7), perhaps the urgent hastening, and they were amazed. Whereas the disciples feared death and only vaguely comprehended the facts, there was no fear in Jesus as He pressed resolutely forward alone. He took the Twelve apart from the crowd, maybe only a pause in the procession He was leading, to inform them a third time

219

(fourth, if the instance returning from the Mount of Transfiguration is included, 8:31; 9:12; 9:31) of the things to happen.

Verses 33-34. Each time Jesus told of His passion and death He revealed new details. In 8:31, He revealed that He would suffer, be rejected, be killed, and after three days rise again; in 9:12, He explained that He would suffer and be treated with contempt; in 9:31, He foretold that He would be delivered up—a hint of betrayal—then killed, to be resurrected the third day. He made no full exposure of the extent of His trial, mockery, and beating. This progressive disclosure might have taken place because the details became clearer as the event approached, or more likely, because Jesus knew the limits of the disciples' ability to receive this revelation.

This pronouncement was the most detailed and sharp. He would be betrayed into the hands of abusive Gentiles—despised outsiders, pagans, without the law. The vivid depiction of the sequence of events must have so captivated the disciples' thoughts until the last phrase—"and the third day he shall rise again"—was lost to their understanding, as subsequently recorded events in Mark and Luke 18:34 indicate.

One commentator identifies this as the twelfth prophecy recorded by Mark, the fourth of Christ's passion, and lists ten specifics given about the crucifixion: Jesus would be (1) taken in Jerusalem; (2) delivered (betrayed) to priests and scribes; (3) condemned to death; (4) delivered to Gentiles; (5) mocked; (6) scourged; (7) spit on; (8) killed; (9) remain dead three days; and (10) arise from death.[3]

This was the first time Jesus mentioned Gentile or

Roman involvement in His death. Although amazed and perplexed before, the disciples had stayed with Jesus, and their resolution remained in the face of this test also. Later tests were to severely try their resolve and faith.

Barclay noted the profound courage of Jesus as He faced this situation.[4] Courage waves two flags. First is the instantaneous, reflex action that enables a person to meet an unforeseen emergency in a heroic manner. Second, there is courage of resolute determination in the face of known crisis with its horrors as it is perceived approaching. Such courage is remarkable because a person of less determination might devise a means to escape. Jesus would have no compromise, no short cuts, nothing but complete and total obedience to the will of God.

7. Problem of Position among the Disciples (10:35-45)

a. Request of James and John (10:35-40)
(Matthew 20:20)

(35) And James and John, the sons of Zebedee, come unto him, saying, Master, we would that thou shouldest do for us whatsoever we shall desire. (36) And he said unto them, What would ye that I should do for you? (37) They said unto him, Grant unto us that we may sit, one on thy right hand, and the other on thy left hand, in thy glory. (38) But Jesus said unto them, Ye know not what ye ask: can ye drink of the cup that I drink of? and be baptized with the baptism that I am baptized with? (39) And they said unto him, We can. And Jesus said unto them, Ye shall indeed drink of the cup that I drink of;

221

*and with the baptism that I am baptized withal shall ye
be baptized: (40) but to sit on my right hand and on my
left hand is not mine to give; but it shall be given to them
for whom it is prepared.*

In the sober atmosphere of approaching doom James
and John made a most astounding request and received
from their Master a most astounding thing. Whether their
request was rooted in complete ignorance or acute per-
ceptivity, Jesus replied tenderly with gentle logic and used
the occasion to instruct all the disciples. The road to glory
was to be marked with hatred, rejection, spit, scourging,
mockery, and murder, yet these two sons of thunder held
their absolute faith in Him so that they saw Him "in thy
glory." Jesus responded by admitting them to the unique
fellowship of suffering. They did comprehend the nearness of the kingdom and wanted to stake a claim on it!

Verses 35-37. It was customary for pupils to ask of
leaders, kings, and those in power certain favors that
would be granted according to the generosity of the king.
(Herod promised "unto the half of my kingdom.") James
and John, through their mother, Salome (Matthew 20:20),
sought such a favor of Jesus. The nature of their request
denoted confidence that Jesus, regardless of His death,
would have a kingdom.

Their thoughts were of sitting on thrones as ministers
of state in victory judging Israel (Matthew 20:25). Why
not? They were part of the "inner circle," they held a kind
of social affluence (their father had servants; Mark 1:20),
they were known to the high priest (John 18:15-16), and if
Salome were Mary's sister, as some supposed, they were
maternal cousins to Jesus and their mother was Jesus'

aunt. Their aims and goals display either a depth of spiritual ambition or merely carnal earthly desire for shared greatness with the Messiah.

Verse 38. Jesus' answer was to the disciples, not Salome. "Ye know not" that My kingdom is spiritual and heavenly, not carnal and earthly; that victory must proceed glory; that blood relationships confer no right of position of merit. To help them think through the request, Jesus used two Jewish metaphors in phrasing His query. "Can ye drink of the cup?" signified the cup of man's portion in life determined by God and handed him to drink. At feasts the king or ruler determined the drink tempered and appointed for each guest (Psalm 75:8; Isaiah 51:17). Jesus' cup was passion and death on a Roman cross, and could they drink of His cup?

The second metaphor is similar: "and be baptized with the baptism?" Baptize (from Greek *baptizein,* a verb, and its participle *baptismenos,* to dip and submerge) meant to go through, endure, or be submerged in rejection, cruel infliction of pain, expressions of hatred, and finally death. He had already stated that this was to be at the hands of Gentiles and on a cross, the most cruel and awful of criminal deaths. His sacrifice was indeed to be salted with fire, for it pleased God "to make the captain of their salvation perfect through sufferings" (Hebrews 2:10).

Verse 39. "We can." Whether they made their affirmation through total ignorance or with spiritual insight is unclear, but James and John had gone too far to back out now. Whatever was in store for Jesus they were willing to accept. Jesus assured them that indeed they would drink of His cup and be baptized with His baptism in the coming days.

Acts 12:2 records the innocent martyrdom of James by Herod's sword for boldly preaching the gospel of the kingdom. John, according to Tertullian, was cast into boiling oil by Emperor Domitian but escaped unharmed.[5] Later tradition depicts John with a cup of poison in hand, and the New Testament records his exile to Patmos for the final revelation.

Verse 40. The gentle appointment followed in response to their request: "I will admit you to My cup and baptism, but to grant a seat on My left or right hand is not My prerogative. It shall be given to them for whom it is prepared." Jesus neither denied nor granted their request and thereby held open a prize for any and all aspiring disciples. Matthew 20:23 indicates that it is the Father's right to appoint to that place those for whom it has been prepared—in the past but with a continuing effect.

The Arians used this verse to claim that Jesus is not of the same substance *(homoousia)* as the Father. Jesus' words related to His humanity, however, and indicated voluntary action. The disciples were appointed to "a kingdom, as my Father hath appointed unto me" (Luke 22:29).

All disciples partake of the cup, an Old Testament symbol for suffering. Jesus referred to it in the Garden of Gethsemane (Mark 14:36). Whether the two sons of Zebedee fully realized the spiritual nature of their desire or the extent of its cost, it is evident that they still believed Him enough to commit themselves. Demonstrated loyalty, faith, and confidence must have provided inspiration for Jesus at this most needed moment. Their spirit was willing though He knew their flesh was weak. It is perhaps ironic that the desired positions on the left and right hand of Christ at the moment of His "glory" were held by two thieves (15:27).

b. Teaching to the Twelve (10:41-45)
(Matthew 20:24)

The request of James and John, its nature, and the interaction stirred a resentment in the other ten disciples. The old controversy of who was greatest, settled at Capernaum, was a divisive wedge to be avoided among the disciples, so Jesus dealt with it immediately. He contrasted Gentile leadership with His own rule and, using Himself as the chief example, set a pattern for Christian service.

(41) And when the ten heard it, they began to be much displeased with James and John. (42) But Jesus called them to him, and saith unto them, Ye know that they which are accounted to rule over the Gentiles exercise lordship over them; and their great ones exercise authority upon them. (43) But so shall it not be among you: but whosoever will be great among you, shall be your minister: (44) and whosoever of you will be the chiefest, shall be servant of all. (45) For even the Son of man came not to be ministered unto, but to minister, and to give his life a ransom for many.

Verse 41. The ten were much displeased, indignant (Matthew 20:24) with James and John at the attempt to steal a position by unfair advantage. Although two made the request, the desire was undoubtedly universal among them and so the remedy had to apply to all.

Verses 42-43. By no means could the disciples at this time be allowed to entertain thoughts leading to disharmony and a lack of unity. If Christ's cause would succeed, these principals of the kingdom needed clear understanding of kingdom principles. Jesus called them to Him for instruction and clarification.

He first explained the manner of lordship practiced by Gentiles, finding no fault with the exercise of authority. Whether civil or religious, it was ordained by God (Romans 13), but He condemned tyrannical and capricious power as the Gentiles implemented and as the disciples conceived of His kingdom. According to the world's standard of greatness a person's authority is measured by the number of subjects governed, servants commanded, or individuals compelled into obedience. Not so among the disciples; the kingdom of God had a different standard and that standard was humble service. Whoever will be great in the kingdom will not be so by reducing others to serve him, but he will minister to (serve) others, concerned about their well-being, happiness, and security. Exaltation in the kingdom is directly related to humble service.

Verse 44. Therefore, "and" as a consequence of this kingdom standard, whoever wants to be chief (Greek *protos*, first, foremost, chief) shall be servant (*doulos*, slave).

Verse 45. The best example is "the Son of man," Jesus' name for Himself—not a son of man but *the* Son of man, suggestive of Messiah to the religious-minded Jews. Others used "Son of man" only one recorded time, and that in a question of identity. Even the Son came not to be served nor to enjoy special favors for Himself but to serve.

The Psalms, Ezekiel, Daniel, and Isaiah present the Son of man as a servant (Isaiah 53:11-12). He came, emptied of ambition and well-being, to serve God by ministering to humanity. There was no concern for Himself or His will, no compelling of lesser people (and all were) to serve Him. He made no attempt to extract joy or pleasure as the expense of service to others, or to alleviate His own suffering and sorrow. He came divested of heavenly status, as a lowly, meek, humble servant.

Christ's ultimate service to humanity was to "give his life a ransom for many." The term "ransom" (Greek *lutron*) means the redeeming price to secure a person's freedom, loose him, or set free from being a slave. To whom was this redeeming price paid? Some ancient writers said the ransom was paid to the devil, but this view is flawed. Neither God nor the Son of man (God incarnate) bargained with the devil, but in every instance rebuked, resisted, and defeated him. Salvation is on God's terms, and the cost was the shedding of innocent blood to satisfy the requirements of God's holy law.

Christ died for all, not only the elect. Everyone has the means necessary for salvation, but only those who believe and obey the gospel actually experience the benefits.

Jesus dealt gently with the two sons of Zebedee for their desire and rebuked all for their misconception. Christian lordship is a contradiction of terms. He starkly contrasted the standards for greatness in the world and in the church: being served versus serving. While people desire to do as little as possible to become as great as possible, the Son of man came to do the maximum—give His life—so that people could have the freedom to choose.

8. Healing of the Jericho Beggar (10:46-52)
(Matthew 20:29; Luke 18:35)

(46) And they came to Jericho: and as he went out of Jericho with his disciples and a great number of people, blind Bartimaeus, the son of Timaeus, sat by the highway side begging. (47) And when he heard that it was Jesus of Nazareth, he began to cry out, and say, Jesus, thou son of David, have mercy on me. (48) And many charged him that he should hold his peace: but he cried the more a great deal, Thou son of David, have mercy on me. (49) And Jesus stood still, and commanded him to be called. And they call the blind man, saying unto him, Be of good comfort, rise; he calleth thee. (50) And he, casting away his garment, rose, and came to Jesus. (51) And Jesus answered and said unto him, What wilt thou that I should do unto thee? The blind man said unto him, Lord, that I might receive my sight. (52) And Jesus said unto him, Go thy way; thy faith hath made thee whole. And immediately he received his sight, and followed Jesus in the way.

This passage reveals the conditions for a miracle and that faith, not need, wrought the miracle for blind Bartimaeus. Jesus restored sight to the blind on six recorded occasions (Matthew 9:27; 12:22; 21:14; Mark 8:22; 10:46; John 9:1). This Jericho beggar might have heard of the other occasions and so determined not to miss his opportunity.

Verse 46. Jericho was the setting. Jesus crossed the Jordan River a few miles from Jericho and entered Judea en route to the Jerusalem feast a few days away. The ancient city of Jericho was famous even in Joshua's time when the Israelites captured it while entering Canaan. Known for its pleasant climate, palm groves, and balsam gardens, it lay fifteen to seventeen miles east-northeast of Jerusalem and at much lower elevation, about eight hundred feet below sea level. Many of the twenty thousand priests and thousands of Levites who attended the Temple in Jerusalem "by course" made this city their home when off duty. Now as Passover approached when all served, they traveled in procession along the rocky wilderness road up to Jerusalem.

Many other travelers—"a great number of people"— left Jericho that day; those who could not attend Passover would line the central roadway to wish travelers godspeed. Among those "by the highway side" was the blind beggar Bartimaeus, the son of Timaeus.

Details vary in the Synoptics. Matthew 20:29 records two blind men "as they departed from Jericho," and Luke 18:35 says the event occurred "as he was come nigh unto Jericho." Mark gives one man, gives his name, and notes the miracle occurred "as he went out of Jericho." It is possible Matthew refers to another instance altogether, or that Mark focuses only on one of two men. Moreover, in the time of Jesus there were actually two Jerichos: the site of Old Testament Jericho lay about one mile northwest of the modern city; New Testament Jericho, built in the Roman style by Herod the Great as winter quarters, was nearby. Jesus was apparently between the two locations, leaving the one and entering the other when the call from the blind beggar came.

Verse 47. When Bartimaeus heard the noisy procession approaching and heard that it was Jesus of Nazareth, he began to "cry out" loudly for mercy. "Son of David" was a Messianic title disputed in Mark 12:35-37 and used to denote one of the lineage of King David who would deliver Israel. It reflected Bartimaeus's concept of Jesus and His mission as a deliverer, not an uncommon concept at the time.

Verse 48. The crowd repeatedly rebuked his loud crying—perhaps because it disturbed those who listened to Jesus as He walked along and spoke. Bartimaeus's response was to persevere and cry out even more with renewed vigor.

Verses 49-50. Jesus stopped and called for the crier. The crowd's attitude changed. Rebukes turned to cheers now that this beggar was the subject of the Lord's interest. Thus highly favored, Bartimaeus cast off his loose outer robe or cloak, rose to his feet, and came to Jesus with expectant faith.

Verse 51. Although Jesus knew his need and the persistence of his cry for mercy, He wanted the request specified and articulated. Vague requests receive only vague responses. Bartimaeus's desire was intense and focused. "Lord" (*rabboni* or *rabbouni;* "My Master," a term of great respect among Jews), "that I might receive my sight"—literally *anablepso*, to see again, implying that Bartimaeus had not always been blind.

Verse 52. Jesus responded, "Go thy way; thy faith hath made thee whole." "Immediately," instantaneously, sight was restored. Bartimaeus received because of faith, persistence in calling out to Jesus, and expectancy of receiving. Too often people entreat God out of need and desire but not in faith, believing the work will be accomplished. Faith, not need, effected this cure.

We can identify the conditions of this miracle as follows: (1) desperate need and desire for renewed vision; (2) immediate, eager response to Jesus' call; (3) specific request; (4) absolute faith and trust in the face of the discouraging crowds; and (5) gratitude expressed by loyally following Jesus in the way.

Notes

[1]Barclay, 246.
[2]R. Alan Cole, *Mark* (Grand Rapids: Eerdmans, 1989), 159.
[3]Dake, marginal note on Mark 10:33.
[4]Barclay, 262.
[5]*Pulpit Commentary*, 65.

D.
Ministry in Jerusalem
(11:1-13:37)

D. Ministry in Jerusalem (11:1-13:37)
1. Preparatory Events (11:1-26)

Chapter 11 records the triumphal entry of Jesus into Jerusalem one week before Passover. All the Gospels record this event. Prior to this time Jesus had resisted talk of Him as Messiah or King of Israel (8:27-33), but now, as predicted by the prophets and in a premeditated manner, He accepted praise and acclaim as their King—not as a warrior, but peacefully, thus dramatizing His Messiahship.

a. Entry into Jerusalem as Messiah (11:1-11)
(Matthew 21:1; Luke 19:28; John 12:12)

(1) And when they came nigh to Jerusalem, unto Bethphage and Bethany, at the mount of Olives, he sendeth forth two of his disciples, (2) and saith unto them, Go your way into the village over against you: and as soon as ye be entered into it, ye shall find a colt tied, whereon never man sat; loose him, and bring him. (3) And if any man say unto you, Why do ye this? say ye that the Lord hath need of him; and straightway he will send him hither. (4) And they went their way, and found the colt tied by the door without in a place where two ways met; and they loose him. (5) And certain of them that stood there said unto them, What do ye, loosing the colt? (6) And they said unto them even as Jesus had commanded: and they let them go. (7) And they brought the colt to Jesus, and cast their garments on him; and he sat upon him. (8) And many spread their

garments in the way: and others cut down branches off the trees, and strawed them in the way. (9) And they that went before, and they that followed, cried, saying, Hosanna; Blessed is he that cometh in the name of the Lord: (10) blessed be the kingdom of our father David, that cometh in the name of the Lord: Hosanna in the highest. (11) And Jesus entered into Jerusalem, and into the temple: and when he had looked round about upon all things, and now the eventide was come, he went out unto Bethany with the twelve.

Verses 1-3. The last stage of Jesus' approach to Jerusalem came to a close. From Jericho to Jerusalem is about fifteen to seventeen miles, requiring a seven-hour walk. About a Sabbath day's journey from the capital, two villages about a mile apart lay on the road to Jerusalem: Bethany, "house of dates," and Bethphage, "house of figs." As Jesus reached the Mount of Olives, He sent two disciples into a village "over against you," probably Bethphage, where there was tied a colt that had never been ridden.

Matthew says a donkey and a colt (foal of a donkey), and Mark adds that the colt was tied "where two ways met" (verse 4). Customarily, colts remained free near their mothers since they rarely wandered away, but to assure availability this colt was tied. This and the signal words "the Lord hath need of him" suggest a prearrangement by the Lord for this occasion. If so, these arrangements must have escaped the disciples' notice and taken place before the withdrawal from Judea. Of course, Jesus had the divine ability to reveal out-of-sight things as easily as He prophesied events to come (cf. Mark 14:13).

For three years Jesus walked over Palestine, but as

Zechariah 9:9 predicted, this day He would be a peaceful conqueror and ride into the city as King.

Verses 4-7. The disciples found the colt, explained to "them" its use and return, and then brought it to Jesus, where they cast garments on the animal's back to form a kind of saddle or cushion.

Verse 8. Many people saw the procession and spread their garments in the way, realizing the dramatic symbolism. (In the East, princes and judges rode white donkeys and their sons rode on colts.) Casting garments and branches from palm trees in the path provided evidence of honor and devotion. Undoubtedly many of these people were strangers staying in Bethany and Bethphage for the Passover, as were Jesus and His disciples.

This triumphal entry was patterned after a reigning monarch returning home from battle leading his subdued conquests, but it differed in several important ways. No instruments of war, swords, spears, bows, armor, horses, or soldiers were evident, only garments and palm fronds. This monarch sat on a colt symbolic of dignity and humility of a spiritual kingdom, and not on a horse symbolic of war, oppression, and physical conquest.

At Passover time, Jewish fervor for a deliverer reached a peak, reminiscent of the triumphal entry of Jehu, the man of blood (II Kings 9:13), or Judas Maccabeus during the intertestamental period, who was welcomed with harps, cymbals, viols, and branches of palms because he had overthrown the oppressor's yoke. This day Israel sought a conquering hero to deliver them from Rome.

Verses 9-10. The Jews expressed their expectation of a divine deliverer by the cries of "Hosanna" that preceded and followed the spiritual Messiah. Hosanna, best rendered "O save" or "save us now," was a cry of hope for deliverance of the Jewish victims of war and oppression. "Blessed be the king that cometh, the king of our father David" was the song of pilgrims coming for the Passover festival commemorating Israel's deliverance from Egypt, and not from the mob of residents who clamored for Christ's death (Luke 23:21). Jesus was to them the expected coming One (Matthew 11:3), king of Davidic lineage about to set up His throne. Even the disciples after the resurrection held this idea (Acts 1:6).

Jesus was never discredited as an heir of David through genealogy. Had His lineage been in question, His enemies in high places would have denounced His right to the throne and Messiahship.

Pilgrims returning to the Temple on feast days used the greeting "Blessed is he that cometh in the name of the Lord" to denote the Messiah as One who is coming. It is a quotation from Psalm 118:26.

People used it to refer to the intertestamental deliverance of Israel from the wicked Syrian despot Antiochus, who forced on the Jews Greek culture and idols. In 167 B.C. Jews could be killed for having a copy of the law or for circumcision of male children. Antiochus desecrated their place of worship by substituting Zeus for Jehovah and swine for a burnt offering. The chambers of the Temple were used as a brothel until Judas Maccabaeus drove him out in 163 B.C. and repurified and reconsecrated the site for the pious Jews. "Hosanna in the highest" was not merely a cry of praise but a cry to God to "break in" for them as Messiah from realms of glory where salvation is perfected and once again deliver and save (II Samuel 4:4; II Kings 6:26).

Verse 11. Amid the crowd's clamor and Pharisees' protests, Jesus courageously led the way to the Temple. This was not the *naon* (house) but *hieron* (courts)—not the Temple proper but the Temple courtyard. His purpose appeared to be to inspect the proceedings. This entry was peaceful and gentle.

Jesus' humble yet bold action sent a clear message to both Romans and Jews. First, the Romans expected trouble and fortified the garrison with soldiers at this time of year. Religious tolerance was allowed, and Rome interfered little with the Jews in the practice of their strange religion. All was to be done in quiet dignity and decency; the well-manned post saw to that.

Second, Jesus chose to ride a donkey, fulfilling an Old Testament prophecy (Zechariah 9:9). The prophecy described a deliverer coming to Zion (Jerusalem, and by extension, the church), just and having salvation (vindicated and victorious), lowly (coming in peace, nonmilitant), riding a donkey. Donkeys were used by royalty and officials upon civil duties; horses denoted battle or war. The message Jesus sent that day was: "Yes, I am Messiah, but not your sort of Messiah. I lead a rebellion, not against Rome, but against your own traditions. I come to attack the grip the opposition has on all humanity. I am not the warrior Messiah you seek." (In Revelation, by contrast, Jesus returns on a white horse in battle array, coming to attack and deliver.)

Many biblical scholars believe that this day fulfilled Daniel's prophetic pronouncement of the Prince Messiah's coming (Daniel 9:24-27). The opposition sought to still the voices of praise and cries of hosanna, shouts of triumph, and prayers for help. To their demands, Jesus declared that if crowds failed to declare Him Messiah, stones would cry out. Prophecy must be fulfilled; He would be declared Messiah in Israel on this day. Jesus undoubtedly was keenly aware of the exact day in history and it being the termination of the period of Daniel's prophecy.

Only Mark indicates this preliminary inspection of the Temple, after which Jesus retired to the peace and quiet of Bethany. Away from the crowds Jesus and the disciples were free to seek God in open solitude. Although Lazarus, Mary, and Martha lived in Bethany (John 11:1) and Jesus spent the nights of this last week in the village, none of the Gospel accounts indicate whether He stayed in their home.

b. Cursing of the fig tree (11:12-14)
(Matthew 21:17; cf. Luke 13:6)

(12) And on the morrow, when they were come from Bethany, he was hungry: (13) and seeing a fig tree afar off having leaves, he came, if haply he might find any thing thereon: and when he came to it, he found nothing but leaves; for the time of figs was not yet. (14) And Jesus answered and said unto it, No man eat fruit of thee hereafter for ever. And his disciples heard it.

Cursing a fruitless fig tree presents expositors with a difficult problem. Some feel the act to be unworthy of the Lord and uncalled for under seasonal circumstances. Some explain that the fig tree was cursed because it represented hypocrisy—leaves without promised fruit— while others emphasize that it was a lesson in faith for His followers, as the text bears out. This is the only time Jesus cursed and destroyed anything. The duty remains to discover what Jesus taught with this lesson.

The incident was separated into two parts by yet another dramatic event of the last week of Christ's earthly life, the cleansing of the Temple. The fig tree incident occurred on two successive days and was treated as an acted parable.

Verse 12. The next day was after Palm Sunday, Monday, Nisan 11, or March 21. The night in Bethany spent outdoors or the early departure left Jesus hungry (Matthew 21:18), revealing His complete humanity amid miracles attesting His deity.

Verse 13. A fig tree alone and conspicuous was not an uncommon sight around Bethany, "the house of figs." Jesus saw a fig tree afar off—Matthew says "in the way"—because of its lush foliage. It seemed in advance of the season as a harbinger of nearing summer (Luke 21:29-30). Peculiarly, some figs mature on the tree before leaves and well before the expected fruit-bearing season. Jesus found nothing but leaves because "the time of figs was not yet."

Verse 14. Jesus spoke to the tree a curse: "No man eat fruit of thee hereafter for ever." This curse seems severe if it was based on an expectation of figs before they were due. Passover season was mid-April; figs normally ripened in late May or early June.

It appears that the curse was symbolic and served as a dramatic and acted parable. The fig tree represented the Jewish nation professing hope and promise but providing only fruitless deception and hypocrisy. Israel was the reservoir of spiritual hope, a promise without fulfillment, and the curse resulted from uselessness. Israel's favored position, early growth, familiarity with God's covenants, and early emphasis on religion but with no fruit cost Israel her place "for ever" (Matthew 21:43-45).

Another lesson on faith comes later (verses 20-25), but the disciples must have wondered at the grace and obedience of this One who was able to curse a fig tree and cause it to wither, yet would endure patiently without any exhibition of inherent latent power the destructive humiliating torment of His enemies.

c. Cleansing of the Temple (11:15-19)
(Matthew 21:12; Luke 19:45)

(15) And they come to Jerusalem: and Jesus went into the temple, and began to cast out them that sold and bought in the temple, and overthrew the tables of the moneychangers, and the seats of them that sold doves; (16) and would not suffer that any man should carry any vessel through the temple. (17) And he taught, saying unto them, Is it not written, My house shall be called of all nations the house of prayer? but ye have made it a den of thieves. (18) And the scribes and chief priests heard it, and sought how they might destroy him: for they feared him, because all the people was astonished at his doctrine. (19) And when even was come, he went out of the city.

This passage, typical of Mark, depicts Jesus as a man of words and action, righting wrongs, claiming His own. His indignation again erupted against corrupt "religious" Temple practices and unfair and partial treatment of pil-

242

grim worshipers. Both His actions and words revealed authority as Messiah and show His reverence for the sacred things of God that people defiled. The response to this purging was a plot to destroy Him, from which Jesus once again retreated.

Verses 15-16. Entering Jerusalem, Jesus went to the Temple and found what He undoubtedly observed the previous evening: buying, selling, and merchandising in the name of religion. The area known as the Temple included four major courts or areas each within the other. Two Greek terms describe key differences: *hieron* means the whole Temple area, with its three courts; *naos* means the Temple proper within the Court of the Priests. (See Figure 2.)

The outermost Court of the Gentiles was open to all people, Jew or Gentile, but the latter could not pass beyond a low wall with its instructive tables under penalty of death. The next area, the Court of the Women, restricted Jewish women from going further unless they bore a sacrificial offering. Congregations met on special occasions in the third area, the Court of Israel, where the priests received offerings. The innermost court or *naos*, the Court of the Priests, was considered the Temple proper because the primary Temple structure stood in this court. It was off-limits to all but priests.

The cleansing took place in the Court of the Gentiles, where dedicated prayer and meditation was quite impossible due to secular merchandising. Activities included three transactions, all dishonest and aimed to take advantage of worshiping pilgrims.

First, the priests themselves sold sacrificial animals at exorbitant prices. The family of the high priest owned the "market," and frequently they deemed as unfit the animals brought by worshipers for sacrifice and sold a sheep or an ox as a substitute. The unfit animal became fit for sale later. In this way people were swindled of their animals and money.

Second, the Temple tax of one-half shekel per year due at Passover had to be paid in special coinage, the sanctuary shekel. The exchange rate was two denarii but if their coin—Greek, Roman, Syrian, Phoenician, Egyptian—exceeded the amount of the Temple tax, an additional fee of two denarii was exacted.

Third, women dealt in doves. Outside the Temple a pair of doves cost nine denarii, but when these birds were condemned for sacrifice (Leviticus 12:8; 14:22; 15:14), a pair from the ladies' Temple stalls cost fifteen denarii. Jesus referred to this all as "a den of robbers."

The Mishnah declared that a man could not enter the Temple Mount with a vessel, staff, wallet, sandals, or dust on his feet, or use it as a pass-through for street traffic seeking a shorter path. In reality, the Mount had become a thoroughfare for commerce. Priests permitted those laden with goods to pass to the city or east to the Mount of Olives, further adding to the confusion in the Court of the Gentiles. This was too much. Jesus, moved to anger, corrected the abuse.

Verse 17. In this cleansing four days before His death (Matthew 21:12), Jesus pointed to the law and prophetic writings (Isaiah 56:7; Jeremiah 7:11). The reverence of "My house shall be called of all nations the house of prayer" had been violated by exclusion of some and by the religious cloak of thievery that transpired in the sacred place. "Thieves" should be more aptly rendered "robbers" as in John 10:1.

Temple Area at the Time of Christ.

A. Court of Gentiles, dimensions:
   north wall, 1,041 feet
   east wall, 1,556 feet
   south wall, 929 feet
   west wall, 1,596 feet

B. Balustrade warning Gentiles not to enter the sacred area

C. Court of Women, 135 cubits square

D. Court of the Israelites, at least 11 cubits beyond the Court of the Priests on all sides, 198 cubits long east to west, 157 cubits wide north to south

E. Court of the Priests, 187 cubits long, 135 cubits wide

F. Holy Place, 20 cubits wide, 40 cubits long

G. Holy of Holies, 20 cubits square

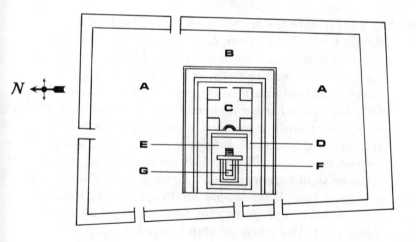

Verse 18. By cleansing the Temple, Christ exercised authority that scribes and chief priests said belonged only to God, the Messiah, a prophet, or the Sanhedrin. "My house" (verse 17) identified Jesus as claiming ownership as well as declaring His identity, which insulted and angered the Temple officials. People consciously or unconsciously destroy what they fear, and from this point on Jesus was the object of an open plot to destroy Him. Religious leaders could not tolerate among them a Man so admired by the people, so powerful with God, and so authoritative over them and their wicked practices.

Verse 19. As every evening before in this final week, Jesus left the city at night to spend time in Bethany or isolated areas on the Mount of Olives.

d. Lesson from the withered fig tree (11:20-26)
(Matthew 21:20)

(20) And in the morning, as they passed by, they saw the fig tree dried up from the roots. (21) And Peter calling to remembrance saith unto him, Master, behold, the fig tree which thou cursedst is withered away. (22) And Jesus answering saith unto them, Have faith in God. (23) For verily I say unto you, That whosoever shall say unto this mountain, Be thou removed, and be thou cast into the sea; and shall not doubt in his heart, but shall believe that those things which he saith shall come to pass; he shall have whatsoever he saith. (24) Therefore I say unto you, What things soever ye desire, when ye pray, believe that ye receive them, and ye shall have them. (25) And when ye stand praying, forgive, if ye

*have ought against any: that your Father also which is
in heaven may forgive you your trespasses. (26) But if
ye do not forgive, neither will your Father which is in
heaven forgive your trespasses.*

Verse 20. This event occurred on the third day of the
final week of Jesus' earthly life. On the first day He
entered the city in triumph amid much public acclaim,
noted the activities at the Temple, and retired at evening
to Bethany. On the morning of the second day He and the
disciples returned to the city, He cursed the fruitless fig
tree, then He cleansed the Temple. As before, He departed
the city at evening. The third day Jesus again returned to
the city, and the disciples commented on the cursed fig
tree being "dried up from the roots."

Verse 21. Peter called attention to the tree as being the
one cursed and withered away so soon. Jesus offered no
explanation of why He cursed the tree but used it to teach
a lesson on petition and faith.

Verse 22. "Have faith in God." This tree reminded them
to have faith—complete, perfect, and effectual—in God.
Forthcoming events would confuse and perplex their
understanding, but they needed to have faith in God and
not in the nation of Israel. The Jews might flourish fruitless for a while, but their nation would soon wither.

Verses 23-24. The scope of the lesson extends to the
potential limits of a person's faith as well as a gentle repri-
mand for lack of faith in Him, for they were astonished at
the sudden, drastic result. The rabbinic phrase "uprooting
a mountain" emphasized the concept of faith in prayer.

Similar expressions in Matthew 17:20 and Luke 17:6—
one pertaining to moving a mountain, the other to plucking

up a mulberry tree—leave the impression that Jesus taught the need for faith in prayer on different occasions. Faith brings people into the presence of God (Hebrews 11:6), allows them to be accepted and justified by God (Romans 4:13-25), begins their redemption, and is essential to continue (Galatians 3:1-6). Prayer is acceptance of God's will, favorable to our will or not, because faith is in a God who knows best.

Jesus promised that we would receive answers in prayer when we believe. God is not limited when we ask in faith, without wavering. The emphatic nature of these promises is evident by Christ's authoritative statements: "For verily I say unto you . . ." (verse 23) and "Therefore I say unto you . . ." (verse 24).

Much modern-day "faith" dogma of "name it and claim it" has been built on these and related verses of Scripture. Such a dogma would have a believer simply state his desires, wants, wishes and needs, holding that God is compelled to provide them because "he shall have whatsoever he saith." The true promise is that a gracious Father will grant the prayerful petitions from a trusting, believing, faithful heart who seeks God's will and acknowledges that God knows best the real needs of His true children.

Verses 25-26. The lesson continues to probe the heart for relationship toward God, a relationship most often expressed in our relationship to our fellow man. Jesus identified a forgiving spirit as a condition for answered prayer.

The typical Eastern prayer posture was to stand humbly with head bowed reverently. Christ looked for a bowed heart, humble, forgiving, and conscious of the grace received of God in forgiveness of sins. Only when we are willing to forgive others does God desire to forgive us.

Verse 26, omitted in several manuscripts, adds weight by means of a logical deduction from the preceding verse. God is not capricious or arbitrary in refusing to forgive, but our unforgiving attitude renders it impossible for us to receive what God freely offers.

2. Public Teaching in Jerusalem (11:27-12:44)
a. Questions by enemies (11:27-12:34)
(1) Question of authority (11:27-12:12)

Now Jesus' authority was questioned as a means to bring specific charges against Him, whether heresy, blasphemy or sedition, because His enemies sought to destroy Him (verse 18). Jesus heard their questions, then posed His own question on the condition that if they truthfully answered His question, He would answer theirs. They could not safely answer Him so Jesus felt no compulsion to answer them. The entire scene from this point until the crucifixion shows Jesus sitting in judgment against religious leaders who rejected His message and person.

(a) Questioners silenced (11:27-33)
(Matthew 21:23; Luke 20:1)

(27) And they come again to Jerusalem: and as he was walking in the temple, there come to him the chief priests, and the scribes, and the elders, (28) and say unto him, By what authority doest thou these things?

*and who gave thee this authority to do these things?
(29) And Jesus answered and said unto them, I will also
ask of you one question, and answer me, and I will tell
you by what authority I do these things. (30) The baptism of John, was it from heaven, or of men? answer me.
(31) And they reasoned with themselves, saying, If we
shall say, From heaven; he will say, Why then did ye not
believe him? (32) But if we shall say, Of men; they
feared the people: for all men counted John, that he was
a prophet indeed. (33) And they answered and said unto
Jesus, We cannot tell. And Jesus answering saith unto
them, Neither do I tell you by what authority I do these
things.*

Verses 27-28. Jesus with the disciples proceeded to
the Temple, where great religious teachers walked among
the cloisters and arcades. A deputation of chief priests,
scribes, and elders arrived, probably sent by the Sanhedrin of which they were a part. They were within their
rights as Temple guardians to question His authority to
"do these things." "These things" doubtless refer to the
casting out of the merchandising, teaching the people,
accepting their "hosannas," healing, casting out spirits,
and the like.

Their aim was to establish His claim to authority as
either inherent or derived. If inherent—that is, of His
own—they could arrest Him on the charge of blasphemy.
If He claimed derived authority, they could arrest Him as
one without credentials or authorization, because they
represented God and never allowed anyone to disturb the
sacredness of their religious institutions.

Verses 29-30. Jesus did not refuse to answer their

question but countered with a question that when answered would answer their own. In essence, Jesus said, "You do not accept My word that I am from God; do you believe John, who declared that I came from God as the Lamb and your Messiah?" The actual question was a literary synedoche, in which a part is used to represent the whole: "Where did John get his authority to baptize and teach? If his authority came from God, so does Mine, because as a forerunner, servant, and friend of the Bridegroom, he testified of Me."

This counterquestion made them reflect, since John pointed everyone to the Messiah: "One comes after me whose shoes I am not worthy to unloose; he shall baptize you with the Holy Ghost and with fire." This they found unsafe to believe, though true, because their intellect was subordinate to stubborn will.

Certainly Jesus did not receive authority from John or act under John's authority, but besides Himself, John was the only human reference who could attest to the source of His authority. He had done so, publicly and forcefully, only to be denied. To this inescapable logic Jesus demanded, "Answer me."

Verses 31-32. All Israel knew John was a prophet of God; they knew his lifestyle, sacrifice, and ultimate martyrdom, and to answer required cautious reason. The questioners' selfish reasoning was aimed to promote the security of their own position and not to discover or admit revealed truth. Their reasoning allowed two possible answers. (1) From heaven. This would be a tacit admission that they had not obeyed God, for they refused to heed John's message to repent or in any way alter their religious hypocrisy. Christ would respond, "Why then did

251

ye not believe him?" (2) From men—here Mark uses a broken sentence with powerful effect. The people respected John as a prophet, and since the deputation desired the people's good will, they could not openly speak against John.

Verse 33. They answered with a lie: "We cannot tell," meaning they would not admit the truth. The logic of their reasoning betrayed them and exposed that they did know. If they answered truthfully about John then they would answer their own question about Jesus, because the answer was the same. They stood accused as blasphemers and heretics, refusing John as the prophet of God and Jesus as the Son of God. Indirectly but conclusively Jesus answered their question.

Again they refused to accept His words, and this denial set the stage for the revealing parable to follow.

(b) Questioners exposed (12:1-12)
(Matthew 21:33; Luke 20:9)

(1) And he began to speak unto them by parables. A certain man planted a vineyard, and set an hedge about it, and digged a place for the winefat, and built a tower, and let it out to husbandmen, and went into a far country. (2) And at the season he sent to the husbandmen a servant, that he might receive from the husbandmen of the fruit of the vineyard. (3) And they caught him, and beat him, and sent him away empty. (4) And again he sent unto them another servant; and at him they cast stones, and wounded him in the head, and sent him away shamefully handled. (5) And again he sent another; and him they killed, and many others; beating some,

and killing some. (6) Having yet therefore one son, his wellbeloved, he sent him also last unto them, saying, They will reverence my son. (7) But those husbandmen said among themselves, This is the heir; come, let us kill him, and the inheritance shall be ours. (8) And they took him, and killed him, and cast him out of the vineyard. (9) What shall therefore the lord of the vineyard do? he will come and destroy the husbandmen, and will give the vineyard unto others. (10) And have ye not read this scripture; The stone which the builders rejected is become the head of the corner: (11) this was the Lord's doing, and it is marvellous in our eyes? (12) And they sought to lay hold on him, but feared the people: for they knew that he had spoken the parable against them: and they left him, and went their way.

This eighth parable recorded by Mark contains more than the usual number of specifically identifiable events, persons, and places, making it appear almost as an allegory. The husbandmen (tenant farmers) represent Israel, while the householder (owner) represents God. The parable illustrates the Jewish rejection of Jesus, the Son of God (verses 10-11).

Verse 1. Jesus directed His words to the questioning chief priests, scribes and Pharisees, but the entire assemblage heard. Jewish familiarity with agriculture, vineyards and Old Testament imagery allowed them to readily identify characters of the story. Isaiah 5:1-7 identifies Israel as the vineyard. Psalm 80:8-13 clearly identifies Israel as the vine; the "certain man" who "brought the vine out of Egypt" was none other than God. The vine represents the kingdom of God planted to be fruitful.

253

A vineyard was the highest-yielding land investment, but it also demanded the greatest protection and unceasing care. Part of the care is indicated in Mark's narrative. The planter set a hedge about it; either an actual hedge of prickly plants or a stone fence or wall. This wall marked the property boundary and kept out wild animals, boars,[1] and robbers. The vineyard was equipped with a winepress to tread out the grapes with the feet and a vat ("winefat") underneath to catch the juice.

The owner built a tower four cubits square and ten cubits high from which the overseer watched the vineyard. It also served as a storage place for wine and a lodging. Finally, the owner leased the vineyard to tenants and went into a far country for a long time (Luke 20:9).

Verse 2. "At the season" for profitable fruit bearing, recognized as five years or the fourth season after planting (Leviticus 19:23-25), the owner sent a servant (*doulon*, a bond slave) to receive the vineyard's fruit as rightfully expected. All vineyard imagery is from the Old Testament, but the absentee owner and tenant farmer are New Testament Palestine phenomena. Many landowners chose to live outside Palestine, lease their land, and receive a share in harvest profits.

Verses 3-5. Servants represent the prophets (cf. Amos 3:7; Jeremiah 7:25; Zechariah 1:6)—spokesmen for God such as Moses, Aaron, and David who were treated scandalously by the cultivators, that is, the rulers of Israel. One servant they caught, beat, and sent away empty; another they cast stones at, wounded in the head, and sent away shamefully handled. Still another they killed. Others sent in succession received similar treatment: beating and murder. Admittedly, Israel's treatment of their prophets was harsh and unfeeling. Jesus spoke woe to them because they built fine tombs for dead prophets yet denied responsibility for their deaths (Matthew 23:29-32). One generation killed prophets, another buried them; thus both shared in the crime, and their blood was required of the present generation (Luke 11:48-51).

Verses 6-8. The owner had yet one—a beloved son—to send to the tenants. This son they would surely respect. But the tenants reasoned otherwise: kill the heir and the vineyard was theirs. They acted on their thoughts, took the son, killed him, and cast him out of the vineyard. In actuality, Jesus was cast outside the city walls and there killed.

Why the rulers felt they could kill the Son and take over the inheritance is speculative. Perhaps they believed that God's favor to the Jews through the Abrahamic Covenant was irrevocable and forever assured. Perhaps they felt God was too far away to interfere, or had given the religious operation over into their hand. They failed to realize that refused privileges and responsibilities pass on to others. Jewish rejection led to the Gentiles being brought into fruitfulness (Romans 11:12-15).

The Son's coming had a finality about it that bespoke a last effort of God to reconcile the rebellious tenants. He was God's ultimate word to the cultivators. There would be no more effort at securing a yield from these robbers. In light of this they chose to kill Him. Cole remarked, "It was not through their failure to recognize the Son that they killed him; that would have been pardonable. It was, as in the parable, precisely because they recognized Him for who He was that they slew Him."[2]

Verses 9-11. The parable of the wicked husbandmen is

in reality a parable of refusal and doom for Israel and a parable of the rejected Son. No nation ever had greater privilege and responsibility to do a service for God.

This parable speaks much about the nature of God, His providential care, and His expectations. As owner of the vineyard, God generously provisions and equips the vineyard to produce efficiently and profitably. Nothing is spared; only the best is given. God is also trusting: just as the owner left tenants to operate in his absence, so God allows us to run our lives as we choose. God is patient, waiting long for His harvest, but also sending servant after servant to seek what is His. People have many chances to pay a longsuffering God their debt to Him.

Finally, the parable reveals a God of eventual triumph and justice. Generation after generation of people may presume upon the patience, mercy, and longsuffering of the grace-giving God, but in the end there is just retribution. God will come to claim what is His. He will put down disobedience, cruelty, and rebellion by a just judgment.

This parable provides insight about how Jesus thought of Himself. First, He regarded Himself as more than just another prophet in a line of successive servants sent to Israel. He was the Son, beloved, begotten, greater than any prophet. This was a deliberate affront to the Jews who viewed Abraham (father), Moses (lawgiver), Solomon (wisdom), and David (king) as Israel's greatest. But a greater than Solomon walked among them (Matthew 12:41-42).

Second, Jesus knew He was about to die. John pronounced the death sentence when declaring Him to be the Lamb bearing the world's sins. Lambs were sacrificed. In the face of impending doom, His courage and resolution never wavered.

Third, Jesus was certain of triumph. Death by crucifixion after cruel torture and humiliation was not the end; after rejection would come glory. The Son would become the chief cornerstone in a new and glorious establishment, the church. In pronouncing ultimate victory He quoted Psalm 118:22.

Verse 12. The religious rulers understood the meaning of the parable. They desired to kill Jesus for indicting them in this manner, but they knew the people supported Him, so they left.

(2) Question of tribute (12:13-17)
(Matthew 22:15; Luke 20:20; cf. Matthew 17:24)

(13) And they send unto him certain of the Pharisees, and of the Herodians, to catch him in his words. (14) And when they were come, they say unto him, Master, we know that thou art true, and carest for no man: for thou regardest not the person of men, but teachest the way of God in truth: Is it lawful to give tribute to Caesar, or not? (15) Shall we give, or shall we not give? But he, knowing their hypocrisy, said unto them, Why tempt ye me? bring me a penny, that I may see it. (16) And they brought it. And he saith unto them, Whose is this image and superscription? And they said unto him, Caesar's. (17) And Jesus answering said unto them, Render to Caesar the things that are Caesar's, and to God the things that are God's. And they marvelled at him.

The question of tribute money is one of four types of questions asked of Jesus designed to entrap, expose, and reveal His position.[3] The religious leaders determined to destroy Him and sought proper grounds to do so. Their questions took the form of (1) rabbinic or legal questions (verses 13-17); (2) mocking or teasing questions (verses 18-27); (3) moral principle or issue questions (verses 28-34); and (4) religious questions that conflicted with or contradicted Scripture.

Each question was steeped in Jewish history, which must be comprehended to gain full impact. The questions might have been sincere since His position on political, civil, and ecclesiastical matters of importance to the Jews was unknown, but Mark states that the questions were to "catch him in his words" (verse 13). Jesus' answers revealed kingdom principles and operation and are more than rhetoric or disputation.

When Herod the Great died in 4 B.C., his Palestine kingdom was divided among his sons, Antipas (Galilee, Perea), Philip (Trachonitis, Iturea), and Archelaus (Samaria, Judea). In A.D. 6, Rome replaced the inept Archelaus and made the southern kingdom into a province ruled by a procurator who answered directly to the emperor. While other kingdoms paid tribute to Philip or Antipas, Judea and Samaria paid tribute to Caesar under the governor.

The first governor, Cyrenius, made a census to enable fair taxation but the Jews resisted, led by Judas the Gaulonite. Josephus records a teaching that only God could be Lord and ruler of the Jews and that taxation was the first step toward slavery.[4] This was Judas's position, and though his rebellion was crushed, the sentiment and resistance to provincial taxation remained: "No tribute to the Romans."

Three taxes were exacted: an agrarian produce tax (one-tenth of grain and one-fifth of wine and fruit, paid in kind or money), an income tax of one percent on all earnings, and a poll tax, the *tributum capitis*. The poll or head tax so opposed by Jews was assessed of every male age fourteen to sixty-five and every female age twelve to sixty-five. It paid simply for the right to exist and had a special coin minted for the purpose, a *denarius* (a day's wage for a laborer).

Verse 13. The Pharisees and the Herodians, a sect of Herod supporters that drew adherents from across many other sects, approached Jesus with questions to entrap and discredit Him with the people or with Rome, depending on His answer.

Verse 14. They began with flattery, attempting to allay suspicions, with words phrased that if true made it all but impossible for Jesus not to answer their question. The question itself pertained to paying tribute or taxes to Caesar and could have been informational except that those asking represented two groups: one opposed to paying, the other supportive. "Yes, it is lawful to pay tribute" would lose support of the people, Pharisees, and staunch Jews. "No tribute" would lose the Herodians and protection of the Roman civil authorities; His enemies could then have Him arrested by Rome. The question posed an inescapable dilemma much like that asked by Jesus Himself (11:30-33).

Verses 15-16. Matthew 22:18 says Jesus perceived their evil intent and named them hypocrites. They flattered to gain cause to destroy; He rebuked in order to save. His request for a penny suggests that He possessed none of these coins Himself and not that He refused to pay tax. The coin named was the denarius, which bore on one side the inscription of "Pontifex Maximus—the high priest of the Roman Nation" and on the obverse the image "Tiberius Caesar—the divine Augustus." Since coins signified a monarch's power and rulership and were valid wherever the king's power and influence reached, the coins actually belonged to the individual whose image and superscription was borne. To possess and use these coins was to admit acceptance of the imperial rule of Caesar.

Verse 17. Then followed the irresistible logic: the coin is his, render (give) it to him. In essence Jesus said, "You Jews are subject to Caesar; here is the positive proof. His coin is in your pocket; you are obligated."

The latter part of the statement provides a strong contrast between earthly and heavenly servitude, for Jesus continued "and to God the things that are God's." Tertullian taught to "give to Caesar his image stamped upon his coin and give to God His own image stamped upon you."[5] Give to Caesar and to God—you owe both. There is no conflict; neither tribute can be interchanged for the other. God's image was stamped upon His creation (Genesis 1:26-27), and certain tribute is due: praise, worship, obedience.

Because the reign of God is universal, eternal, and absolute, He is the first source and order of authority in a person's life. God granted to the state authority to establish political units and economic order (Romans 13:1-7). Where conflict arises over jurisdiction of ecclesiastical matters, we ought to obey God (Acts 5:29).

In this passage Jesus elevated their question high above petty politics and squabble. His answer transcends the controversy of the moment to establish a kingdom principle of natural and spiritual obligation that belongs to all people at all places in all generations. The principle of Christian citizenship conserves civil and religious authority and gives rulers a sacred call never before acknowledged. The New Testament teaching of Christian relations asserts both the rights of the state and liberty of conscience.

Both man and the state with its rulers belong to God (Matthew 28:18). Kings are in His hand. Jesus rightfully said to Pilate, "Thou couldest have no power at all against me, except it were given thee from above" (John 19:11). Man has God's image on him and he too belongs to God. When claims of state and God conflict, loyalty to God comes first.

Christians, by accepting state benefits (roads to travel, security of law enforcement, protection, justice of the courts, economic order, commerce, business, utilities, and so on), should accept responsibility and support the agencies that God has given jurisdiction to govern lawfully.

(3) Question about the resurrection (12:18-27)
(Matthew 22:23; Luke 20:27)

(18) Then come unto him the Sadducees, which say there is no resurrection; and they asked him, saying, (19) Master, Moses wrote unto us, If a man's brother die, and leave his wife behind him, and leave no children, that his brother should take his wife, and raise up seed unto his brother. (20) Now there were seven brethren: and the first took a wife, and dying left no

seed. (21) And the second took her, and died, neither left he any seed: and the third likewise. (22) And the seven had her, and left no seed: last of all the woman died also. (23) In the resurrection therefore, when they shall rise, whose wife shall she be of them? for the seven had her to wife. (24) And Jesus answering said unto them, Do ye not therefore err, because ye know not the scriptures, neither the power of God? (25) For when they shall rise from the dead, they neither marry, nor are given in marriage; but are as the angels which are in heaven. (26) And as touching the dead, that they rise: have ye not read in the book of Moses, how in the bush God spake unto him, saying, I am the God of Abraham, and the God of Isaac, and the God of Jacob? (27) He is not the God of the dead, but the God of the living: ye therefore do greatly err.

This next question was a mocking or teasing one posed by an odd sect of the Jews, the Sadducees. Jesus answered their question in kind, showing them their error and then proceeding to instruct in immortal truth the nature of the kingdom of God. He was at His best as rabbi and prophet.

Verse 18. The Sadducees, a group of prominent, wealthy priests and leaders, here make their sole appearance by name in Mark's record. They composed one of three sects at the time of Judas Maccabaeus, according to Josephus and other scattered notes; what is known of them was written by their opponents.[6] The Sadducees disappeared after the Temple was destroyed in A.D. 70. They were dangerous enemies, politically and religiously conservative supporters of Rome. Many were landowners with little real concern for religious matters though their name meant "just and righteous."

They believed that only the Pentateuch (five books of Moses) was binding, rejected oral law and tradition, and chose a strict and literal interpretation of Moses' law. They denied the existence of spirits and angels. Their most famous doctrine was the denial of life after death, immortality, or resurrection. They claimed to be spiritual descendants of Zadok, a priest of Solomon's time (I Kings 1:38-39).

Verses 19-23. Their question pertained to the law of levirate marriage given by Moses. (See Genesis 38:8; Deuteronomy 25:5-6; Ruth 3:9-4:12.) The purpose of this law was to assure the perpetuation of a man's name and estate. Family was at the heart of the law.

The question was based on a hypothetical caricature of one woman marrying seven brothers in succession. It was intended to expose the idea of resurrection as ridiculous. "Whose wife shall she be?" had in the past successfully stumped opponents. To answer that any one husband would have her, would create envy and discount the value of the other six. To answer that she would be wife to all was more absurd. Jesus ignored both pat answers as illogical and offered the third, true option that they in their limited mentality had overlooked.

Verse 24. Jesus responded, "Do ye not therefore err, because ye know not the scriptures, neither the power of God?" Matthew makes the response declarative: "Ye do err" (22:29). They erred in two ways, first in not knowing the Scriptures. The Scriptures they spurned taught the resurrection (Job 19:25; Isaiah 26:19; Daniel

12:2). Second, they failed to appreciate the power of God.

Verse 25. Jesus affirmed resurrection, saying that when people rise from the dead there will be no marriage. He affirmed angels' existence by stating they will be as angels in heaven: in purity, in spiritual existence, in glory, in happiness, in perpetual existence.

Marriage is God's institution to assure progeny, children to replace the generations by succession. Succession is made necessary by death, and where there is no death there is no need of replacement children nor marriages to produce them. Their absurd caricature was meaningless in heaven. The Sadducees' error was to create heaven in an earthly image. According to Isaiah 64:4 and I Corinthians 2:9-10, knowledge of heaven requires revelation by the Spirit.

Verse 26. Jesus referred to Moses' writings (to which they held) to expose the second mistake. From the bush God spoke to Moses in self-revelation, stating "I am" the God of Abraham, Isaac, and Jacob (Exodus 3:5-6). God, who is life, cannot be a God of the dead. If He was God of these long-dead patriarchs in Moses' day, then they must have been living somewhere then; and if then, still now. The Sadducees, like the Epicureans, denied immortality of the soul as well as resurrection, both of which are in the Pentateuch. What is a soul without a body? Hence the body will resurrect to unite with the spirit. What is dead to us is alive to God.

Verse 27. Jesus pointed out that God is the God of the living and not the dead. Their great error was to believe that death could sever the relationship between God and man. Fellowship with God is spiritual, perpetual, and cannot be broken by the body's demise.

(4) Question about the first commandment (12:28-34)
(Matthew 22:34; cf. Luke 10:27)

(28) And one of the scribes came, and having heard them reasoning together, and perceiving that he had answered them well, asked him, Which is the first commandment of all? (29) And Jesus answered him, The first of all the commandments is, Hear, O Israel; the Lord our God is one Lord: (30) and thou shalt love the Lord thy God with all thy heart, and with all thy soul, and with all thy mind, and with all thy strength: this is the first commandment. (31) And the second is like, namely this, Thou shalt love thy neighbour as thyself. There is none other commandment greater than these. (32) And the scribe said unto him, Well, Master, thou hast said the truth: for there is one God; and there is none other but he: (33) and to love him with all the heart, and with all the understanding, and with all the soul, and with all the strength, and to love his neighbour as himself, is more than all whole burnt offerings and sacrifices. (34) And when Jesus saw that he answered discreetly, he said unto him, Thou art not far from the kingdom of God. And no man after that durst ask him any question.

Next there came a question about the greatest commandment from a scribe with sincere motive. The exchange ended with the scribe's admiration for Jesus and Jesus' encouragement for the scribe's astuteness and candor.

Verse 28. The Jews followed one of two trends concerning law interpretation. One was to proliferate the law endlessly into many precepts; the other was to condense all law into concise statement. As Barclay related, Shammai taught that Moses received 613 precepts—365 negative precepts for the number of days in a year and 248 positive precepts for the number of generations. David reduced the 613 to eleven (Psalm 15), Isaiah reduced the eleven to six (33:15), Micah reduced the six to three (6:8), Isaiah reduced three to two (66:2), and Habakkuk condensed the two to one (2:4).[7]

Verses 29-30. Jesus gave the first commandment from Deuteronomy 6:4-5, known as the *Shema*, from the Hebrew word meaning "hear." Devout Jews repeated this creedal statement three times daily as the foundation of Jewish monotheism. The full Shema was quoted from Deuteronomy 6:4-9, 11:13-21, and Numbers 15:37-41. In prayer it was worn in phylacteries (frontlets, *tefillin*) on the forehead and wrist (Matthew 23:5). It was affixed as the *mezuzah* to the entrance doorway of the house and at the doors inside as a constant reminder of God.

Verse 31. This command Jesus combined with Leviticus 19:18, which Jesus here extended to all people, even Gentiles. Absolute love for God encompassed the first four commands in the Decalogue; absolute love for man encompasses the final six commands. We must love God above all others—people, angels, created things. After God, we are to love our neighbors, offering them the same quality of affection we reserve for ourselves—a sincere, sensitive desire for them and the best for their body and soul. On these hang the law and prophets (Matthew 22:40).

Verse 32. This verse means, "Truly, Master, you have well said that He is one."

Verses 33-34. These verses indicate that the manner in which Jesus put these verses of Scripture together offered new insight to the earnest-hearted scribe, who now perceived the superiority of moral law to ceremonial. To this enlightenment Jesus gave most tender encouragement. Jesus read everyone and found this one "not far from the kingdom" in his understanding of the nature of the kingdom of God.

b. Counterquestion by Jesus (12:35-40)

Having stopped the questioners, Jesus now asked a question of His own. He aimed to make them acknowledge the Messiah as uniquely anointed by God. His descent was no ordinary human-derived event, even if from David's royal line. Psalm 110, assumed to be written by King David, direct ancestor of the Anointed One, addressed the future Messiah as "My Lord." The question was how could Messiah be both "Lord" and yet son to David. Thus it involved the deity (Lord) and humanity of Christ (Son) and implied Messiahship and the mystery of the Incarnation.

(1) Question concerning Messiah's Sonship
(12:35-37)
(Matthew 22:41; Luke 20:41)

(35) And Jesus answered and said, while he taught in the temple, How say the scribes that Christ is the Son of David? (36) For David himself said by the Holy Ghost, The Lord said to my Lord, Sit thou on my right hand, till I make thine enemies thy footstool. (37) David

therefore himself calleth him Lord; and whence is he then his son? And the common people heard him gladly.

Verse 35. Jesus put the question to scribes in the Temple. (Matthew 22:41 says "Pharisees," but since "scribe" is a title of function and not a sect, there is no discrepancy.) The argument is rabbinic in form and christological in nature. The Hebrew word *Messiah* and Greek word *Christ* have the meaning of "Anointed One." Since the definite article ("the") precedes "Christ" in verse 35, the meaning is "the Christ" or "the Anointed One," and since people were made kings by anointing, the title was kingly. The question can be rephrased as follows: "How can the scribes say that God's anointed king who is to come is the son of David when David called Him his Lord?"

The expected Messiah was to be a descendant of King David (Isaiah 9:2-7; 11:1-5; Jeremiah 23:5; 33:14-18; Ezekiel 34:23; 37:24; Psalm 89:20). The crowds as well as individuals addressed Jesus by the Messianic title of "Son of David" (Mark 10:47; Matthew 9:27; 12:23; 15:22; 21:9, 15). The genealogies of Matthew 1:1-17 and Luke 3:23-38 provide detailed documentation of the fact, and Paul, the apostle to the Gentiles, was convinced of the indisputable evidence (Romans 1:3; II Timothy 2:8).

Verses 36-37. There can be no doubt about the inspiration of David's writing in Psalm 110; "by the Holy Ghost" gives the passage unique authority that even the scribes could not deny. "The Lord [Greek *kurios*, a translation of the Hebrew *Yahweh* or *Jehovah*] said to my Lord [the Anointed One, Messiah], Sit thou on my right hand." This was the exalted place to which Christ would ascend after

His passion, burial, and resurrection, when He would be exalted above all principality and power to a reigning throne.

The argument is neither to affirm nor deny that He is the Messiah or the son of David, but to point out that the coming One is much more than David's son; indeed He is David's Lord, as David himself stated. Undoubtedly Jesus still combatted the Jews' popular notion that the son of David, their Messiah, would come in militancy to conquer foes and break earthly dominion. Jesus attempted to realign their inadequate concepts to His real purpose, to turn people's hearts to God. "Until" the enemies become a footstool will be realized in the judgment.

The common people gladly heard Jesus, as He put the questioners in their place. This statement is connected closely to the next section, for common people are more likely to listen when those who defraud and cheat are denounced.

(2) Condemnation of the scribes (12:38-40)
(Matthew 23:1; Luke 20:45)

(38) And he said unto them in his doctrine, Beware of the scribes, which love to go in long clothing, and love salutations in the marketplaces, (39) and the chief seats in the synagogues, and the uppermost rooms at feasts: (40) which devour widows' houses, and for a pretence make long prayers: these shall receive greater damnation.

These brief verses contain a scathing denunciation of six sins of the scribes and religious leaders. It is likely that the gladness of the common people in verse 37b related more to these words than to the rabbinic theological question of Messiahship. The Stephanus verse divisions of the sixteenth century might have more accurately assigned that statement to this text.

Jesus charged His followers, who were not immune to the danger (Luke 22:24), to be wary of pious behavior of professional religionists because it may point to inner desires at odds with humility and true piety. The satire, condensed by Mark, is elaborated by Matthew 23 as a series of woes, perhaps because of the more Jewish audience of Matthew and the more Gentile audience of Mark.

Verses 38-40. Jesus' teaching was His doctrine, and doctrine transcends calendar, place, and people. The warnings and charges to the disciples are no less appropriate today than at the time they were first voiced. The marks of scribes and Pharisees are detailed in Matthew 23:1-33, Mark 7:1-20, 12:38-40, and Luke 11:39-52. The six marks given here denoted religious hypocrites. Jesus described the behavior first.

1. *The scribes loved to parade about in long robes.* The *stole,* long clothing, was worn by dignitaries such as kings, government officials, and priests. In these garments one could not hurry or work, giving the impression of a leisure and honored class. Matthew 23:5 speaks of enlarging the borders of garments and adding tassels. The Jews wore tassels at the edge of the outer robe as a reminder of their relationship to God (Numbers 15:38-39). This practice was no doubt exaggerated in some, an ostentatious display.

2. *They loved marketplace salutations.* Eastern greet-

ings are likely to be long, expressive, and ceremonial. Jesus instructed His disciples on one occasion not to engage in excessive greetings (Luke 10:4). The marketplace assured a greater audience to give the vain and pretentious religionists the recognition they so coveted.

3. *They loved the chief seats.* The word *thelonton* carries the meaning "the ones wishing for" the chief seats. In the synagogues beyond the sacred volumes, a bench facing the crowd was reserved for seating distinguished dignitaries in full view of the congregation. The "chief seats" were highly desired as places of honor and respect.

4. *They loved the uppermost rooms at feasts.* "Rooms" meant couches on which Easterners reclined to eat at banquets, those set in highest places. At feasts protocol fixed the positions of the guests at the table in proximity to the host. The most favored place was immediately to the right of the host, the next was to his left. Positions alternated right, then left, and so on around the table; the seating indicated the host's esteem for the guest. For such occasions Jesus taught His disciples a rule of modesty to follow (Luke 14:7-11).

5. *They "devoured" (took possession of) widows' houses.* This charge was possibly against the priestly group, who accepted property for services and made lengthy prayers. Religious experts in interpretation of the law were not to accept pay for teaching but were to make a living by a skilled trade. However, the religionists of Jesus' day had convinced people that it was a special privilege with eternal merit to support their rabbi in comfort, even when it meant taking over the homes of helpless widows (Exodus 22:22; Psalm 146:9).

6. *For a pretense they made long prayers.* This charge is a natural extension of the previous one and suggests that prayer was used to cover the covetous behavior. It could also serve to cover up any of the foregoing behaviors since one who prays often may in the human mind be excused from demands and responsibilities of others. Jesus indicated that the spirit of prayer matters more than its length (Matthew 6:7). (See also James 5:16.) Their prayers were pretentious, a display designed to draw attention to personal piety. In location, time, and manner, they offered prayers so that people might hear. Hence, one might conclude that they offered prayer to people and not to God.

The passage ends with a proclamation of "greater damnation" for those involved in such hypocritical behavior. Greater knowledge and opportunity bring greater responsibility, resulting either in great reward or great condemnation (Luke 12:47-48).

Condemnation and warning come against three things common to human nature. First is the desire for prominence and recognition. Religion offers titled positions, offices and privileges easily compromised. Christianity offers work, jobs, and a yearning to serve responsibly.

Second is the desire for deference, for entitlements. These Jews desired to be treated with honor and respect because of their position. Christ-likeness on the other hand, makes a person small, unassuming in service to God.

Finally there was the charge of making religion an enterprise. Religion for self-gain and personal advancement is contrary to the principles and practice of true religion. Christianity has no respect of persons (Romans 2:11; Colossians 3:25; Ephesians 2:9). Christianity cares for widows and orphans and is unspotted by the world (James 1:27). Christianity is concerned with doing the things of God for the people of God. Too often people serve the things of man and not the things of God, resulting in partiality, self-promotion, self-aggrandizement, and nepotism. Many people make Christianity an enterprise, holding name, rank, class, and affluence as more significant than piety.

c. Commendation of the widow's giving (12:41-44)
(Luke 21:1)

(41) And Jesus sat over against the treasury, and beheld how the people cast money into the treasury: and many that were rich cast in much. (42) And there came a certain poor widow, and she threw in two mites, which make a farthing. (43) And he called unto him his disciples, and saith unto them, Verily I say unto you, That this poor widow hath cast more in, than all they which have cast into the treasury: (44) for all they did cast in of their abundance; but she of her want did cast in all that she had, even all her living.

Chapter 12 ends with Jesus' observance and teaching about the offerings of common people, in sharp contrast to the avarice and pomp of priests. Mark and Luke record the incident of a poor widow who, in giving an offering of the smallest monetary value, actually made a greater sacrifice and hence a greater expression of gratitude to God than the wealthy who gave generously of their larger

273

store. The lesson seems to be that the value of how much we give is less important than the value of what we retain. The fine ideal of giving should be to give sacrificially.

Verses 41-42. Jesus, finished with a strenuous day of debate, rested near the Temple treasury and observed people casting in money. The treasury, located in the Court of the Women, consisted of thirteen "shofar chests" or trumpet-shaped collection receptacles, each for special donations. Revenues offset Temple expenses in purchasing oil, corn, wine, and wood for sacrifices and for the priests or the poor. Several receptacles were for undesignated free-will offerings, and it appears that the offerings were under the priests' scrutiny so the relative amounts given were known.[8] Hobbs noted that the least amount legal to give was the amount presented by this widow.[9]

This widow drew special notice because she was very poor, a "pauper" who cast in but two mites. While the wealthy were "casting in" of their store, she "cast in" all she had. The actual coins were two *lepta* (singular *lepton*, "thin coin"); a *lepton* was the smallest Greek copper coin, about one-fifth of a cent. Two of these equaled a farthing, *kodrantes*, the smallest Roman brass coin. Thus, two mites was about one-tenth of a denarius and unworthy of special attention except for the motive.

This poor widow, who supported herself by her own labor, gave all her living for that day. People procured food almost daily since cold-storage preservation and extended protection was impossible. Likely she sacrificed by going without basic necessities in order to give, trusting God for providence.

Verses 43-44. Jesus called His disciples and noted that

this widow cast more in than the wealthy. He made no remark about rich gifts but gave the disciples and all mankind the ideal for charity. The rich gave "of their abundance"; she "of her want," or lack. They gave much, a comparative term; she gave all, superlative.

Clearly Jesus weighed the mind and motive of the giver and not the value of the gift, the motive being the greater gift (II Corinthians 8:12). What we give in sacrifice, humility, and devotion is more highly esteemed than what we proudly present. The priests counted money; Jesus measured gratitude. The rich gave spare change; the widow sacrificed. They gave extra money; she gave "need" money. They had plenty left; she had nothing left.

It is doubtful if the treasury receipts for that day were greatly affected by the widow's mite; it is certain that her life was. That offering, unseen, unheralded and probably unappreciated by the Temple officials, made a great impact upon the liberality of all humanity. One cannot give the "widow's mite" until he gives all he has. The large amounts and ambitious pledges church leaders often seek have no place beside the widow's mite until they represent all.

Perhaps ironically, this lesson quite appropriately follows the denunciation of the leaders for their avarice in religious service where widows' houses were devoured (verses 38-40). The poor often are more generous givers in resources, time, hospitality, affection, and service than the rich. No less ironic is that Jesus here gave history a champion of generosity whose gift was half a farthing. Such a historic lesson encourages expressions of charity and provides great hope to the masses of poor who have so little in actual amount to give.

3. Eschatological Discourse to the Disciples (13:1-37)

Chapter 13 contains Mark's account of the Great Olivet discourse also presented in Matthew 24-25 and Luke 21. It began with a prediction of Jerusalem's destruction (Mark 13:1-2; Matthew 24:1-2) and provided answers to two questions posed by the disciples (Mark 13:3-4).

This chapter contains signs, warnings, and prophecies pointing to the Jews' coming tribulation and the second advent of Christ. It instructs Jews and Gentiles, Christians and non-Christians. It relates events at the close of our age, that of the Gentile church, which had its inception at Pentecost (Acts 2) and that usher in the peaceful Millennium. Between come the cataclysmic events foretold by Daniel (8:9-25; 9:27; 12:1) and other prophets (Zechariah 12-14; Isaiah 24; Ezekiel 39) and foreseen by John (Revelation 1-4; 13:14), as well as the *parousia*, or catching away of the church (I Thessalonians 4:13-18; I Corinthians 15:50-55; Romans 8:23).

This chapter is historical since it pertains to recorded events in Christ's life; it is present since Jesus' foretelling of the future is current media headlines; it is also future in its immediacy of fulfillment to be witnessed during the next few years or decades. Because of its eschatological nature (dealing with the last days), it is wise to proceed with prayerful caution in the interpretation and exegesis of this passage of Scripture.

Chapter 13 is referred to as the "little apocalypse," from a Greek word meaning unveiling or revelation. The Jews had a history of apocalyptic literature. The Old Testament record of Daniel is heavily apocalyptic in nature.

The longest New Testament writing of this nature is John's Revelation. Other sections of certain books are apocalyptic: II Thessalonians 2, Luke 21, and Matthew 24 are parallels to this chapter.

a. Prediction about the Temple (13:1-2)
(Matthew 24:1)

(1) And as he went out of the temple, one of his disciples saith unto him, Master, see what manner of stones and what buildings are here! (2) And Jesus answering said unto him, Seest thou these great buildings? there shall not be left one stone upon another, that shall not be thrown down.

In an effort to appease the Jews who resented his Idumean origin and Roman affiliation, and to promote himself as their leader, Herod the Great built the lavish and magnificent Temple on top of Mount Moriah in 20-19 B.C. To fill in and level the summit, vast retaining walls were constructed underground with supporting piers, on top of which was constructed a platform. Massive stones, some as large as forty feet long by eighteen feet wide by twelve feet high, formed the foundation. A bridge 354 feet long and 50 feet wide arched 225 feet above the Tyropeon Valley at the southwest entrance leading to the south, facing the Royal Porch with its double rows of 162 Corinthian columns 37.5 feet high.

Josephus wrote:

Now the outward face of the Temple in its front wanted nothing that was likely to surprise men's minds or their eyes for it was covered all over with plates of gold of great weight, and at the first rising of the sun, reflected back a very fiery splendor and made those who forced themselves to look upon it to turn their eyes away just as they would have done at the sun's own rays.[10]

The Temple was a wonder of the Roman world that to the disciples could not be destroyed.

Verses 1-2. According to Luke, Jesus spent the nights of His final week on the Mount of Olives; it is probable that He left this final time (He was never to return except as a prisoner) via the Golden Gate as the east sun produced its fiery splendor.

With pride of Jewish patriotism the disciples commented on the "manner of" carved Herodian stones and the magnificent buildings displayed behind them. The comment was natural since Jesus had previously spoken of its destruction. Here Jesus specifically declared that not one stone would be left upon another. Indeed, after the destruction of A.D. 70 only the foundation stones remained. These are visible today at the southeast corner of *Harem esh Sherif* and the Western Wall (Wailing Wall), left to depict the greatness of the Roman conquest. The present wall is constructed on the foundation stones of the Herodian structure. Verses 14-20 of this chapter provide details of the city's destruction.

b. Question by four disciples (13:3-4)
(Matthew 24:3; Luke 21:7)

(3) And as he sat upon the mount of Olives over against the temple, Peter and James and John and

Andrew asked him privately, (4) Tell us, when shall these things be? and what shall be the sign when all these things shall be fulfilled?

Verse 3. Although Matthew and Luke give the questions, only Mark names the asking disciples. Andrew is admitted to the inner council in this scene, and since he was first disciple Jesus called, one wonders why he was omitted on other occasions. Accounts in the Gospels and Acts indicate that Peter and John were the more forceful and pivotal individuals among the pairs of brothers.

Verse 4. They had privately discussed Christ's remark about the Temple; to speak openly about it would incur the scribes' and Pharisees' opposition. Evident from their questions is that the disciples associated the destruction of the Temple and Jerusalem with Jesus' return and the end of the age. "When shall these things be?" referred to the Temple's destruction and is answered in Luke 21:12-24. "What shall be the sign when all these things shall be fulfilled?" concerned events at the age's consummation, for Matthew 24:3 adds a third related question ". . . and of the end of the world?" The answer to the former question is found in Mark 13:5-23, Matthew 24:4-27 and Luke 21:8-11, 25-26. Christ's answer to the latter question is given in Matthew 24:27-25:46, Mark 13:24-37 and Luke 21:27-38. His answers are specific but spiritual instruction of what to expect and prepare for concerning these events or "signs."

c. Prophetic answer to the disciples (13:5-37)
(1) Warning to the disciples (13:5-13)
(a) Perils from the character of the age (13:5-8)
(Matthew 24:4; Luke 21:8; Revelation 8-9)

(5) And Jesus answering them began to say, Take heed lest any man deceive you: (6) for many shall come in my name, saying, I am Christ; and shall deceive many. (7) And when ye shall hear of wars and rumours of wars, be ye not troubled: for such things must needs be; but the end shall not be yet. (8) For nation shall rise against nation, and kingdom against kingdom: and there shall be earthquakes in divers places, and there shall be famines and troubles: these are the beginnings of sorrows.

Jesus responded to the question about signs of His coming first, then signs of the age. His answer reinforced the basic Jewish imagery of the "day of the Lord." He did not attempt to provide a means of mapping a future timetable. His answer appears to mingle references, signs, and events of time in such a way that believers could stand prepared to embrace and participate in a spiritual kingdom and spiritual warfare regardless of international affairs.

There would come on the earth a progressive succession of alarming crises, each more devastating than the previous, beyond which a believer should look, never wavering in faith, ever trusting in Jesus. Only by acting in faith could the church survive the Roman circle of death around Jerusalem in A.D. 69-70. Only by refusing the claims of false leaders (e.g., Bar Cochba) and false worship could the church remain free of idolatry and heresy. The aim is to note the events around and with confident assurance know that He will come again and that the Day of the Lord is certain.

The signs provided will begin Jewish sorrows, and in

view of Daniel 9:24, must occur in order for God to put in motion earthly events that set the stage and form the backdrop to achieve His marvelous purposes. God works through earthly events and circumstances within man, kingdoms, nations, and Spirit-filled believers to accomplish His purpose of obliterating the impact of Satan.

These are two possible views concerning the nature of the events that make up this prophecy: (1) primary marked chronological happenings and (2) a gradual but continuous worsening sequence of events. These views are not mutually exclusive. This analysis will look first at the events named, then at the supporting scriptural evidence.

Verses 5-6. The first sign of Christ's coming, of the end, and of the Day of the Lord is deception. The enemy's attempts to sidetrack believers include the rising of false leaders claiming to be Christ, the Anointed One, the Son of God. In New Testament times this was fulfilled by Theudas and Simon (Acts 5:36; 8:9-10). Against such the Scripture is replete with warning, anticipation, and instruction (Acts 20:29; Titus 1:14-16; 3:10-11; I Timothy 1:3-4; 4:16).

Today, deceptions arise from compromising leaders who expound messages of false peace, prosperity, and a better humanistic world. Departures from Christian dogma are prominent in history through councils that led away from the apostolic doctrines of the first-century church established in Acts 2:1-42 and to which people now look for direction. Deception extends further into sectarian and charismatic cult leaders who deceive and enslave people by psychological and metaphysical means.

Verse 7. A second sign Jesus noted was wars and rumors of wars, increasingly worse, an alarming plague on humankind. Threats of wars, especially in the shadow of nuclear explosives, provide adequate reason to be fearful and troubled in spirit. Immediately, there were early wars in the Roman Empire, such as during Caligula's reign, and others over the next three and a half centuries. For Christians, physical oppression and persecution continued until the Edict of Milan, A.D. 311. At that time a worse malady befell, that of doctrinal impurity.

Jesus offered words of comfort with "Be ye not troubled," for such things must be expected before the end. War and turmoil were distinct parts of the Jewish expectation for their Messiah's appearance. Jesus' words were to encourage faith in the face of despairing conditions that the gospel's work be first and steadfastly advanced. The succession of calamities would serve to indicate the need to be prepared, patient, hopeful, and confident. (See also II Thessalonians 2:1-12.)

Verse 8. "Nation shall rise against nation, and kingdom against kingdom" refers back to Isaiah 19:2, indicating internal strife and opposition of brother against brother. This sign crosses physical, geographic, political, and social boundaries as each party contends for rulership and authority.

Earthquakes, a biblical sign of God, here mark the end time with increasing frequency in diverse places. Wim Malgo gives the numbers of major earthquakes from the Strasbourg observatory:[11]

Century	Number of Major Earthquakes
12th	84
13th	118
14th	137
15th	174
16th	258
17th	378
18th	640
19th	2,119

Historically, earthquakes devastated Laodicea; famines came in the reign of Claudius (Acts 11:28); Vesuvius erupted, burying Pompeii; and the Parthians came against Rome during the decades immediately after this prophecy, all of which reinforced the image of a returning Savior. The Day of the Lord was remembered as a certainty with the appearance of each calamity.

(b) Personal danger amid persecution (13:9-13)
(Matthew 24:9)

Verses 9-13 provide disciples and believers a personal warning and identify signs to come during Israel's sorrows (Matthew 24:9). These signs, easily traced and verified in Acts and the Epistles, warned of persecution to come as the disciples glimpsed mounting hostility; full realization came in Acts 8:1. Each test cut deeper until even personal family ties were severed (verse 12). The disciple must count the cost (Luke 14:28) and be resolved in mind so that he will not stumble but endure as only a true disciple can.

(9) But take heed to yourselves: for they shall deliver you up to councils; and in the synagogues ye shall be beaten: and ye shall be brought before rulers and kings for my sake, for a testimony against them. (10) And the gospel must first be published among all nations. (11) But when they shall lead you, and deliver you up, take no thought beforehand what ye shall speak, neither do ye premeditate: but whatsoever shall be given you in that hour, that speak ye: for it is not ye that speak, but the Holy Ghost. (12) Now the brother shall betray the brother to death, and the father the son; and children shall rise up against their parents, and shall cause them to be put to death. (13) And ye shall be hated of all men for my name's sake: but he that shall endure unto the end, the same shall be saved.

Verse 9. Jesus left no doubt that the gospel and His cause would be unpopular, a hard way with rejection and hostility. To face this the disciples needed to take heed and expect certain opposition. They must watch, guard against weaknesses, and not endanger themselves as they preached the kingdom message. Jewish enemies would deliver them up to the council (Sanhedrin) for judgment; they would be beaten in synagogues, which had their own courts for local judgment of offenders. (See Deuteronomy 25:1-3.) This Jewish persecution persisted until A.D. 70. Paul was flogged five times (II Corinthians 11:24).

Gentile persecution included being hailed before rulers, governors, and kings. Luke records Paul on trial before Governors Felix and Festus (Acts 23:31-25:12), as well as before King Herod Agrippa (Acts 25:23-26:32).

Paul even appealed to Caesar (Act 25:10-12).

Verse 10. All nations (more literally, all Gentiles) must hear the gospel; then shall the end come. Israel was no longer the favored nation for the gospel. This statement is more than hyperbole since within fifty years Christian churches and influence had touched the entire Western civilized world.

This is the single historic sign Jesus gives as to the end of the age, and it pertains not to chronology but to condition. Has this condition been met? The gospel has reached all nations. The Bible is an international bestseller, read in more language translations than any other book, and proclaimed in communication technology throughout the world.

Verse 11. For defense after sudden arrest and prosecution, the disciples were to rely on the Holy Spirit for inspiration in speaking (Luke 21:15). This does not mean one should not prepare thoughtful and prudent responses, but simply that a disciple would never be alone in his witness. This is one of Mark's sparse references to the Holy Spirit. (See also Mark 1:8.) An enactment of this prophecy is found in Peter's defense before the elders (Acts 4:8).

Verse 12. The last great danger, or *skandalizo* (Matthew 24:9-10), is persecution from within one's family. Brother would oppose brother, father would oppose son over the gospel. Natural ties, usually strong, would be severed. A person's enemies are often those of his own house (Micah 7:6), but the love for God proves greater than love for family.

Verse 13. Pagans falsely accused Christians of cannibalism, because they took the sacrament of the "body and blood" of Christ. The Jews, who had their law, and Gentiles, who had their idols, both opposed the gospel. All found reason to persecute and oppose this new doctrine and its converts. Tacitus records that Christians were hated for their abominations, and their religion was a "most mischievous superstition."[12]

I Peter 4:12-16 shows that the early church endured persecution because of His name. The early disciples were not rescued from tribulation but were faithful unto death to inherit a crown of life (Luke 21:19; Revelation 2:10).

"Endure" means as in a marathon race or campaign, not a mere sprint or battle. "To the end" is to the end of one's lifetime, or the termination of persecution and not to the end of the age. Even death surrenders to the power of Christian resurrection. When one endures, bearing up under severe trials, the end is definite and assured.

(2) Sign of the end and the Second Advent (13:14-27)

(a) End-time crisis (13:14-23)
(Matthew 24:15-17, 21-24; Daniel 9:27; 12:1;
Revelation 12-19)

(14) But when ye shall see the abomination of desolation, spoken of by Daniel the prophet, standing where it ought not, (let him that readeth understand,) then let them that be in Judaea flee to the mountains: (15) and let him that is on the housetop not go down into the house, neither enter therein, to take any thing out of

his house: (16) and let him that is in the field not turn back again for to take up his garment. (17) But woe to them that are with child, and to them that give suck in those days! (18) And pray ye that your flight be not in the winter. (19) For in those days shall be affliction, such as was not from the beginning of the creation which God created unto this time, neither shall be. (20) And except that the Lord had shortened those days, no flesh should be saved: but for the elect's sake, whom he hath chosen, he hath shortened the days. (21) And then if any man shall say to you, Lo, here is Christ; or, lo, he is there; believe him not: (22) for false Christs and false prophets shall rise, and shall shew signs and wonders, to seduce, if it were possible, even the elect. (23) But take ye heed: behold, I have foretold you all things.

End-time signs immediately preceding the Second Advent are Jewish tribulation and sorrows. This is the time of Jacob's trouble forecast by Daniel 9:24-27 as the final of seventy weeks of years. Daniel spoke of sixty-nine weeks (of years) from the command to restore and rebuild Jerusalem to the cutting off of Prince Messiah. These events are marked historically by the return of Nehemiah to rebuild Jerusalem and by Jesus Christ Himself. The Jewish rejection of their Messiah, followed by the destruction of Jerusalem in A.D. 70, marked the close of the sixty-nine weeks of years determined upon the Jews and their city. The final (seventieth) week of seven years will begin with a covenant between the Jews and Antichrist (Daniel 9:27). It will endure for three and a half years before great tribulation. This time of crisis between the Jews and the Antichrist is the tribulation Jesus here unfolded for His disciples.

Some interpreters ascribe this passage to the destruction of Jerusalem, which occurred about four decades from the time of the prophecy. Others hold that it pertains to the Second Advent. Many utterances parallel the Jerusalem destruction and can be verified in historical accounts of events. Some scholars say these words do not apply to a tribulation at the end of the age[13]; however, others apply the verses to the Tribulation.[14] Jesus spoke to the Jewish disciples, the first Christians, relating events that could apply to either time. Fulfillment of prophecy in one era does not necessarily preclude additional fulfillment at a later date.

The weight of evidence favors a futuristic interpretation because of Daniel's prophecy of a covenant between regathered Jews and a coming prince for a period of one week (seven years) (Daniel 9:26-27). In the middle of the week the coming prince breaks the treaty, enters the Temple, and causes sacrifices to cease by appointing himself God and "standing where it ought not" (Mark 13:14). This move precipitates a time of wrath against the Jews, which terminates Daniel's seventieth week and ushers in a time of unparalleled blessings for Israel's survivors during the reign of their Messiah. His return to govern Israel is the Second Advent.

Verse 14. "Abomination of desolation" is a Hebrew idiom, a guarded and cryptic term because of many enemies of the Jews. It means the abomination or sacrilege that makes desolate the Temple of the Jews. It was prophesied in Daniel (9:27; 11:31; 12:11) as a "profanation that appalls."[15]

In this passage Jesus mingled thoughts of Jerusalem's doom with past events and end-time events yet to be fulfilled. The Syrian ruler Antiochus Epiphanes had defiled the Holy Place of the Temple in the intertestamental period in 168 B.C. by setting up a statue (idol) of the Greek god Zeus and offering swine on the altar of sacrifice. (See the apocryphal book *I Maccabees* 1:54.) In A.D. 40 the mad Emperor Caligula insisted that he was god and attempted to provide an image of himself for the Jews. Fortunately his death aborted the plan and prevented Jewish insurrection. Again in A.D. 135, with Jerusalem rebuilt as the Roman city Aelia Capitolina, a statue of Zeus stood in the spot of the Holy Place.

The parenthetic expression "let him that readeth understand," appears to be editorial and calls for the reader to use his imagination.

The abomination is spoken of in II Thessalonians 2:4, Revelation 13, 14:9-11, 15:2-4, 16:10, 20:4-6, and Matthew 24:15, evidently having an expected future fulfillment. The remainder of verse 14 relates to the siege of Jerusalem and the Christians' flight to Pella and freedom, whereas orthodox Jews flocked to their Holy City and died by the tens and hundreds of thousands (1,100,000 died; 97,000 were captured).[16]

The adverb "when" strongly implies a futuristic sign for the Jews to mark the beginning of the final half (three and a half years) of the seventieth week of tribulation to come.

Verse 14 carries three distinct thoughts beginning with end-time events (denoted by "when" and proceeding on to "then" in verses 14, 17, 19-22, 24, 26-27), a parenthetic admonition, and the imminent siege of Jerusalem, resulting in those with understanding fleeing the doomed city.

Finally, the people had to abandon Judea for the mountains of Transjordan if they were to escape. Historically, Eusebius noted an oracle to the church to flee to Pella.[17] This event prophetically parallels Revelation 12:6, 14, the flight of the woman to refuge in Moab and Edom.

In conjunction with no exact time for the Second Advent (verse 32) and the general signs of the times, we should note that time has existence and meaning only in the temporal order of fulfillment of God's preordained plan. Inasmuch as time is the stage on which events and actions by people, kingdoms, governments, wars, and so on occur, it is to events rather than to chronological time or calendar that we should look for a fulfillment or ripeness of God's conditions.

Before the end the Jews expected the revelation of an evil incarnate, antigod. Paul spoke of him as the "man of sin" (II Thessalonians 2:3).

Verses 15-18. The housetop or flat area of the roof was a living space from which one could descend on an outside stair or ladder to enter the house or move from house to house along the adjoining rooftops. As the Antichrist dominated Jerusalem there would be sudden urgency to escape from the roof without even entering the house for valuables, or from the field without turning back for cloak or tunic, the *pallium* or *himation*—garments laid aside to free the body for labor. The situation would bring woe (distress) to nursing mothers or expectant women encumbered by their children or condition, and people should pray that it would not occur in winter when survival would be further encumbered by unfavorable weath-

er. Matthew 24:20 adds "neither on the sabbath" for benefit of the pious Jews who would rather die than to exceed
a Sabbath day's journey.

Verse 19. The underlying reason for the prayers,
urgency, and sudden abandoning of Jerusalem is next
revealed. "For in those days" will occur cruel affliction so
intense that Jesus denoted the period as the time of tribulation. Neither has there been since creation nor will
there ever be anything like this time under the godless
and evil Antichrist. The Flood, destruction of Sodom and
Gomorrah, deliverance from Egypt and the drowning of
Pharaoh's armies, conquest of Jericho, famine in Samaria,
destruction of Nineveh, fall of Babylon, or even the overthrow of Jerusalem by Titus to come in A.D. 70 cannot
compare to the end-time Tribulation. Tribulation is a herald of the Second Advent.

Verse 20. The Lord set the events and time frame and
only He can alter it. Again we can infer a dual application.
First, in A.D. 70 the Roman general Titus offered the
besieged Jews clemency, shortening the starvation,
agony, and deaths. Jews are God's elect, noted here
because Jesus answered questions of the Jews on this
occasion. In the second application, the "chosen" can
refer to believers who escape into Transjordan in the days
of the Antichrist.

Verses 21-23. Jesus referred back to verses 3-6 ("many
shall come in my name") for this end-time sign. "Then" if
any say Christ is "here" or "there," God's people should
not believe it. These are signs that Deuteronomy 13:1-3
warns about.

Immediately after the Roman destruction of Jerusalem, pseudo-Messianic claims began to arise to regather

the scattered Jews. In other times Simon of Gergasa, Eleazer, and John the Zealot gained confidence of the Jews in order to plunder their sacred traditions. The church in the first century and later saw the rise of Gnostic heresies and men claiming divine status.

The warning comes in advance of the seducers, false Christs, and false prophets with their signs and wonders. Their intent is to seduce, to lead astray (Revised Version), to deceive, or pull away even the elect as the end approaches. They will manifest lying signs and wonders (Acts 8:9; II Thessalonians 2:9-12; Revelation 13:13). These powers will be satanic (Daniel 8:24; II Thessalonians 2:7-12; Revelation 13:1-18; 16:13-16; 19:20).

Jesus emphasized the need to "heed" what He foretold. Three other verses call for "taking heed": 5, 9, and 33. All Christians should soberly study and reflect on these signs and prophesies.

This brings to a close a difficult section that commentators have applied to two time periods: the destruction of Jerusalem (then four decades away), and the end time leading up to the Second Advent. Interpreted in light of history, some of Christ's words refer to the A.D. 70 destruction and some to end-time events. Further refinement is necessary and possible as we see the day approaching.

We can identify the following teachings relative to the Second Advent:

1. It will occur after the Tribulation Christ described in answer to their questions (Matthew 24:30; 25:31; Revelation 19:11-19).

2. It will usher in the Millennium (Revelation 19:11-21; 20:1-10), and mark a time of peace and unprecedented earthly productivity (Isaiah 35).

3. It will follow the three-and-a-half-year reign of terror under the Antichrist (Revelation 13:5) and result in his overthrow and defeat (Revelation 19:11-21).

4. It will occur after the age of the Gentile church (II Thessalonians 2:7-11; Acts 15:13-20; Jude 14-16; Zechariah 14:5).

5. It will occur after the resurrection and translation of the "dead in Christ" (Jude 14; I Thessalonians 4:13-17; I Corinthians 15:51-55).

6. It will see Israel restored and converted and Christ enthroned on the throne of David to reign over Israel forever (Isaiah 9:6-7; Ezekiel 36:23-28; 37:16-28; Hosea 3:4-5; Luke 1:32-33).

The signs of verses 21-23 (false prophets showing fake signs) evidently take place during the Tribulation but have precedent earlier in history. Likewise, abominations occurred at different times throughout history. However, the end-time abomination is evidently not a statue but a person (verse 14), and the "affliction" of "those days" supersedes any abomination or cruelty known to that point (verse 19). It is apparent that these prophecies may have recurrent or parallel fulfillment.

(b) Return of the Son of man (13:24-27)
(Matthew 24:27)

(24) But in those days, after that tribulation, the sun shall be darkened, and the moon shall not give her light, (25) and the stars of heaven shall fall, and the powers that are in heaven shall be shaken. (26) And then shall they see the Son of man coming in the clouds with great power and glory. (27) And then shall he send his angels, and

293

shall gather together his elect from the four winds, from the uttermost part of the earth to the uttermost part of heaven.

Jesus continued to answer the disciples' questions about when these things would be. In verses 24-27 He foretold His return and provided signs to watch for.

Verse 24. In those days, that is, after the Tribulation, conflict between Jews and the Antichrist will lead to the Second Advent. These signs are universal phenomena of the heavens themselves that bespeak of a new age (Matthew 24:29). Terminology remains apocalyptic and specific to the Jews. Between first and second advents but only indirectly tied to Jews lies the period called the church age. Jesus now turns full attention to the Jews as Messiah.

The sun will darken and the moon, a body reflective of the sun, will of course provide no light. Many other passages of Scripture similarly relate astronomical happenings before the Second Advent. (See Isaiah 13:10; 24:23; 34:4; Ezekiel 32:7-8; Joel 2:10, 31; 3:15; Amos 8:9; Matthew 24:29; Luke 21:25-26; Revelation 6:12-14.) There appears no reason to suppose a nonliteral interpretation for events noted here. They are natural disturbances in the heavens among the planetary system of which Earth is a part. They do appear to be part of a series of events composing the backdrop of the Second Advent.

Verse 25. Physical changes in heavenly bodies and falling stars (meteorites) denote the coming of Christ (Matthew 24:29; Revelation 6:12-17). The phrase "powers that are in heaven shall be shaken" could mean a trembling of unexplained forces that unite in universal laws

294

balancing the solar system. Such would result in changes in the moon, sun, and stars. Job 26:11 speaks of pillars of heaven that shake at God's reproof, and Isaiah 34:4 speaks of heavens rolled together as a scroll. Some commentators apply these words metaphorically to human or demonic powers being shaken.

Verse 26. "Then" is emphatic, a time after the foregoing events. Matthew 24:30 speaks of the "sign of the Son of man." It is the Son Himself returning as He went away, on clouds, as promised (Acts 1:9-10). It is no secret coming; on earth "shall they see" the rejected One return, this time in power and great glory.

Verse 27. The Son will waste no time but will initiate His everlasting kingdom. He immediately will send His special messengers to gather in His own (Daniel 7:10). The earth, from the "four winds" and the "uttermost," will be scoured for the elect—a search from earth to heaven. They will be taken from horizon to horizon, from all quarters of the universe; every nation, kindred, and tongue will be represented. The angelic harvest results in separation of the just from the evil and a regathering of the elect, a common Old Testament theme (Isaiah 11:11-12; 27:13; Psalm 147:2). God's regathered people form an eternal nation according to the prophets (Isaiah 60:2-9; 65:9, 22; 66:19-24; Jeremiah 31:36-40; 33:17-26; Ezekiel 36:8-24; 37:21-28; 39:25-29; Amos 9:11-15; Luke 1:31-33; Acts 15:14-18).

(3) Concluding instructions (13:28-37)

This section brings to a conclusion the Olivet discourse to the disciples. It includes a lesson from the parable of the fig tree (verses 28-29), denial of any knowable fixed date for the consummation (verses 30-32), and admonition to watchfulness in light of the many preceding signs (verses 33-37). This summary includes things near (Jerusalem's fall) and things distant (Christ's return). Each can be anticipated in its generation by observing "these things" (verses 14-20).

(a) Lesson from the fig tree (13:28-29)
(Matthew 24:32; Luke 21:29)

(28) Now learn a parable of the fig tree; When her branch is yet tender, and putteth forth leaves, ye know that summer is near: (29) so ye in like manner, when ye shall see these things come to pass, know that is nigh, even at the doors.

Verses 28-29. This is the ninth parable recorded by Mark. The fig tree, a favorite example, was a common and conspicuous deciduous tree in Palestine. Its growth pattern set forth a simile for comparison to events. Leaves appear in late spring, April or May, just preceding long, hot summer days. In response to summer, the fig fruits begin to appear and quickly ripen. The lesson is that "in like manner, when ye shall see these things come to pass," that is, events of verses 14-20, it is "at the doors," an idiom for "about to enter."

The fig is a traditional national symbol of Israel, just as the vine and olive represent spiritual Israel in the Old Testament. It is unnecessary to read the Jews as a nation into this parable, however, because every biblical use of the fig does not refer symbolically to Israel. Here it appears to be a common-sense parable and simile. Luke 21:29 adds "and all the trees." Matthew 24:33 uses "so likewise," indicating that as fig leaves on a tender shoot are harbingers of summer, these foregoing signs will indicate the nearness of Jesus' return.

(b) Date of the consummation (13:30-32)
(Matthew 24:34; Luke 21:32; cf. Luke 17:26)

(30) Verily I say unto you, that this generation shall not pass, till all these things be done. (31) Heaven and earth shall pass away: but my words shall not pass away. (32) But of that day and that hour knoweth no man, no, not the angels which are in heaven, neither the Son, but the Father.

Verse 30. The declaration of signs turned to admonition as Jesus soberly relegated the events to a single generation. Although He carefully avoided date setting, this solemn affirmation suggests that Jesus held the traditional Jewish view of eschatology. He clearly predicted the Temple's demise and the fall of Jerusalem but drew the line at more specific signs to precede His return. The coming kingdom of God is God's prerogative and known only to Him. The important thing is to be ready at all times.

"This generation" means all people alive at a particular time. Many people alive in Christ's day would live to see the destruction of Jerusalem in A.D. 70. Wider application to mean the entire Jewish nation is unfounded. The generation of Jews alive during Jesus' earthly ministry lived to see the siege and fall of their city, obviously not the Second Coming.

The early church must have wondered at these sayings as each apostle passed away and still there was no return. The delay affected the Thessalonian church, prompting Paul to write of the end (I Thessalonians 4:13-17). II Peter 3:4 and John 21:23 refer to the soon return. The church taught that each generation should eagerly and expectantly await His return (II Peter 3:12; I Thessalonians 4:13-17). The first and second advents appear on the landscape of time as two mountain peaks viewed as close together from afar but actually separated by a wide valley. With regard to the Second Coming, perhaps Jesus' words indicate that the generation seeing the fulfillment of the signs will also see His return.

Verses 31-32. The present universal order will perish and pass away to be changed and refashioned (II Peter 3:13). Science predicts a climax, a burnout, for spaceship Earth to be polluted and exhausted. "My words" relate to prophecies and revelations of truth of God provided in His self-revelation to man; these are eternal and will persist beyond time into eternity.

We can easily understand how humans and angels would remain ignorant of the day and the hour of Christ's return, but here Jesus added "neither the Son." Could Jesus, God incarnate, full deity and omniscient, not know the day or the hour of His coming? Contrary to tritheistic views, this phrase does not affirm that Christ was less than full deity, had limited knowledge, or was a subordinate individual in the Godhead during the days of His incarnation. He was then, as now, fully human and fully divine. The date of His second return was left in the hand of God, who was fully incarnate in the Son. As God, Jesus knew all things. As the Son of David, as the human king of the Jews, however, He would be unaware of the day and hour. The point is that no human has the ability to know the time of the Second Coming.

God reckons chronological time not by hours or calendar days, but by marker events. (See the discussion of verse 14.) Hence when chronological time brings a completion of all predicted events (the times of the Gentiles, regathered Jerusalem, rise of the Antichrist, completed tribulation), then will the Son appear.

(c) Need for watchfulness (13:33-37)
(Matthew 24:42; Luke 12:36;
cf. Matthew 25:1; Luke 19:12; Acts 1:7)

(33) Take ye heed, watch and pray: for ye know not when the time is. (34) For the Son of man is as a man taking a far journey, who left his house, and gave authority to his servants, and to every man his work, and commanded the porter to watch. (35) Watch ye therefore: for ye know not when the master of the house cometh, at even, or at midnight, or at the cockcrowing, or in the morning: (36) lest coming suddenly he find you sleeping. (37) And what I say unto you I say unto all, Watch.

The purpose for the preceding discourse becomes clear with the final verses of chapter 13. Only if an exact day and hour remain unknown but eagerly anticipated will the disciples, the church, and even sinful people know the conviction of events. If the date were fixed, people of the final generation would attempt to wait until the last possible moment to be converted. To know the date removes the need for the perpetual vigilance called for by Christ's words to take heed, to watch, and to pray.

Verse 33. The warning "take heed" is sounded in verses 5, 9, 23 and 33, and comes from *agrupneo*, meaning to watch sleeplessly. (See Ephesians 6:18; Hebrews 13:17.) Jesus here called for the most difficult mark of discipleship—perpetual watchfulness, being ever "on the alert." Christians are to be busy spreading the good news and establishing conditions for the return, but leave the time to God. The message clearly rebukes timetable setting.

Verse 34. Jesus offered the final parable of Mark to illustrate as a master teacher His pronouncement of expectant watchfulness. An absentee householder on a far journey gave authority to his servants, assigned work to everyone, and commanded the porter (doorkeeper) to watch. Here it is a porter, not a steward, who sits at the gate of the walled courtyard to intercept and challenge those who would enter. He must be watchful, vigilant, keeping alert and awake. The word used, *gregorite*, meaning to be wakeful, became the popular Christian name Gregory. Servants entrusted with authority and specific duties are to perform alertly.

Verses 35-36. Jesus applied names to the four principal watches fixed by the Romans: "even," sunset until 9:00 P.M.; "midnight," 9:00 P.M. until midnight; "cockcrowing," midnight until 3:00 A.M., and "morning," 3:00 A.M. until sunrise. Certainly one watch would witness the Master's return, calling for *gregoreuo*, vigilant watchfulness and alertness (I Peter 5:8). Matthew 24:43-44 compares the event to a thief coming and admonishes us not to sleep as the foolish virgins of Matthew 25:1-13.

Verse 37. The final discourse of Mark 13 emphasizes the spiritual value of doctrine. Only by knowing can one be expectantly alert. The price of Christian liberty, as all freedoms, is constant vigilance. Christ's abiding command is to "watch."

Chapter 13, difficult as it is, offers strong admonition and great hope for the disciples and later generations of Christians. First, only to people who know God are revealed the secrets of history. Christians can alertly expose false Christs, false moral teachings, and false doctrines that secular leaders need guidance even to see.

On the timing of the Second Coming it is useless to speculate; history reveals foolish and false attempts. Events in history lead us to conclude that many things Jesus named have occurred and continue to intensify as the end approaches.

Finally comes the powerful message that even though the Son of man is away in a far journey, it is foolish to discount His involvement in earthly affairs. His words "watch and pray" (verse 33) and "watch ye therefore" (verse 35) summon obedience in the heart of every true child of God.

Notes

[1]The papal bull issued against Martin Luther in 1520 began with the words, "Arise, O Lord, a wild boar has entered the vineyard." (See Psalm 68:1; 80:13.)

[2]Cole, 185.

[3]Johnson, 196.

[4]Josephus, 18:1; 1.6.

[5]*Pulpit Commentary*, 155.

[6]Josephus, 18:1; 4-8.

[7]Barclay, 307.

[8]Johnson, 207.

[9]Hobbs, 61.

[10]Josephus, 15:2, 3-7.

[11]Wim Malgo, *There Shall Be Signs in Heaven and on Earth* (Columbia, SC: Midnight Call, 1980), 1948-82.

[12]Tacitus, *Annals*, 15:44.

[13]Hobbs, 64.

[14]Johnson, 215.

[15]Barclay, 324.

[16]*Ibid.*, 325.

[17]Johnson, 216.

III.

Self-Sacrifice of the Servant
(14:1-15:47)

III.

Self-Sacrifice of the Servant
(14:1-15:47)

All the Gospels relate Jesus' passion. Characteristically, Mark's narrative is brief, action-filled, and unembellished. Luke edits and explains the martyrdom, Matthew focuses on Christological features significant to Jews, and John supplements and illumines the story independently.

Mark relates the shameful story of the cross, more than biography or history, to reveal God's purpose for a Savior. We are not to glorify or worship the cross itself, however, for the story does not take its spiritual victory from His death but from the resurrection of Jesus Christ and the fulfillment of His promise to return. Without a resurrection there would be no Savior and the hopelessness of man would remain (Luke 24:19-27). The risen Lord expounded Moses and the prophets and gave the gospel its true nature and power.

Before the writing of the New Testament, the early church apparently related Christ's suffering and death in a story cycle at Easter time. The stories included Old Testament references to Christ and the fulfillment of Christ as a Passover type. With this in mind, Mark describes the Last Supper with the disciples as a Passover.

A.
Foes and Friends of Jesus
(14:1-11)

A. Foes and Friends of Jesus (14:1-11)
1. Plotting of the Sanhedrin (14:1-2)
(Matthew 26:3; Luke 22:1)

People attempt to destroy what threatens them or what they fear, and the only recourse to unanswerable logic is violence. This is what the Jewish leaders decided to do. The time was just prior to the start of two major Jewish feasts that blended together: the Passover and the Feast of Unleavened Bread.

(1) After two days was the feast of the passover, and of unleavened bread: and the chief priests and the scribes sought how they might take him by craft, and put him to death. (2) But they said, Not on the feast day, lest there be an uproar of the people.

Verse 1. "Passover" is the rendering of a Hebrew term *Pehsach*, commonly *Pasch*, or *Paschal* in Christian liturgy and song. It occurred on Nisan 14 (April) and commemorated Israel's historic deliverance from Egyptian bondage (Exodus 12). The Feast of Passover was one of three compulsory feasts (along with the Feast of Tabernacles and the Feast of Pentecost) for every Jewish male within fifteen miles of Jerusalem. They kept the Passover day like a Sabbath, observing similar restrictions.

On this day Jews recalled stories of God's miraculous affliction of Egypt with plagues, Pharaoh's promise to release them, then Pharaoh changing his mind as the latest plague abated. The final plague came when at midnight a death angel swept through Egypt killing the firstborn of every household. The Jews escaped by using hyssop to splash the blood of a sacrificial lamb on the lintel and doorposts of their homes. The destroying angel "passed over" any house displaying the blood of the lamb. The Jews, packed for imminent departure, ate the roasted lamb with unleavened bread. Hence, the festival of unleavened bread began the same day as the Passover and continued for seven days.

At the Passover the Jews sacrificed lambs in the Temple and feasted on them throughout Jerusalem. Usually, they made leavened bread by adding a piece of yeast dough from yesterday's baking to today's dough, a practice perpetuated throughout the year. However, at this festival they used no yeast, symbolizing a clean break with the past and with sin. These festivals marked the beginning of a new year (Exodus 12:2).

This time also marked the ingathering of the barley harvest when a sheaf of barley was waved before the Lord (Leviticus 23:10-11). After this ceremony, the new crop of barley could be made into flour or sold in shops.

Preparation for the Passover included study in the synagogues and lessons so that no one would be ignorant of its significance. Routes entering Jerusalem and bridges over chasms or streams were repaired; wayside burial places, tombs, and sepulchers along the road were whitewashed to prevent travelers from casually touching a burial place and becoming ceremonially unclean for the great festival.

Travelers often sang Psalms 120-134, psalms of degrees en route to the feast. Traditionally, they sang Psalm 122 while climbing the hill to the Temple entrance.

The burning desire of every Jew was to eat at least one Passover in Jerusalem before death. Lodging was free in the city, and in neighboring villages such as Bethany, Bethphage, and environs every house was filled.

Josephus related that thirty years later (A.D. 65) a total of 256,000 lambs were slain. The law required the lamb to be totally consumed, and one lamb fed a minimum of ten people; hence, we can estimate that 2,560,000, or almost three million people, were in Jerusalem.[1] If the Passover lambs were killed on one day only, 256,000 lambs would require that 10,666 die per hour. If a lamb could be processed every three minutes, 533 priests would be on duty for the twenty-four hours of Passover. (The traditional time for killing the lamb was at the evening sacrifice.)

Undoubtedly, the story of deliverance from Egypt made the strong-willed Jews long for deliverance from Rome. The Romans, conscious of the fervor of patriotic nationalism, sent extra detachments of troops from their garrison in Caesarea to Jerusalem at this time. These troops quartered in the Tower of Antonia overlooking the Temple. At Passover, the most bustling time of year when Jews crowded into Jerusalem from everywhere (Acts 2:5-11), God's deliverer was to be offered.

Two days before the celebration, the chief priests and scribes (Matthew 26:3 says elders of the people), key leaders of the Sanhedrin, eagerly sought with intense desire to capture Jesus with craft.

Verse 2. Their concerns were twofold: they feared that He might again escape their net (they were evidently afraid of Him and alarmed by His unusual power), and they feared an uprising of the people, for Jesus was popular in areas where their own influence was not strong.

They probably also desired to avoid at this time a confrontation with the Romans, which would surely ensue if all were not peaceful in the city.

These verses make clear that Christ's death was decided; all that was needed was opportunity with a moderate degree of self-protection. The religious leaders' callous nature revealed itself in their care for self-preservation but lack of concern for the holy day. Fear of riot or of Rome weighed greater than the fear of God with these leaders. Here divine omnipotence overrode the course of events and plans were hastily changed, assuring a paschal offering of the "Lamb of God, which taketh away the sin of the world" (John 1:29). Matthew 26:3 gives the name of the high priest, Caiaphas, and mentions the gathering at his court.

2. Anointing in Bethany (14:3-9)
(Matthew 26:6; John 12:1; cf. Luke 7:36-50)

(3) And being in Bethany in the house of Simon the leper, as he sat at meat, there came a woman having an alabaster box of ointment of spikenard very precious; and she brake the box, and poured it on his head. (4) And there were some that had indignation within themselves, and said, Why was this waste of the ointment made? (5) For it might have been sold for more than three hundred pence, and have been given to the poor. And they murmured against her. (6) And Jesus said, Let her alone; why trouble ye her? she hath wrought a good work on me. (7) For ye have the poor with you always, and whensoever ye will ye may do them good: but me ye have not always. (8) She hath done what she

could: she is come aforehand to anoint my body to the burying. (9) Verily I say unto you, Wheresoever this gospel shall be preached throughout the whole world, this also that she hath done shall be spoken of for a memorial of her.

The Gospels give several of perhaps many instances of Jesus being anointed. All accounts have in common a woman, an alabaster box of ointment, and occurrence at mealtime in the home of a specifically named individual. In Eastern custom, perfumed ointment was placed on special guests upon entry into the home or at mealtime. The extra anointing here served other purposes: to anoint Christ's body (Matthew 26; Mark 14; John 12) and to express due affection for Him and thankfulness for His forgiveness (Luke 7).

At each anointing, special lessons were caught as well as taught. In Luke 7:36-50 a sinner woman with an alabaster box anointed Jesus' feet, shed tears, and wiped them with the hairs of her head. This occurred at Nain in the home of Simon, a Pharisee.

Matthew 26 and Mark 14 recount a second anointing. The anointing in John 12 is commonly treated as the same account.[2] However, differences in details are difficult to reconcile, leading some to conclude that there were three distinct anointings rather than two.

Verse 3. As noted before, Jesus retired from the city at night, usually to Bethany, and returned in the morning. Thus, the setting for the anointing was Bethany in the house of Simon the leper—former leper, now probably cleansed since the law forbade contact with lepers, especially so near the festival when the seven days required for cleansing could not be fulfilled before the Passover. At Eastern meals guests reclined on low couches on the left side and elbow and took food with the right hand from a common dish. In this manner, the full length of Jesus' body was accessible when approached from the back.

Alabaster is soft marble (or a cheaper substitute) named for Alabaster, Egypt, that can be hollowed out into various designs and shapes for holding ointment. This mineral stone used for vases and bottles had the property of preserving spiced oils for long periods without absorbing or changing the ingredients. In this case the flask contained expensive ("very precious") spikenard, or spiked nard, a pure fragrant medicinal oil derived from roots of the north Indian bearded plant "nardi spice," *Nardostachys*, probably *N. jatamansi*.

Instead of the customary few drops of ointment applied upon arrival or at mealtime, here the woman poured all. If the vessel held about a pint of fluid as usual, Jesus' head would have been saturated and His body genuinely anointed. By breaking the vial instead of merely pouring out the liquid, the women adhered to the ancient custom of breaking the cup or glass used by a person of great honor, thus preventing the hand of a lesser individual from holding it later. Anointing the head was a distinct mark of honor.

Verses 4-5. "Some" people objected with inner indignation, vexed at this waste of precious ointment. Matthew names the "some" as disciples, and John names Judas Iscariot as the chief one. Discontent is contagious and the reason offered—it would be better to sell the ointment and give the proceeds to the poor—seemed logical, so they murmured, literally growling and glowering at the women. Economically the flask and contents were valued at three hundred pence. One pence *(denarion)* represented a day's labor wage, so the sum represented almost a year's wages for a workingman.

One condemned practice that never pleased God was murmuring. Regardless of how justified, ill-treated, frustrated, or betrayed one might be, murmuring never pleases God. Jesus never murmured. Murmuring ex-presses an attitude of discontent, inability to cope or overcome, and God desires that we be overcomers. Hence, God condemned murmuring (Exodus 15:24; 16:2-12; Numbers 14:2-37; 17:5-10; Joshua 9:18; Matthew 20:11). It is tantamount to criticism of the path God has given and belittles His ability to deliver or see one through all kinds of difficulty.

Verse 6. Jesus spoke emphatically: "Let her alone," taking the woman's side in this good work wrought on Him. The Greek text uses two terms, *agathos* and *kalor*, for good works or acts of charity. The former, *agathos*, indicates moral precision and correctness in describing moral good. It may be stern, hard, and demanding, yet morally correct. The second term, *kalos*, means good and lovely or sweet, generous, and kind motivation of good. Jesus used this word to describe this woman's act. Her "good" was an altogether lovely, kind, un-selfish, generous, sweet, tender, compassionate, and extravagant personal work not often witnessed. (See Luke 7:44-47.)

Verse 7. A further reason the woman was justified is that "ye have the poor with you always." It was never inappropriate to help them, but the privilege of helping a passing guest, especially one sent by God, was greater.

Jesus was not indifferent to the poor, but all cannot be helped all the time. The Old Testament states that the poor never cease in the land (Deuteronomy 15:11).

Here Jesus' words emphatically counter the dogma of transubstantiation. If His body were present always, as transubstantiation holds, it might at any time be anointed—or taken in a sacrament. This was not the case.

Verse 8. Jesus put the woman's action in proper perspective by a preburial acknowledgement of impending death. Ointment with spices was customarily employed on dead bodies before burial, and at His statement the woman as well as the disciples must have been shocked. Certainly the disciples failed to fully recognize what Jesus was facing and undoubtedly felt shame as they argued about who should be "greatest" (Luke 22:24-27). This humble lady honored the One who was truly the "greatest." The anointing was for burial, not kingship.

Verse 9. The act was to become a memorial of her wherever the gospel is preached. The verse contains a prophecy of the spread of the gospel "throughout the whole world." The cross was in view, yet He assured them that the good news for all generations would transmit this story.

This second anointing came just two days prior to Passover, whereas anointing at Lazarus' house was six days prior to Passover (John 12:1-8). It was an anointing for burial "aforehand" (Mark 14:8). It was a genuine act of love, unselfish, sacrificial, and without hope or thought of recompense. "God loveth a cheerful," not a careful, "giver" (II Corinthians 9:7). This lavish gift was no waste when put on Jesus Christ, nor are our lavish gifts of sacrifice wasted now.

316

3. Treachery of Judas (14:10-11)
(Matthew 26:14; Luke 22:3)

(10) And Judas Iscariot, one of the twelve, went unto the chief priests, to betray him unto them. (11) And when they heard it, they were glad, and promised to give him money. And he sought how he might conveniently betray him.

The scene of beauty and of generous love rapidly shifts to ugly and selfish malice, for following the anointing and rebuke Mark shows the betrayal plot. Judas was undoubtedly hardened by the rebuke and resolved to profit as much as possible, seeing that Jesus was about to die. John 11:57 hints that there might have been a reward to the man who made possible His arrest.

Verse 10. Mark pointedly shows Judas as "one of the twelve" most trusted followers of Jesus. Speculations as to the motive of Judas for betraying His Master include avarice, covetousness, jealousy, ambition, and an attempt to force Jesus to use His great powers in self-defense and thus usher in His kingdom. Since Judas undoubtedly smarted under the rebuke of verses 6-9 and John 12:4-8, anger and vengeance would be natural. To whatever initial cause is preferred we can add the true underlying reason: the devil himself. Both Luke 22:3 and John 13:27 declare that the devil entered Judas. His intent was clear: he went to the chief priests "to betray him unto them."

Verse 11. The chief priests were elated at this sudden unexpected stroke, first because of the opportunity to take Jesus, and second because one of the chosen Twelve "sought" to betray Him. Betrayal by an insider would go far in formulating propaganda to discredit His teachings.

In their gladness they promised to give Judas money for delivery. Matthew 26:15 quotes Zechariah 11:12, giving the exact amount, thirty pieces of silver. Thirty silver shekels of the sanctuary were less than half the worth of the precious ointment and were the blood price for death of a servant (Exodus 21:32). After the deal was struck, only one thing remained: to find a convenient place and time when Jesus was alone or away from the crowds when He could be arrested.

The treachery of Judas, like the anointing by the unnamed woman, has become known wherever the gospel is preached, providing two distinct, contrasting relationships.

Notes

[1]Barclay, 340.
[2]Hobbs, 66; *Pulpit Commentary*, 229.

B.
Passover Observance
(14:12-25)

B. Passover Observance (14:12-25)

1. Preparation for the Passover (14:12-16)
(Matthew 26:17; Luke 22:7)

(12) And the first day of unleavened bread, when they killed the passover, his disciples said unto him, Where wilt thou that we go and prepare that thou mayest eat the passover? (13) And he sendeth forth two of his disciples, and saith unto them, Go ye into the city, and there shall meet you a man bearing a pitcher of water: follow him. (14) And wheresoever he shall go in, say ye to the goodman of the house, The Master saith, Where is the guestchamber, where I shall eat the passover with my disciples? (15) And he will shew you a large upper room furnished and prepared: there make ready for us. (16) And his disciples went forth, and came into the city, and found as he had said unto them: and they made ready the passover.

Verse 12. The first day of unleavened bread beginning at 6:00 P.M. on Nisan 14 was the day for killing the Passover lamb. Mark treats this "last supper" as a Passover meal. Although there are objections (see John 18:28), it appears that Jesus and the disciples prepared and ate the lamb before Jesus was Himself sacrificed as the paschal lamb (I Corinthians 5:7). The actual crucifixion occurred on Friday, at Passover (John 19:14).

The disciples' question concerned the intent to prepare and eat the Passover meal: where, at what house? Some feel that Jesus had made prior arrangements for a

321

place and that the disciples were sent to make final preparations.

Verse 13. Jesus sent two disciples, John and Peter (Luke 22:8), to prepare. The signal was a man they would meet carrying a water pitcher, which was usually carried by women. They were to follow him to the designated place.

Verses 14-15. Where this servant went in they were to ask the master of the house about the guest chamber. The name of the man of the house was withheld, perhaps for fear of the Jews even at the time of the writing of Mark. Tradition holds it to be the home of John Mark, also the place where the disciples congregated just before the Resurrection, and where the Spirit fell at Pentecost. It appears that the man was a believer and the two disciples were known to him since their message "the Master saith" was sufficient to secure the upper room guest chamber furnished and prepared with tables, couches, rugs, and necessities for a Passover meal.

Verse 16. They found the foreknowledge of Jesus to be accurate "as he had said," and there they made ready the Passover. If Jesus died at the time the Passover lambs were slain, then He had to eat the meal a day early, before the usual Passover time. If so, could a Passover lamb be obtained from the priests at the Temple before the designated time?

Johnson has presented evidence that the Last Supper was probably not the actual Passover meal but preceded it, because Jesus was offered as the paschal lamb at approximately the time the lambs were being slain in the Temple.[1] However, the disciples evidently expected to eat the Passover and the preparations noted by Mark point to this supper as a Passover, which nowhere is contradicted by the words or actions of the Master. If so, perhaps they were able to eat the Passover a day earlier. The usual Feast of Unleavened Bread officially began one day after Passover, but pious Jews began to eat unleavened bread on the day of preparation.

Preparation was a ritual that included the ceremonial searching of the house with a lighted candle for leavening, the symbol of rottenness and putrefaction. This exercise was prefaced and ended with solemn prayers: "Blessed art Thou, Jehovah, our God, King of all the Universe, who hast sanctified us by thy commandments and commanded us to remove the leaven." "All the leaven that is in my possession, that which I have seen and that which I have not seen, be it null, be it accounted as the dust of the earth."

Peter and John would take a lamb to the priests at the Temple for sacrifice and join the throng of worshipers there. The worshipers presented the lamb to the priest, who cut its throat, catching the blood in a silver or gold bowl before casting it upon the altar. The carcass was flayed, its entrails and fat removed, and returned to the worshipers for roasting at home over an open flame. The carcass was cooked on a spit of pomegranate wood extending through the body. It could not touch even a pot or vessel and had to be roasted whole—head, legs, and tail with the body.

Other preparations at Passover reminded the Jews of Egypt. Included were a bowl of salt water reminiscent of tears and the Red Sea; bitter herbs (horseradish, chicory, endive, horehound) depicting bitter slavery; a pastelike sauce of apples, dates, pomegranates, and nuts to remind the Jews of the clay for bricks; and sticks of cinnamon to

323

represent straw for the clay bricks. The meal was taken in courses with four cups of three parts wine to two parts water being introduced at different times to correspond to the four promises of Exodus 6:6-7. Thus each detail commemorated the events of the great deliverance from Egypt.

2. Announcement of the Betrayal (14:17-21)
(Matthew 26:20; Luke 22:21; John 13)

(17) And in the evening he cometh with the twelve. (18) And as they sat and did eat, Jesus said, Verily I say unto you, One of you which eateth with me shall betray me. (19) And they began to be sorrowful, and to say unto him one by one, Is it I? and another said, Is it I? (20) And he answered and said unto them, It is one of the twelve, that dippeth with me in the dish. (21) The Son of man indeed goeth, as it is written of him: but woe to that man by whom the Son of man is betrayed! good were it for that man if he had never been born.

Verse 17. On the evening the lamb was to be eaten, the beginning of Nisan 15, Jesus came with the Twelve to the prepared room in Jerusalem.

Verse 18. As they ate Jesus announced what must have been a bombshell: one of you will betray Me.

Verses 19-20. The disciples were shocked, then sorrowful, even at this normally joyous occasion, and desired to know who it would be. They questioned, one by one, "Is it I?" (The last phrase of verse 19, "and another said," is omitted from some manuscripts.) Jesus answered by a general statement: "one of the twelve that dippeth with

324

me in the dish." Jesus referred to the centrally located dish of charoseth sauce (paste) into which several men reached simultaneously, so the exact identity of the culprit was not divulged.

Other evangelists noted that Jesus pointed out that "the hand . . . is with me on the table" (Luke 22:21). Peter motioned for John, who was seated nearest Jesus, to ask Him for more specific identification (John 13:24-26). Jesus indicated that the betrayer would receive of Him a sop. Apparently Judas reclined near Jesus at the supper, well within arm's reach.

One difference between the commemorative Passover and the initial one in Egypt was that the first Passover was eaten standing, wearing sandals, with staff in hand, as slaves ready to run. Here the Passover was consumed reclining in a house as free men.

Psalm 41:9 previewed this scene. Jesus, well knowing what was coming, continued to appeal to Judas. Undoubtedly the disciples were never able to zero in on the betrayer, because had they done so they would surely have intervened. All the Gospels affirm that Jesus knew who would betray Him and made no effort to save Himself from the "cup" prepared for Him.

Verse 21 refers to Christ's departure from mortal life by death, as God foreordained from the foundation of the world. It is noteworthy that the predetermined nature of Christ's suffering and death made the betrayer no less guilty of his deed. Jesus stated a woe so severe that it would have been better for the betrayer not to have ever been born. To this Judas answered, "Master, is it I?", choosing to call Him rabbi instead of Lord (Matthew 26:25). The significance of Jesus' response escaped the notice of all, for still no action was taken against Judas (John 13:26-30), who departed without eating the Lord's Supper.

3. Institution of the Lord's Supper (14:22-25)
(Matthew 26:26; Luke 22:8; I Corinthians 11:23-29)

Although the identity of this supper as the Passover itself can be questioned, it is clear that the resources present were prepared for a Passover (verse 12). The nearness of the great feast dominated the thoughts of the disciples. Mark indicates that the Lord's Supper followed the meal, the revelation of a betrayer, and the departure of Judas from the group. The institution of the Lord's Supper presented certain elements that occurred in the orderly course of the Passover feast, here taken and uniquely adapted with special meanings for the church.

(22) And as they did eat, Jesus took bread, and blessed, and brake it, and gave to them, and said, Take, eat: this is my body. (23) And he took the cup, and when he had given thanks, he gave it to them: and they all drank of it. (24) And he said unto them, This is my blood of the new testament, which is shed for many. (25) Verily I say unto you, I will drink no more of the fruit of the vine, until that day that I drink it new in the kingdom of God.

Verse 22. The course of a Passover meal included three times of breaking bread and partaking. Exactly which one was meant in this case is not known, but customarily a grace was offered with the second. Jesus gave the broken bread with the words "Take, eat: this is my body." The bread was symbolic and not intended as a transubstantiation (in which bread becomes literal flesh) or consubstantiation (in which literal flesh is present with the bread). The eating of the bread represents Christ's broken, lifeless, and bloodless body—broken and offered for people. Motivated by Old Testament prohibitions concerning blood, the Jews had earlier turned away horrified at Jesus' statements concerning the eating of flesh and drinking of blood (John 6:53-66).

Verses 23-24. No account of the Lord's Supper uses the word "wine." Verse 25 identifies the contents of the cup of which they all drank as the "fruit of the vine." Because the feast called for bread without leaven and leaven symbolized corruption and putrefaction to Jews, it is reasonable to assume that the fruit of the vine was not "wine" resulting from fermentation. Leavening of dough and fermentation of sugars in fruit juices occurs by metabolism of yeast microorganisms. One byproduct of this metabolism is carbon dioxide gas, which causes dough to rise; a second byproduct of yeast metabolism is ethanol, the alcohol present in fermented wine.

Jesus's intent was to seal a covenant ("new" in verse 24 is absent from important texts) with the fruit of the vine representing His blood. This covenant parallels the one God gave to Israel at Sinai (Exodus 24:8), but was better and complete, fulfilling both Sinai and the early promise implied in Genesis 3:15. The promise of redemption was not just for the Twelve or for the Jews, but His blood was "shed for many."

Verse 25. Jesus added a solemn, self-imposed restriction and made a pronouncement of great eschatological significance. First, He would no more drink of fruit of the vine (He refused wine with myrrh while on the cross) until that "day" in the kingdom of God when He would drink it anew. Second, He implied His certainty of death ("no more"), but equally His certainty of resurrection and life after death and burial. The words speak of the restoration and fulfillment that the Jews expected in the Millennium.

Until then, His disciples were to feed upon and draw strength from the body and blood of Christ, which He gave as evidence of God's love and care. Because Jesus resurrected, so assuredly will God resurrect all believers to dine once again with Jesus at His heavenly table. The Lord's Supper prophetically symbolizes the marriage feast of the lamb (Revelation 19:9).

Paul used the pledge of the kingdom to come and the Lord's Supper as strength and hope: we celebrate "the Lord's death till he come" (I Corinthians 11:26). Jews in foreign lands have their own expression at Passover: "This year we keep it here, next year in the land of Israel; this year as slaves, next year as free."

The Last Supper revealed several noteworthy surprises. First, the disciples, who normally partook of the feast as head or members of their family, chose to do so with their Master. Jesus' prophecy of commitment to Him being stronger than family ties had already been realized.

Second, Jesus took elements of the Passover and attached to them special significance, commemorating, not hyssop, lamb's blood on doorposts, or escape from death, but a cross smeared with His own blood. He walked into the fiercest of wrath that we might escape death. Jesus actually became the Passover lamb for all humanity.

Third, Jesus renounced (in Nazarite fashion, Numbers 6:2-4) further drinking of the fruit of the vine until the kingdom be fulfilled. This must have caught the disciples' attention and impressed them of the finality of this meal. The vow and the covenant voiced to His chosen disciples would provide strength and courage for facing the trying ordeal about to break forth upon Him.

Note

[1]Johnson, 226.

C.

Garden of Gethsemane
(14:26-52)

C. Garden of Gethsemane (14:26-52)
1. Revelation on the Way (14:26-31)
(Matthew 26:30; Luke 22:31; John 13:36)

After adjourning from the upper room, Jesus led the disciples to the Garden of Gethsemane on the Mount of Olives, where the second act of the betrayal drama occurred. Along the way Jesus made astounding pronouncements.

(26) And when they had sung an hymn, they went out into the mount of Olives. (27) And Jesus saith unto them, All ye shall be offended because of me this night: for it is written, I will smite the shepherd, and the sheep shall be scattered. (28) But after that I am risen, I will go before you into Galilee. (29) But Peter said unto him, Although all shall be offended, yet will not I. (30) And Jesus saith unto him, Verily I say unto thee, That this day, even in this night, before the cock crow twice, thou shalt deny me thrice. (31) But he spake the more vehemently, If I should die with thee, I will not deny thee in any wise. Likewise also said they all.

Verse 26. The hymns sung at Passover were from the Psalter, the Hillel psalms (Psalms 113-118). Every Jewish schoolboy committed these psalms to memory, and with the words fresh in their minds the band left the upper room. The Mount of Olives arose from the ravine through which the Brook of Kidron flowed; Gethsemane adorned the western slope. Apparently the pattern of other days and nights during the final week varied little. Jesus taught in Jerusalem during the day, retreated to Bethany to sup in the evening, then returned to the Mount of Olives to spend the entire night in prayer (Luke 21:37). Knowing the hour was at hand and also aware that Judas knew His habits, Jesus proceeded with great courage like Daniel to follow His pattern. He deliberately and voluntarily set Himself up for the traitor (John 18:2).

Verse 27. Jesus' first pronouncement was that all of them would be offended ("because of me this night" is omitted from important texts), as written in Zechariah 13:7. Like sheep, when their Shepherd was smitten the disciples would scatter. The word translated "offended" (fall away) is the Greek term *skandalon*, meaning a bait in a trap or the snare itself.

Verse 28. The second prophetic announcement was that He would regroup the "scattered sheep" and lead or precede them into Galilee. This must have carried notes of reassurance since many if not all of the disciples were Galileans. Home, friends, warmth, and family would be welcome after a week of hostile stares and rude treatment by the religious Jews in Jerusalem. The scattering was only temporary; the regrouping was permanent (Ezekiel 34:11-16). Scattering was not due to persecution but to the stumbling on His account; Jesus thus became a "stone of stumbling" (Isaiah 8:14; I Peter 2:8).

Verse 29. Peter, forgetting the *skandalon*, immediately fell into the snare created by his own flesh. Although his heart was right and his spirit willing, his flesh was weak. "All the others, yes, but not me" expresses the invincibility of youth still resident in Peter. He failed to take heed and thought he could stand against his own constitution as well as the truth of Jesus' words.

Verse 30. In a rejoinder Jesus emphasized what falling away would mean for His chosen disciple: to disown his Master three times. It was easy for Peter to believe what Christ said of others, but he could not see how it could apply to him. Jesus prophesied more than a mere stumble for Peter; he would miserably fail and fall flat. Only Luke 22:31-32 records Jesus' words about Satan's attempt to winnow the big fisherman and the prayer for him.

Christ's words were verified with the second crowing of the rooster, which only Mark notes. The crowing depicted a change in the night watches. It was probably the sound of the final one after a night of trial that reminded Peter of his boast and exposed to himself his own weakness.

Verse 31. Peter had the audacity to reassert loyalty even to death, as did all the disciples, even discounting the words of Jesus Himself. Peter in his simple loyalty undoubtedly meant what he said but in the moment of test was unable to follow through. So every Christian is warned, when facing trial and persecution, to beware of the snare of the flesh. There is also encouragement in the tragic fall: the love of God provides forgiveness and restoration for every penitent individual in his utter failure.

Each Christian stands where Peter stood. The contrast between Peter and Jesus was sharp at this point. Peter, big, strong and vocal, appeared well able to face any trial, test, or challenge. Jesus, slight, meek and quiet, appeared so tender, so helpless, that the disciples and His friends, especially the women, tried to look out for Him. Yet it was Jesus who had prepared Himself for this moment. He steeled Himself to face the opposition, the rejection, the misunderstanding, the hate and anger of hostile leaders. He anticipated the agony, pain, and cruelty at the hands of His "own" as Calvary loomed nearer. He was prepared for the denial of Peter, the scattering of His chosen band, and the utter forsakeness of the cross. He was also prepared to reassemble the disciples to initiate His work through them.

2. Agony in the Garden (14:32-42)
(Matthew 26:36; Luke 22:39; John 18:1)

Christ's darkest hour became for sinners' the most glorious hour. Here in the solitude of a garden—not on the tree—He fought and won His internal battle. The betrayer worked, the disciples slept, but Jesus prayed.

(32) And they came to a place which was named Gethsemane: and he saith to his disciples, Sit ye here, while I shall pray. (33) And he taketh with him Peter and James and John, and began to be sore amazed, and to be very heavy; (34) and saith unto them, My soul is exceeding sorrowful unto death: tarry ye here, and watch. (35) And he went forward a little, and fell on the ground, and prayed that, if it were possible, the hour might pass from him. (36) And he said, Abba, Father, all things are possible unto thee; take away this cup from me: nevertheless not what I will, but what thou wilt. (37) And he cometh, and findeth them sleeping, and saith unto Peter, Simon, sleepest thou? couldest not thou watch one hour? (38) Watch ye and pray, lest ye enter into temptation. The spirit truly is ready, but the flesh is weak. (39) And again he went away, and

prayed, and spake the same words. (40) And when he returned, he found them asleep again, (for their eyes were heavy,) neither wist they what to answer him. (41) And he cometh the third time, and saith unto them, Sleep on now, and take your rest: it is enough, the hour is come; behold, the Son of man is betrayed into the hands of sinners. (42) Rise up, let us go; lo, he that betrayeth me is at hand.

Verse 32. The Mount of Olives east of Jerusalem was the site of many gardens and groves. Gardens outside the crowded city (whose sanctified soil could not be polluted with dung) belonged to the city's more affluent people, one of whom allowed Jesus to use the Garden of Gethsemane. The name means "the place of the olive press," perhaps because oil was pressed from the olives grown on Mount Moriah. The garden had before fulfilled Jesus' need for fellowship with God, and in this darkest hour it again became His retreat. This time the disciples came.

Verse 33. He selected three disciples, Peter, James and John, to fill the craving for human fellowship as the time of arrest approached.

Jesus began to be "sore amazed," *ekthambeo* (to throw into terror, alarm, or distress). It appears that His flesh did not fully comprehend why all the foreseen suffering and death was necessary. Jesus' flesh did not want to die, yet even what is not understood must be accepted if it is the will of God.

Verses 34-35. Christ's deep sorrow was not due merely to the thought of the pain of physical death; He had faced death before. Neither was He afraid of murder in the garden, for the cross was part of His cup. There was no question about resurrection or even of the welfare of His disciples. The sorrow and agony arose from the absolute purity of a sinless Christ being made sin for humanity (II Corinthians 5:21). He was having placed upon Him the "iniquity of us all" (Isaiah 53:6); hence the condition of being "exceeding sorrowful unto death."

After further separation, "a stone's cast" (Luke 22:41), He fell to the ground prostrate, the supreme position of supplication. Ordinary prayers were offered standing with uplifted hands (Luke 18:11; I Timothy 2:8). Jesus, prostrate, prayed intensely for the passing of the terrible hours of testing.

Verse 36. He repeated "Abba," a tender Aramaic word for "Father." While omnipotence knows no impossibility, the omnipotent God was bound by self-imposed divine law to satisfy wrath for sin, so the appeal to seek another way was at once subordinated to the divine will. Humanly, He desired deliverance by the removal of the awful cup— the lot or portion appointed by God; spiritually, He desired only to accept the position and please God. The garden scene of the Gospels shows a fully human will surrendering to a fully divine will. To trust enough to call God Abba speaks of a relationship that makes all things bearable.

Verses 37-38. Jesus paused to check on the disciples; their sleep brought a rebuke in which Jesus singled out Peter, using his old name, Simon. His boast of staying even unto death seemed shallow when he could not even remain awake one hour. "Watch"—reminiscent of the doorkeeper in Mark 13:34-37—and "pray" became watchwords for every disciple.

Jesus accepted that trials, tests, and temptations

belong to the human life, that they are not necessarily sent by God, and that prayer for deliverance or courage to endure them is the rightful remedy. The contrast of an eager, willing spirit and a failing, weak flesh is lessened by prayer, watchfulness for snares, and dependence on the Father.

The disciples' temptation was to deny Christ because of fear. Because they failed to heed His counsel, they fell, as He knew they would. Christ understood their weakness of flesh and noted their willingness of spirit.

Verses 39-40. Jesus again prayed the same words, affirming His willingness to submit to the will of God and thus set the example by adhering to His own advice to "watch and pray." Only the physician Luke recorded the unusual perspiration (Luke 22:44).

With the battle won, Jesus returned to find His companions once again sleeping, their eyes "heavy." This time there was no answer for their slumber.

Verses 41-42. Jesus must have prayed again, then returned a third time to the sleeping men. This time, victory was won: "It is enough" *(apechei);* the betrayer had done his work, received his money, and was ready. The Son was betrayed. There must have been a short space of time between the "sleep on" of verse 41 and the "rise up" of verse 42.

"Sinners" probably refers to Judas as well as the other participants. A Jewish traitor revealed Christ's whereabouts to religious leaders, who in turn maneuvered Rome into a position to kill Him, since they lacked the power to impose the death penalty.

The passage produces an interesting question, although moot due to divine inspiration: if the disciples slept, who heard and reported Christ's actual words? There is further interest in the repetition of threes: three disciples, three times sleeping, three prayers, then Peter's three denials.

The words "Abba, Father" reflected a costly submission to the will of God and gained usage by submitted Christians in the first century (Romans 8:15; Galatians 4:6). Finally, it is significant that we can discuss the human spirit and its will distinct from the flesh, for flesh has desires of its own.

3. Betrayal and Arrest (14:43-50)
(Matthew 26:47; Luke 22:47; John 18:1)

For the complete story with all its drama and details one must read all the Gospel accounts of the betrayal and arrest. Mark evidently had reservations in naming the sword bearer (verse 47) and the fleeing young man (verse 51). Perhaps it was unwise at the time of Mark's writing to name the former, for John, writing forty years later, gave names (John 18:10).

(43) And immediately, while he yet spake, cometh Judas, one of the twelve, and with him a great multitude with swords and staves, from the chief priests and the scribes and the elders. (44) And he that betrayed him had given them a token, saying, Whomsoever I shall kiss, that same is he; take him, and lead him away safely. (45) And as soon as he was come, he goeth straightway to him, and saith, Master, master; and kissed him. (46) And they laid their hands on him, and took him. (47) And one of them that stood by drew a sword, and

*smote a servant of the high priest, and cut off his ear.
(48) And Jesus answered and said unto them, Are ye
come out, as against a thief, with swords and with
staves to take me? (49) I was daily with you in the temple teaching, and ye took me not: but the scriptures must
be fulfilled. (50) And they all forsook him, and fled.*

Verse 43. Judas, identified in shame as one of the
Twelve (verses 10, 20), went before the multitude. It
appears that Judas used careful forethought. He came
upon the garden at an hour when the disciples were sleeping (verse 42) and, when awakened, would be confused
and disoriented and therefore offer little resistance. He
probably knew who in the band held the two swords
(Luke 22:35-38) and had with him soldiers armed with
swords and civil officers or Temple police of the Sanhedrin armed with staves (cudgels) since a priest could
not shed blood. John 18:3 adds that they came with
lanterns and torches, even though the moon was full.

Verses 44-49a. Judas was anxious to identify and
secure Jesus properly lest He hide or miraculously escape
and he, Judas, would lose his reward. The signal was a
kiss, as one would give in Eastern salutations or among
the Romans. Barclay noted that the betrayal kiss was not
the customary *philein* but an intense *kataphlein*, a kiss of
endearment that one might deliver to a rabbi's hand or
head.[1] The hateful nature of this betrayal is made even
worse by the absolute moral bankruptcy of the one who a
few hours before accepted the sop of friendship from the
Man he now kissed.

The events in the garden drama fall into a sequence as
follows: Judas reached Jesus, called Him rabbi (not Lord),

and kissed Him. Jesus stepped forward with "Whom seek ye? . . . I am he" (John 18:4-6). The mob momentarily fell backward to the ground before His power and majesty.

As they rose and surged forward, "one of them" (John 18:10 names Peter), encouraged to fight, drew a sword and struck a slave of the high priest. Again John provides a name, Malchus, whose ear was severed. With medical precision, Luke noted that it was the right ear (Luke 22:50). Jesus restored the ear, a miracle of compassion, delivering a rebuke to the disciples and sharp stinging words for the priests: "Are ye come out, as against a thief?" They could have arrested Him in the Temple any day during the past week but now they took the cowardly way at night away from His supporters.

Verse 49b. This statement is a sentence fragment made complete by Matthew 26:56. Either the evangelist or Jesus could have said it, probably Jesus, but exactly which verse of Scripture is fulfilled is uncertain. Isaiah 53:12 has been suggested.

Verse 50. At this point the disciples' nerves cracked, and they scattered like sheep when their Shepherd was smitten. They fled.

If Peter and perhaps another disciple with a sword was supposed to guard Jesus (i.e., watch, verses 37-38), their reactions were too slow to be effective. Peter, freshly awakened and startled into action, did what he thought he should do, but this was no time for swordplay. Like Moses' blow to the Egyptian (Exodus 2:12), the force of man fails in God's plan. Besides, in the entire exchange it is the Master who is serene, confident, in charge, commanding, even directing the affairs of His own arrest (verse 48). He is at peace, after the agony of prayer, in following the will of God. Even "seized" He is not a prisoner of man but a victim for man.

4. The Young Man Who Fled (14:51-52)

(51) And there followed him a certain young man, having a linen cloth cast about his naked body; and the young men laid hold on him: (52) and he left the linen cloth, and fled from them naked.

Verses 51-52. Mark is the only Gospel that tells the story of the fleeing *neaniskos*, teenager or young man. The description is vivid and detailed except for a name. Some believe the young man was Lazarus or the rich young ruler. Most believe that it was John Mark himself. The *sindon*, or fine linen cloak, as sleeping apparel bespoke certain family affluence since the fabric was expensive and manufactured in Sidon of Phoenicia. It was also used for burial wraps. Being spied by the soldiers, the young man who followed left the cloth and fled. The incident might have been added to suggest the rage that all followers of Jesus met. The disciples would no doubt have been seized had they not resorted to flight.

If the youth was John Mark then, in spite of sleeping disciples, the Gethsemane narrative had a reverent eyewitness hiding in the shadows. Perhaps Judas led the mob to the upper room first and in the process awakened John Mark, whose home hosted the meal. Mark fled in haste to warn Jesus, robed only in his night clothes, but arrived too late and was nearly arrested himself. Papias said that Mark neither heard the Lord nor was he a follower, which, if reliable, would seem to eliminate Mark.[2] The incident is of interest only to Mark, since Matthew and Luke omit it. The facts speak for themselves; naming the person is speculation, though he was probably known to the early church.

Notes

[1]Barclay, 363.
[2]Johnson, 238.

D.
Trials of Jesus
(14:53-15:20a)

D. Trials of Jesus (14:53-15:20a)
1. "Trial" before the Sanhedrin (14:53-65)
(Matthew 26:57; Luke 22:63; John 18:12, 19)

The trial before the Sanhedrin was far from an attempt at justice. Jesus was never considered innocent. His enemies' hatred and expressed desire to kill Him made the illegal proceedings nothing but an attempt to find suitable cause to elicit the Roman death penalty. The Messiah was in the hands of angry and irrational men. Through them the words of the prophets were fulfilled (Isaiah 53) and God's wrath for sin appeased. The entire action proceeded hastily to avoid infringing upon the national religious holiday and lest something should arise to again allow Jesus to slip through their grasp.

(53) And they led Jesus away to the high priest: and with him were assembled all the chief priests and the elders and the scribes. (54) And Peter followed him afar off, even into the palace of the high priest: and he sat with the servants, and warmed himself at the fire. (55) And the chief priests and all the council sought for witness against Jesus to put him to death; and found none. (56) For many bare false witness against him, but their witness agreed not together. (57) And there arose certain, and bare false witness against him, saying, (58) We heard him say, I will destroy this temple that is made with hands, and within three days I will build another made without hands. (59) But neither so did their witness agree together. (60) And the high priest

347

stood up in the midst, and asked Jesus, saying, Answerest thou nothing? what is it which these witness against thee? (61) But he held his peace, and answered nothing. Again the high priest asked him, and said unto him, Art thou the Christ, the Son of the Blessed? (62) And Jesus said, I am: and ye shall see the Son of man sitting on the right hand of power, and coming in the clouds of heaven. (63) Then the high priest rent his clothes, and saith, What need we any further witnesses? (64) Ye have heard the blasphemy: what think ye? And they all condemned him to be guilty of death. (65) And some began to spit on him, and to cover his face, and to buffet him, and to say unto him, Prophesy: and the servants did strike him with the palms of their hands.

The procedural details of the account are difficult to reconstruct. Mark indicates three meetings: the Sanhedrin at night, again in early morning (15:1), then before Pilate (15:2-15).

Verse 53. The high priest at that time was Joseph Caiaphas, in office from A.D. 18-35. John 18:13 informs us that Jesus was taken from the garden to the house of Annas, father-in-law of Caiaphas and an influential voice on the council. Annas and his five sons held the high priest's position in succession, with Caiaphas serving between the terms of the first and second sons. Judas Iscariot evidently received his commission from Annas.

Verse 54. The stage was set for Peter's denial, as John, known to the high priest (John 18:15), entered and admitted Peter to the court area where servants and guards assembled. Jesus was arraigned before the council in a larger inside room. The late night air was cold, and Peter, warming at the fire, was identified.

Verse 55. The Sanhedrin council of seventy scribes, elders, Sadducees, Pharisees and heads of families was presided over by the seventy-first man, the high priest. Procedures for operating provided in the Mishnah were suspended in this case.[1] The council's authority was primarily over religious matters. The Sanhedrin sat in a semicircle so that every member could see every other member, with the high priest at the center point, resembling a trial before grand jury. The court wanted to prepare a charge that would lead to the death penalty from the Roman governor. According to the Talmud, the Jewish high court could execute by stoning, fire, beheading, or strangulation. Rome had curtailed their powers, however, and it was not lawful for Jews to implement capital punishment (John 18:31).[2] Since Jesus was crucified, His execution was implemented by Rome but instigated by the Jews.

Consistent with their system of judgment, the court sought witnesses against Jesus. None could be found whose testimony agreed or whose charge would warrant the death penalty. It was necessary to have at least two witnesses.

Verses 56-59. The false witnesses contradicted each other and could not agree. The court tolerated no witnesses on behalf of Jesus, however.

There arose two people (Matthew 26:60) who offered false witness. Hobbs thinks that witnesses were primed or prepared to offer testimony but were late in arriving due to the hasty arrest and court proceedings.[3] Even then their testimonies conflicted. They accused Jesus of seeking to destroy the Temple, but Jesus' actual words were:

"Destroy this temple, and in three days I will raise it up" (John 2:19). Verse 58 affirms their perjury. Jesus did not offer to destroy, only to rebuild, as a sign to the Jews (John 2:18-19). John 2:21 shows that He did not refer to their sacred Temple but to the temple of His body, wherein dwelt the fullness of the Godhead (Colossians 2:9; cf. I Corinthians 3:16; 6:19; II Corinthians 6:16). Even if misunderstood, His words would seem little more than an empty boast and hardly worth punishment, let alone a death penalty.

Verses 60-61. Seeing that the witnesses were incompetent, the high priest attempted to draw Jesus into argument of self-defense by which His own words would condemn. Jesus refused to answer. Answer to what? At this point there was nothing but vague and inaccurate charges and disagreement by witnesses who discredited themselves. Flanked by hostile and bloodthirsty men, He would receive no fair hearing, only a twisting of His words. His silence, golden and dignified, spoke loudly to the hearts of men on the court.

The high priest, confronted with silence, commanded Him under oath (Matthew 26:63) and asked a leading question.[4]

Verse 62. To this question Jesus responded with all the power and dignity of the position He now filled. He was the Messiah, Son of God, and not ashamed of it. To the world this truth needed to be established once again. His confession included an affirmation and placed in condemnation and judgment those who judged Him. His judgment would be from "the right hand of power" at His coming in the clouds of heaven.

Jesus's answer was powerful, majestic, yet humble. It

was emphatic: "I am." Jesus answered out of respect for the office of the high priest and out of respect to the blessed divine name invoked by the high priest. His words drew a sharp and quick response.

Verses 63-64. The high priest rent his clothes, literally his garment. People of position wore two tunics, the outer one open at the neck to be slipped over the head and worn over the shoulders and upper body. As a sign of anguish, grief, or indignation this garment would be violently torn from the chin downward in a swift violent motion. A high priest could not lawfully tear his garment for private grief (Leviticus 10:6).

The high priest pronounced Jesus' words, heard by all, as "blasphemy."[5] Now the council rendered a collective decision, which was illegal since decisions were to be reached independently. All there opposed Him, and any of Jesus' friends on the council, such as Joseph of Arimathea or Nicodemus, were either silent or not present at this meeting. The council found Him guilty of blasphemy, punishable by death.

Verse 65. Now further illegalities began as Jesus was physically abused. Some spat on Him. They covered His eyes (face) and struck (buffeted) Him. Servants smote Him with the palms of their hands (Matthew 26:67) and mocked with the taunt, "Prophesy who struck you." He bore the physical and mental cruelty of His tormentors in the silence of a lamb led to the slaughter (Isaiah 50:5-7).

2. Three Denials by Peter (14:66-72)
(Matthew 26:69; Luke 22:54; John 18:15, 25)

Mark's account of Peter's denial must be attributed to

the apostle himself. Although incriminating and shameful, it is lifelike and full of hope. It stands in sharp contrast to what occurred with Judas Iscariot who, under the weight of heavy remorse, sought only death. Peter's behavior and our Lord's tender forgiveness provide a shining ray of hope for all Christians who seek repentance for wrong-doing.

(66) And as Peter was beneath in the palace, there cometh one of the maids of the high priest: (67) and when she saw Peter warming himself, she looked upon him, and said, And thou also wast with Jesus of Nazareth. (68) But he denied, saying, I know not, nei-ther understand I what thou sayest. And he went out into the porch; and the cock crew. (69) And a maid saw him again, and began to say to them that stood by, This is one of them. (70) And he denied it again. And a little after, they that stood by said again to Peter, Surely thou art one of them: for thou art a Galilaean, and thy speech agreeth thereto. (71) But he began to curse and to swear, saying, I know not this man of whom ye speak. (72) And the second time the cock crew. And Peter called to mind the word that Jesus said unto him, Before the cock crow twice, thou shalt deny me thrice. And when he thought thereon, he wept.

Verse 66. As the Sanhedrin sought cause to kill Christ, outside and beneath the court a disciple found cause to deny him. Peter had demonstrated great physical courage in his determination to stick with Jesus but lacked the moral courage to actually own His Savior. It was Peter who voiced his allegiance to Christ repeatedly and then drew his sword to take on an entire mob single-handedly. It was Peter who fled but then followed to the place where he was now challenged to keep his word. Temptation came because of his loyalty.

Verse 67. The light of the blazing fire exposed Peter's features to recognition by a maidservant to the high priest. She called attention to his having been with Jesus of Nazareth.

Verse 68. Peter denied, professing ignorance about what the maid spoke. He went onto the porch or vestibule area between the court and outer gate. (The phrase "and the cock crew" does not appear in all manuscripts but agrees with verse 72.) Still Peter lingered to be near his Christ.

Verse 69. "A maid," perhaps another, caught up with him and declared to the bystanders that "this is one of them."

Verse 70. His denial became more emphatic. The only safe thing to do was to depart, but not Peter. The "rock" stayed and again faced being a disciple. However, bystanders noted that the speech used in his vehement denials betrayed a dialect common to Galileans (Matthew 26:73).

Verse 71. Pulling out all stops, Peter began to curse and swear, *anathatizein,* or call down curses on himself if he were not truthful. Jesus had forbidden such cursing and swearing to members of the kingdom (Matthew 5:33-37), but Peter's predicament outweighed his consciousness of the great sin he had committed.

Verse 72. The cock's crowing as foretold by Jesus loosed upon Peter the overwhelming flood of shame. Some say this was the *gallicinium* or bugle call ending the third and beginning the fourth watch of the night (13:35); others hold that it was an actual rooster that might crow at any time of the night. The Lord turned to look on Peter (Luke 22:61). The sound of the cock coupled with the look in Jesus' eye was more than Peter could stand. These revealed to him an inner state, which he "thought thereon"; as he did, he began and continued to weep.

3. Trial before Pilate (15:1-15)
(Matthew 27:11; Luke 23:1, 13; John 18:28)

(1) And straightway in the morning the chief priests held a consultation with the elders and scribes and the whole council, and bound Jesus, and carried him away, and delivered him to Pilate. (2) And Pilate asked him, Art thou the King of the Jews? And he answering said unto him, Thou sayest it. (3) And the chief priests accused him of many things: but he answered nothing. (4) And Pilate asked him again, saying, Answerest thou nothing? behold how many things they witness against thee. (5) But Jesus yet answered nothing; so that Pilate marvelled. (6) Now at that feast he released unto them one prisoner, whomsoever they desired. (7) And there was one named Barabbas, which lay bound with them that had made insurrection with him, who had committed murder in the insurrection. (8) And the multitude crying aloud began to desire him to do as he had ever done unto them. (9) But Pilate answered them, saying, Will ye that I release unto you the King of the Jews? (10) For he knew that the chief priests had delivered him for envy. (11) But the chief priests moved the people, that he

should rather release Barabbas unto them. (12) And Pilate answered and said again unto them, What will ye then that I shall do unto him whom ye call the King of the Jews? (13) And they cried out again, Crucify him. (14) Then Pilate said unto them, Why, what evil hath he done? And they cried out the more exceedingly, Crucify him. (15) And so Pilate, willing to content the people, released Barabbas unto them, and delivered Jesus, when he had scourged him, to be crucified.

Verse 1. The night trial ended about 5:00 to 6:00 A.M. with the charge of blasphemy. "Straightway," as soon as the group could be assembled, the chief priests, scribes, elders, and "whole council" of the Sanhedrin met together. Their twofold purpose was to (1) legitimize in the light the illegal events done in darkness and (2) decide on a charge to present to the Roman government.

Blasphemy, insult of the Jews' God, was a religious charge that would not persuade Pilate. Their dilemma was that on the one hand they desired to kill Jesus but lacked the authority. On the other hand, they had no cause sufficient to convince the Romans to do their dirty work.

The pious rulers failed in their first purpose because now the trial, sentencing, and execution fell on the same day, equally illegal as a night trial.

Verse 2. The second purpose was evidently more successful and the hearing before Pilate secured. To avoid defilement for entering a house not purged of leaven and belonging to a Gentile, the careful religious leaders had Pilate meet them outside the palace (John 18:28). Frank Morison suggested that the high priest had gone to Pilate the night before to forewarn the procurator as to what would confront him in the morning and to persuade Pilate to rule on the case.[6]

Jesus was brought bound and the charges stated as: (1) attempting to pervert the people, (2) forbidding the paying of tribute to Caesar, and (3) claiming to be King of the Jews (Luke 23:1-2). This charge was given when it became evident that Pilate was not going to rubber-stamp the Jews' dirty work, but upon meeting Christ, insisted on a legitimate charge.[7] Thus He was delivered to suffer many things of the Gentiles. To Pilate's question of His kingship Jesus answered with a declarative affirmation: "Thou sayest it," that is, "It is you who says so—you are the judge here."

Verses 3-5. Now the Jews' accusation came on many counts but, just as before the Sanhedrin, Jesus was silent. How could a man being condemned to die not speak in His own defense? Pilate prompted Him to speak to the charges (to hear His plea to escape death), but His hour had come. To speak convincingly would only postpone acceptance of the inevitable drinking of the cup accepted in the garden a few hours before. Jesus was a lamb sacrifice, silently moving to the slaughter (Isaiah 53:7). Pilate marvelled at the eloquence of His silence, which placed weighty doubts on the uneasy conscience of wicked men.

His was not a silence of fear, although He was bound and under guard (Mark 15:1). Not once had He attempted to escape. It was not silence of contempt, for as He had respected the position of the high priest He answered in respect to the governor's position. It was not a silence of grief or sorrow that defied verbal expression. It was more a silence of tragedy; since the die was cast, no defense would suffice. Pilate drew no words from Him to ease in any way the uncomfortable burden settling upon his conscience. The trial before Pilate had become the trial of Pilate.

The Marcan record omits Pilate's quest for a way to rid himself of this innocent man. Discovering that He was a Galilean (Luke 23:5-6), he sent Jesus to Herod Antipas in Jerusalem. Luke 23:7-12 hints at two reasons, one personal and the other political. Politically this move would help absolve the enmity existing between the two rulers. The latter purpose succeeded; the two were reconciled. The former one failed; Herod, after belittling and mocking Him, refused to make a decision and returned Jesus to Pilate.

Verse 6. Pilate next appealed to a Jewish custom to mercifully receive back into society a prisoner or criminal of the people's choice at feast time.

Verse 7. The choice between a murderer and Jesus was apparently meant to assure the release of Jesus, whom Pilate knew to be an innocent victim of envious religious rulers (verse 10). Surely the Jews would not want Barabbas. Knowledge of this man comes only from the Gospel records and Acts 3:14. The name Bar Abbas means "Son of Father," but he was a son of whom few fathers would be proud. His record of lawlessness included rebellion and defiance, leading insurrection, murder, and robbery (banditry), for which he was now bound and imprisoned.

Verses 8-11. The multitude cried for Pilate to offer one for release and in a question he offered them the King of the Jews. Pilate underestimated the religious leaders' venomous hatred against Jesus. They quickly ran among the crowd inciting them to cry aloud, raise their voices in a

roar (Matthew 27:20), to demand the release of the law-
less murderer Barabbas.

Verses 12-13. For the third time Pilate faced the
quandary of what to do with an innocent man. His appeal
to the Jews only propelled him along the path he had tried
to avoid but was forced by political expedience to walk.
His appeal to their patriotic spirit to save their king, even
at the time of Passover only drew the cry, "Crucify him."
The Lamb of God was about to be offered.

Verse 14. Pilate next appealed to reason. "What evil
hath He done?" brought a louder, "Crucify him!" Crucifixion was the Roman execution of criminals for sedition
and treason and a means of death for slaves and foreign-
ers. Stoning was the Jews' punishment for blasphemy.
Here they demanded execution by the Roman method,
probably because of their intense hatred and desire for
vengeance.

Verse 15. Unable through reason or national pride to
get from the Jews any act of clemency, Pilate now resorted to violence, willing to content the clamoring mob and
hoping that the Jews' desire for blood would be appeased
by the cruel act of scourging. Whatever his intent, the
Jews would settle for no less than capital punishment.

Scourging was reserved for slaves and punishment of
condemned men. It was employed before a person was
condemned to crucifixion. The Roman scourge was a
weapon designed to inflict pain. The victim was first
stripped and bound to a low post in front to expose his
back and upper torso. The scourge, a thick leather whip
that ended in several slender thongs studded with pieces
of sharp stone, glass, metal, or bone, would cut a man's
body to ribbons and tear away pieces of flesh. Many failed

to survive at all and hardly anyone remained conscious through the pitiless whipping. Mark mercifully spares any detail, merely stating that Pilate "released Barabbas unto them, and delivered Jesus, when he had scourged Him, to be crucified." A Roman citizen would have been beheaded, except for treason; a Jew would have been stoned for blasphemy. Jesus would die as a slave and foreigner.

4. Mockery by the Soldiers (15:16-20a)
(Matthew 27:27; John 19:1)

(16) And the soldiers led him away into the hall, called Praetorium; and they called together the whole band. (17) And they clothed him with purple, and platted a crown of thorns, and put it about his head, (18) and began to salute him, Hail, King of the Jews! (19) And they smote him on the head with a reed, and did spit upon him, and bowing their knees worshipped him. (20a) And when they had mocked him, they took off the purple from him, and put his own clothes on him.

Verse 16. Loosed from the whipping post, Jesus became sport for the Roman soldiers assigned to carry out the execution. While the cross was prepared and the tablet inscribed they mocked Him as a rival of Caesar. Though cruel, their action appeared as mere child's play compared to the Jews' malice and the governor's cowardly decisions. A bruised, torn, and hurting Savior was led into the Praetorium. The place was the residence of the Roman governor while in the city and also headquarters for his bodyguard of soldiers in Jerusalem to ensure a peaceful Passover.

359

Verses 17-18. Their mockery set Jesus up as king. First He was clothed in a purple robe (John 19:2; Matthew 27:28 says scarlet), likely the purple *sagum* or cloak of a Roman cavalryman. Next a crown was put on Him. The crown was plaited of a thorn-bearing plant, probably *Zizyphus spina christi*, which had long, flexible, thorny branches and was common in the area. This thorn crown may not have been so much to inflict torture as shame, in which case they may have used the upright spirelike spines of *Phoenix dactylifera*, the date palm, resembling projections on a crown.

Verse 19. A reed served to smite His head and became a mock scepter to put into His hand. He was spat upon again and again. To complete the royal pantomime, the soldiers bowed their knees in worship as they would do only for Caesar.

Verse 20a. When the cross was ready, the game ended. The purple robe was retrieved, and His clothes restored. Now Jesus was led out to be crucified. Customarily prisoners carried their own cross to the place of execution, taking the longest route so that people along the way could take notice. The criminal walked in a space flanked by four soldiers and followed a fifth soldier who carried a tablet or board inscribed with the nature of the crime. This was later affixed to the cross. From the Praetorium near the Jaffa Gate to the presently supposed site of the crucifixion is about one-third mile.

Notes

¹They were to meet only in the Hall of Hewn Stone or decisions were invalid; there could be no night sessions, nor at feast time; evidence presented must be by separate individuals and agree in detail; each member of the court reached a decision independently and expressed it from the youngest to eldest; on a verdict of death a night must elapse before execution, as an act of mercy. Obviously, these rules were violated at Jesus' hearing.

²The Sanhedrin would on occasion execute victims, apparently without Rome's approval. Examples include the near death of the woman taken in adultery (John 8:3-11), the beheading of James the Lord's brother (Acts 12:1-2), and Stephen's stoning (Acts 6:12-7:60). Josephus gives other instances (*Antiquities of the Jews*, 14:9.3; 20:10.5; 10:9.1) Did the Jews at this point seek sanction of the governor to avoid a riot and the subsequent wrath of Rome?

³Hobbs, 71.

⁴Justice prohibited such a question because it required Jesus to testify against Himself. "Art thou the Christ, the Son of the Blessed?" The high priest refused to use the name of Jehovah, substituting "Blessed." Jesus had before confessed to being the Son of God; now Caiaphas wanted an admission before the council.

⁵The charge presented by the Jews to Pilate was not blasphemy, since Rome would not act on this charge, but treason and sedition relative to His claim to be "King of the Jews" (Mark 15:2).

⁶Frank Morison, *Who Moved the Stone?* (Grand Rapids: Zondervan, 1930), 41-42.

⁷*Ibid.*, 54-57.

E.

Account of the Crucifixion
(15:20b-41)

E. Account of the Crucifixion (15:20b-41)

1. Road to Golgotha (15:20b-22)
(Matthew 27:31b; Luke 23:32; John 19:16)

(20b) And led him out to crucify him. (21) And they compel one Simon a Cyrenian, who passed by, coming out of the country, the father of Alexander and Rufus, to bear his cross. (22) And they bring him unto the place Golgotha, which is, being interpreted, The place of a skull.

Verses 20b-21. On the route out of the city (the Jews were careful not to execute one inside the walls) Jesus began to weaken and eventually fell near the gate (Matthew 27:32). Simon was compelled (impressed) to carry His cross. Simon, coming out of the countryside, was perhaps a Passover pilgrim from Cyrene, North Africa. Mark identified him as father of Alexander and Rufus. They were perhaps known as Christians at the time of the writing; in Romans 16:13 Paul mentioned a Rufus.

The cross was probably an upright beam fifteen feet in length with a traverse beam *(patibulum)* of eight feet. When carried, the upper portion rested on the shoulders, while the long member dragged behind. Shorter crosses were shaped like the letter T; still others were like an X or a mere upright post.

Verse 22. The escort and procession brought Jesus to Golgotha, an Aramaic name meaning "the place of the skull," probably a hill named for its skulllike geographic configuration. The Latin term is *calvaria*, skull, from *calvus*, bald (Luke 23:33). The site was an elevated, smooth, round knoll or skull-shaped mound that was visible for some distance.

Mark mercifully spares readers the gruesome detail of the crucifixion process and makes no appeal to reader emotion. The crucifixion routine included carrying the cross—if not the whole cross, then the *patibulum* crossbar—to the site of execution, where it was laid flat on the ground, the prisoner stretched upon it, and his outstretched hands nailed in place. A ledge of wood formed a saddle on which the body could partially rest, and this took part of the body weight as the cross was lifted upright. The feet were nailed or tied to the upright beam. In this condition, a victim might live for a few hours to several days, death eventually coming by respiratory failure, exposure, thirst, or internal injuries. The body hung two or three feet off the ground.

2. Crucifixion and First Three Hours (15:23-32)
(Matthew 27:34; Luke 23:34; John 19:18)

(23) And they gave him to drink wine mingled with myrrh: but he received it not. (24) And when they had crucified him, they parted his garments, casting lots upon them, what every man should take. (25) And it was the third hour, and they crucified him. (26) And the superscription of his accusation was written over, THE KING OF THE JEWS. (27) And with him they crucify two thieves; the one on his right hand, and the other on his left. (28) And the scripture was fulfilled, which saith, And he was numbered with the transgressors.

366

(29) And they that passed by railed on him, wagging their heads, and saying, Ah, thou that destroyest the temple, and buildest it in three days, (30) save thyself, and come down from the cross. (31) Likewise also the chief priests mocking said among themselves with the scribes, He saved others; himself he cannot save. (32) Let Christ the King of Israel descend now from the cross, that we may see and believe. And they that were crucified with him reviled him.

These verses describe the undescribable, the humiliation and agony of the Lord in crucifixion. From the previous night Jesus had had no reprieve emotionally or physically. He rose from the Last Supper, proceeded to the garden test, was arrested and tried at night and again in early morning, was taken to Pilate, then went to Herod (omitted by Mark), went back before Pilate, was scourged, and finally traveled the path to Calvary, carrying the cross on which He now hung. His weakened body condition became evident when He fell beneath the weight of the cross; His flesh was weak but His spirit was strong.

It was almost over, but to the very end temptations arose for Him to use His omnipotence to escape the agony and the mocking taunts, and take vengeance on His tormentors. But no, the Son of God must complete His work. He accepted no efforts by well-meaning people even to alleviate the pain. Instead, He sat in judgment, granted a place in paradise to a penitent robber, and prayed God's mercy on His worst enemies.

Verse 23. The women of Jerusalem expressed compassion on helpless victims by providing a wine in which was dissolved "myrrh." The bitter herb, a potion of "gall" (Matthew 27:34), was a strong sedating narcotic, an opiate to render one senseless and thus escape pain until death mercifully came. Such a tonic was offered Jesus, but He refused. Jesus accepted no favors from man, sought no escape from the torture, took the full brunt of the wrath of God for sin. He saw it through in full consciousness for two reasons. First, He had vowed to His disciples at the Last Supper not to drink of the fruit of the vine again until the kingdom be come (Mark 14:25), and second, He must fully participate in all suffering to appease the wrath of God against sin.

Verse 24. "When they had crucified Him" is a plain statement without details. This done, Jesus hung on the cross awaiting death, and His garment became the object of interest. To the executioners went the garments. The Jews typically wore five articles of clothing: sandals, headdress, a girdle (belt), and inner and outer garments. John 19:23-24 shows that the four soldiers took one item each and cast lots for the seamless inner garment, a fulfillment of Psalm 22:18. This Jesus observed from the cross.

Verse 25. Crucifixion came at the third hour, around 9:00 A.M. or thereafter. The Jews reckoned daytime beginning with 6:00 A.M. as the first hour, but there is some indication that they also spoke of blocks of time, so that the "third hour" could extend from 9:00 A.M. to noon. Jesus was on the cross to the ninth hour, about 6:00 P.M.

Verse 26. To the cross above the victim's head was affixed a superscription, or *titulus*, stating the charge of the condemned man. Each Gospel notes the inscription, but in the different terms of Hebrew, Latin, and Greek, the national, official, and common languages respectively. Mark's *titulus* in Latin would be "Rex Judaeorum," reflecting that His true claim of the Jewish Messiahship had been twisted to a claim of treason or sedition against Rome. John 19:19-22 shows that the Jews were insulted by Pilate's inscription but that he refused to change it, his one defiant authoritative act against the cunning leaders who placed him in such a difficult role.

Verses 27-28. Two robbers (perhaps companions of Barabbas) were part of the crucifixion procession and were hung on crosses, one on the left and the other on the right hand of Christ (Luke 23:32). Mark omits that one robber, observing Jesus, acknowledged Christ's innocence and his own guilt in penitence (Luke 23:40-41). The cross that day became a judgment seat: the judge in the middle, the repentant sinner set free, the unrepentant one condemned. This act of clemency from the cross showed that Jesus could still save others.

Verse 28 is omitted in many early manuscripts; scholars think it was probably added from Luke 22:37. It is fulfillment of Isaiah 53:12. It shows that Jesus, although innocent, was treated as an evildoer by God and man.

Verses 29-30. A prophecy in Psalm 22:7-8 was fulfilled as passersby on the thoroughfare leading to Jerusalem became infected with the venom of the chief priests and scribes. The jeering people wagged their heads in an Oriental gesture of scorn (Isaiah 37:22; Jeremiah 18:16) and repeated the false, trumped-up charges concerning the Temple destruction and rebuilding. Undoubtedly the religious leaders instigated these insults to capitalize on this moment to discredit Jesus. Their taunts voiced the earlier wilderness temptation of Satan to seek an easier way to kingship. They challenged Jesus to prove His identity by coming down from the cross.

Verses 31-32. The religious leaders nearby exulted among themselves in mockery: "He saved others; himself he cannot save." Their statement was undeniable—He had saved others, and He would not save Himself so that salvation would be completed. He could not spare Himself and yet be able to save others. To grant Himself a pardon would be to deny all mankind the chance to be pardoned. It was a moral and spiritual impossibility for the Son of God.

Their taunt continued as a challenge—"Let Christ the King of Israel [a reference to the confession of verse 2] descend . . . that we may see and believe." God's way is to believe and then see; first faith, then fact. This was again the voice of Satan, and again, for the fourth time, Jesus repelled the temptation.[1]

3. Last Three Hours and Death (15:33-39)
(Matthew 27:45; Luke 23:44; John 19:28)

(33) And when the sixth hour was come, there was darkness over the whole land until the ninth hour. (34) And at the ninth hour Jesus cried with a loud voice, saying, Eloi, Eloi, lama sabachthani? which is, being interpreted, My God, my God, why hast thou forsaken me? (35) And some of them that stood by, when they heard it, said, Behold, he calleth Elias. (36) And one ran and filled a spunge full of vinegar, and put it on a reed, and gave him to drink, saying, Let alone; let us see whether Elias will come to take him down. (37) And Jesus cried with a loud voice, and gave up the ghost. (38) And the

veil of the temple was rent in twain from the top to the bottom. (39) And when the centurion, which stood over against him, saw that he so cried out, and gave up the ghost, he said, Truly this man was the Son of God.

Verse 33. No eclipse was possible at Passover with the moon full; nevertheless the sixth hour (noon) until the ninth hour came with descent of supernatural darkness. For three hours creation refused to look on or shed light upon the terrible work a creature had wrought on his Creator. Darkness signified a curse (Exodus 10:22).

Verse 34. As the darkness lifted, or perhaps out of the eerie darkness, came the voice of Jesus from the cross: *"Eloi, Eloi, lama sabachthani?"* Mark explains this Aramaic phrase: "My God, my God, why hast thou forsaken me?" It was a quotation of Psalm 22:1. A perfect man who had never known separation from the Father was now facing the unfaceable and unthinkable. Though Jesus knew no sin, He was made sin and bore the wrath of God for crime that was not His (II Corinthians 5:21). His complete faith and confidence was unwavering: *"My* God" (emphasis added).

Verse 35. Even in the darkness, people lingered at Calvary. Now they heard the cry, mistaking "Eloi" for "Elias," thought by Jews to be a forerunner of Messiah.

Verse 36. According to Matthew 27:49, "the rest said, let be"; Mark ascribes the words particularly to the one offering the vinegar-soaked sponge. John 19:28 puts the latter action after Jesus declared, "I thirst." Vinegar, Greek *oxos*, was probably sour wine, water, and egg (Latin *posca*) of the common man, here offered in kindness to a dying man. It was not a drug, and Jesus used it to moisten His lips for one great cry.

Verses 37, 39. Jesus cried loudly—not the groan or moan of a weakened, dying man, but a mighty shout. All the Synoptics record it. John 19:30 gives the phrase: "It is finished." It came after Jesus gave rational and specific instructions concerning His mother (John 19:25-27).

Jesus expired, dismissing His spirit to leave a lifeless corpse hanging cursed on the tree. The eerie darkness, followed by the victorious cry and death after only six hours of agony (a short time for crucifixion), convinced the centurion. This worldly man accustomed to death and hardened to agony saw that Jesus was no ordinary man; rather, He was indeed the Son of God and died a hero's death. His was a shout of triumph—not hopeless, but hopeful. The centurion acknowledged Jesus to be a "righteous man" and "Son of God" (Matthew 27:54; Luke 23:47).

Verse 38. In the Temple between the Holy Place and the Holy of Holies hung a mighty veil or curtain (Hebrews 9:2-3). This tapestry measured sixty feet long by thirty feet wide.[2] It was blue, purple, crimson, and of fine linen, and it carried rich embroidery (II Chronicles 3:14). Its purpose was to conceal and separate the sacred things of God from the common people. Only priests could enter the Holy Place; only the High Priest could enter the Holy of Holies once each year to offer on the mercy seat of the ark of the covenant sacrificial blood for the sins of the people.

Mark inserts what happened in the Temple at the moment of death: the massive veil was torn, ripped in two, from top to bottom. From above, God ripped open the veil, symbolizing that now the flesh of Christ had been rent and that the way to God was uninterrupted by any barriers. Everyone could enter with boldness by the blood of Jesus Christ (Hebrews 10:19-22). He was the sin-bearing paschal lamb (Hebrews 9:28), our curse (Deuteronomy 21:23; Galatians 3:13).

4. Women Watching from Afar (15:40-41)
(Matthew 27:55; Luke 23:49; John 19:25)

(40) There were also women looking on afar off: among whom was Mary Magdalene, and Mary the mother of James the less and of Joses, and Salome; (41) (who also, when he was in Galilee, followed him, and ministered unto him;) and many other women which came up with him unto Jerusalem.

Verses 40-41. Of Jesus' most intimate friends it seems that only the women felt safe enough to be present. Mark names three women, afar; John indicates they stood near the cross. Both observations are correct in that the women likely stood near the cross until the darkness lifted at death, then moved away to watch the proceedings and mark the burial site so they could return and properly prepare the body.

First named is Mary Magdalene (of the town of Magdala), freed of seven demons by Jesus (Mark 16:9; Luke 8:2). Later she was among the women who came to find an empty tomb (Luke 24:10). John 20:1-18 and Mark 16:9 show her meeting the risen Christ.

Also named was Mary the mother of James the Less and Joses. This Mary is thought to have been wife of Cleophas (Clopas) and sister of Mary the mother of Jesus (John 19:25).

Matthew 27:56 notes that the mother of the sons of Zebedee was also present; the comparison with Mark indicates that this was Salome.

It is not strange that these women were present. In a time when women were deeply oppressed, Jesus demonstrated courtesy, dignity, concern and compassion for them. They in turn followed Him and ministered to His human needs in Galilee and even to Jerusalem, showing faith and love, along with many other women. Hobbs calls their presence an island of love in an ocean of hate.[3] These women provided comforting encouragement when viewed from the cross. And their ministry was not over. They shared in burial (verse 47), brought gifts of spices (16:1), heard first of the resurrection (16:5-6), were at Pentecost (Acts 1:14), and opened their homes for consecrated worship of God (Acts 12:12).

Notes

[1] The first time was in the wilderness (Matthew 4:6-7), the second at Caesarea Philippi (Matthew 16:22-23), the third in Gethsemane (Mark 14:36), and now here (15:32).

[2] J. Dwight Pentecost, *The Words and Works of Jesus Christ* (Grand Rapids: Zondervan, 1981), 488.

[3] Hobbs, 75.

F.
Burial of the Body
(15:42-47)

F. Burial of the Body (15:42-47)
(Matthew 25:57; Luke 23:50; John 19:38)

(42) And now when the even was come, because it was the preparation, that is, the day before the sabbath, (43) Joseph of Arimathaea, an honourable counsellor, which also waited for the kingdom of God, came, and went in boldly unto Pilate, and craved the body of Jesus. (44) And Pilate marvelled if he were already dead: and calling unto him the centurion, he asked him whether he had been any while dead. (45) And when he knew it of the centurion, he gave the body to Joseph. (46) And he bought fine linen, and took him down, and wrapped him in the linen, and laid him in a sepulchre which was hewn out of a rock, and rolled a stone unto the door of the sepulchre. (47) And Mary Magdalene and Mary the mother of Joses beheld where he was laid.

Verse 42. The new Jewish day began at 6:00 P.M.; evening at 3:00 P.M. Jesus died at evening, and now a sense of urgency descended upon the pious Jews, for it was the evening before Sabbath, when no work could be done. This then was the day when chores, cooking, and tending livestock were done in preparation for the Sabbath. It was also the time at Passover when the lambs were slain. This Sabbath was no ordinary weekly Sabbath, but the high Sabbath of the feast (Leviticus 23:6-7).

It was customary to entomb the body on the day of death after embalming and proper preparation. To allow a body to hang overnight on a tree would profane the holy

377

body to hang overnight on a tree would profane the holy land (Deuteronomy 21:23), and this was the eve of the high festival (John 19:31).

Verse 43. John mentions Nicodemus, but all the Synoptics mention Joseph of Arimathea (a city about fifteen miles from Joppa). He was now a citizen of Jerusalem and served on the Sanhedrin, or perhaps a lesser council. He was rich (Matthew 27:57) and an honorable counselor who had not agreed to the death penalty (Luke 23:51), so evidently he had not attended Jesus' trial. A secret disciple of Christ in life (Matthew 27:57), he now boldly, courageously stepped forward to retrieve the corpse of a fallen leader who could not help him.

The body would not likely be given to Jesus' women friends, though embalming was women's work. Nor would it likely be given to the fearful disciples. Bodies of crucified criminals belonged to Rome and would be disposed of either in a potter's field, thrown into the Valley of Hinnom, or left to vultures and wild dogs. Only a man of some affluence could secure it, and Joseph made his appeal at the risk of his peers' unfavorable regard.

Verses 44-45. Pilate, surprised that Jesus was dead so soon (many victims hung for days before dying), sought confirmation from his trusted centurion. Pilate's uncertainty adds yet another affirmation of Jesus' death through the testimony of one who had witnessed many such deaths. Himself now sure, Pilate gave Joseph the body.

Verse 46. With help from willing hands (Nicodemus), Joseph himself evidently removed the body from the cross, wrapped it in a grave shroud (Greek *sindon*) of linen, and enfolded myrrh and aloes (John 19:39). He then laid it in his new tomb hewn from the rock and rolled a stone before the door or entrance. Thus Joseph, a silent disciple in life, risked his own life and provided a tomb for Jesus among the wealthy (Isaiah 53:9).

Verse 47. Mary of Magdala and Mary the mother of Joses watched to be certain of where the body was placed. They now knew where to return after the Sabbath and properly prepare the body for burial.

Jesus' funeral was attended by few people—only two men and two women are named—but Luke 23:55 says other women also observed the place where He was laid.

IV.
The Resurrection of the Servant
(16:1-20)

IV.

The Resurrection of the Servant (16:1-20)

A. Women Coming to the Empty Tomb (16:1-8)
(Matthew 28:1; Luke 24:1)

(1) And when the sabbath was past, Mary Magdalene, and Mary the mother of James, and Salome, had bought sweet spices, that they might come and anoint him. (2) And very early in the morning the first day of the week, they came unto the sepulchre at the rising of the sun. (3) And they said among themselves, Who shall roll us away the stone from the door of the sepulchre? (4) And when they looked, they saw that the stone was rolled away: for it was very great. (5) And entering into the sepulchre, they saw a young man sitting on the right side, clothed in a long white garment; and they were affrighted. (6) And he saith unto them, Be not affrighted: Ye seek Jesus of Nazareth, which was crucified: he is risen; he is not here: behold the place where they laid him. (7) But go your way, tell his disciples and Peter that he goeth before you into Galilee: there shall ye see him, as he said unto you. (8) And they went out quickly, and fled from the sepulchre; for they trembled and were amazed: neither said they any thing to any man; for they were afraid.

Jesus' body had been placed in the tomb on Friday

before sunset, then came the Sabbath, a full day, and now it was the day after Sabbath at sunrise, the third day. Jews reckoned any portion of a day as a whole day, so in the briefest amount of time (about thirty-six hours), the three days were fulfilled.

Verses 1-3. When the Sabbath was over the body could be properly prepared for burial, and now the women came to pay last tribute to Jesus' dead body by embalming it with oils and spices. They, unlike the fearful disciples (John 20:19), were preoccupied with one problem. They had marked the tomb site, noting the massive stone over the entrance. The stone, estimated to be the size of a cart-wheel in diameter but oval, six feet long, three feet wide, and eight to twelve inches thick, would be too much for the women to move.

Verses 4-5. The great stone had been rolled away and upon entering the sepulcher the women saw not a body, but a young man sitting on the right side. Mark does not refer to this youth as an angel as do the other Gospels (Matthew 28:5; John 20:12) but notes the long white apparel and the women's response of fear and amazement.

Verse 6. The young man spoke to confirm that they had come to the correct tomb, but that Jesus of Nazareth had risen. The evidence of a resurrection was unmistakable. The stone was not removed to let Jesus out, but to show human witnesses the place where He had lain.

Verse 7. The angel then gave instructions to go tell Jesus' disciples, particularly Peter, that He was going before them into Galilee as He had said (Mark 14:28). The message to Peter was touching and characteristic of Jesus. Peter, after contemptuous and blasphemous denials of his Lord (Matthew 26:70-74), was in self-punishing remorse and sorrow. Jesus sought to comfort Peter and offer forgiveness, not to punish the sin.

Verse 8 relates that the women "went out," fled from the sepulcher trembling and in amazement. Their fear kept them silent about the empty tomb. The initial response to the Resurrection was fear, astonishment, perhaps perplexity as to how it could be. There must occur a transfer of faith from an incarnate Lord to a risen Lord (II Corinthians 5:16) because the glorified Christ was unlike the Christ of the Gospels (Revelation 1:13-16).

B. Ending of Mark (16:9-20)

For a discussion of the textual evidence for this passage, see the Introduction. Since the events and doctrines described in this ending have support in the rest of Scripture, even if someone did not accept this passage, the truth it teaches would still stand.

1. Appearings of Jesus (16:9-14)
(Matthew 28:8, 16; Luke 24:13; John 20:11)

(9) Now when Jesus was risen early the first day of the week, he appeared first to Mary Magdalene, out of whom he had cast seven devils. (10) And she went and told them that had been with him, as they mourned and wept. (11) And they, when they had heard that he was alive, and had been seen of her, believed not. (12) After that he appeared in another form unto two of them, as they walked, and went into the country. (13) And they went and told it unto the residue: neither believed they

them. (14) Afterward he appeared unto the eleven as they sat at meat, and upbraided them with their unbelief and hardness of heart, because they believed not them which had seen him after he was risen.

Jesus appeared to the women, to a pair of disciples on the road, then to a group. The purpose was to convince His followers of the Resurrection. At first the result was just the opposite.

Verses 9-10. Early the first day Jesus appeared to a woman in the garden as she lingered at the tomb. It was Mary Magdalene, who loved Him much and who had been delivered from demons (Luke 8:2). She went to spread the good news to His friends as they wept and mourned for the dead Savior.

Verse 11. They heard her testimony but her credibility as a witness was not convincing. Women's talk to Jewish men was *leros*, rubbish; they refused to believe her story.

Verses 12-13. Afterward Jesus manifested Himself to two disciples as they walked on the road to the country (Luke 24:13-35). At first, they failed to see Christ in the stranger. Finally convinced, they shared the good news with the remainder of the disciples in Jerusalem, only to be disbelieved as Mary had been.

Verse 14. The third appearance of the resurrected Savior was to the eleven as they ate dinner. For their hardness of heart and unbelief or slowness to believe without sense-verified evidence, He upbraided them. This rebuke came because they ought to have believed competent witnesses. Instead, it seemed they almost preferred to grieve, mourn, and weep in disbelief than to become excited in anticipation, joy, and hope of a resurrected Lord. The unbelief and hardness of heart noted in Mark 9:14 was slow to die in the disciples of Jesus Christ.

2. Commission to His Followers (16:15-18)
(Matthew 28:18; Luke 24:47)

(15) And he said unto them, Go ye into all the world, and preach the gospel to every creature. (16) He that believeth and is baptized shall be saved; but he that believeth not shall be damned. (17) And these signs shall follow them that believe; In my name shall they cast out devils; they shall speak with new tongues; (18) they shall take up serpents; and if they drink any deadly thing, it shall not hurt them; they shall lay hands on the sick, and they shall recover.

Verse 15. Mark fails to note any interval of time or locale between the Resurrection and this commission. The commission transpired in Galilee (Matthew 28:16-20) and was repeated just before the Ascension (Acts 1:8). Before the Resurrection the gospel was not complete and could not be preached as such. Jesus' ministry was to Israel (Matthew 10:5), excluding Gentiles except on unusual occasions (Mark 7:26). Now all mankind—"the world," "every creature," Jew and Gentile—was to hear the good news. Paul interpreted the tearing of the Temple veil as uniting Jew and Gentile (Ephesians 2:14), enabling everyone to be reconciled to God, the Jews first and now all (Romans 1:16). The gospel expanded from Judea, to Samaria, to the entire Roman Empire, and ultimately to whole continents not then known. (See Acts 1:8.)

Verses 16-18. "He that believeth and is baptized shall

be saved" does not oppose the New Testament teaching of salvation by grace through faith. Baptism is an act of faith, and if a person truly believes the gospel he will obey this command of the gospel. By obeying he expresses his faith, while a refusal to obey reveals a lack of faith. By faith he will be justified, by disbelief condemned.

This is the first explicit mention of Christian baptism, if we conclude that John 4:1-2 was a baptism unto repentance as a continuation of John's baptism (Matthew 3:11).

The instruction of Matthew 28:19 speaks of baptism in the name of the Father, Son, and Holy Ghost. The apostles enacted this commission after the Day of Pentecost, using the name of Jesus, the only saving name (Acts 4:12) to fully cover all modes of God's manifestation. Thus to be baptized in Jesus' name is to be baptized into the fully revealed Father, Son, and Holy Ghost— Jesus Christ (Acts 2:38). Although a trinitarian who advocates the use of the three titles in baptism instead of the name of Jesus, Cole acknowledged the apostolic practice and its meaning:

> To baptize into the threefold Name of God, then, is not a theological quirk or quibble; it corresponds to a baptism into the fully revealed nature of God, and thus into the fullness of Christian experience. In early unsophisticated days, however, the name of "Jesus" could conceivably stand for all this, especially if the candidates were already Jewish monotheists.[1]

The signs that follow believers of Jesus Christ include new tongues. Here Mark gives an intimation of Pentecost to come. Other signs are expulsion of demons, taking up of serpents, laying hands on the sick, and drinking of toxins. All these were manifested in the early church (Acts 2:4; 16:18; 28:2-8; James 5:14-15), except that the last one has no New Testament parallel. An early second-century writer, Papias, tells of Justus Barnabas (Acts 1:23) who drank poison and was unharmed.[2] Signs are more common to the writings of John and Luke than Mark (John 2:11; Acts 4:16, 22), and the Pharisees hypocritically sought after them. Jesus gave them only one: the sign of Jonah (Matthew 12:39).

Evidential signs are for those in the church as confirmation of the work of God. The taking up of serpents and drinking of poison refer to divine protection in times of danger, not to the deliberate handling of them. Luke 10:19 gives a similar promise of God's keeping power with respect to the danger of snakes and scorpions, associating them figuratively with demons. Neither passage speaks of deliberately exposing oneself to snakes, scorpions, or poisons as a sign of faith. Never could such antics be justified by the New Testament. In fact, Matthew 4:7 and Luke 4:12 expressly forbid testing God in such perilous folly.

3. Ascension of the Lord Jesus (16:19-20)
(Luke 24:50; Acts 1:9-11; See Ephesians 1:20-23; 4:7-10)

(19) So then after the Lord had spoken unto them, he was received up into heaven, and sat on the right hand of God. (20) And they went forth, and preached every where, the Lord working with them, and confirming the word with signs following. Amen.

In this ending, Mark apparently gathered some of the primary postresurrection sayings about Jesus and used them to conclude his narrative. Verse 19 parallels Luke 24:51, Acts 1:9, and Hebrews 10:12; verse 20 is a single statement of the history of the church in Acts.

Verse 19. "So then after" there followed another interval of time before Christ was "received up into heaven." Acts 1:9-11 and Luke 24:50-51 elaborate on this event, and Acts 7:55 provides a glimpse of the outcome. Luke's phraseology is based on the Old Testament, particularly II Kings 2:11 and Psalm 110. The Ascension gradually unfolds through the Gospels: it is absent from Matthew, characteristically brief in Mark, and described with more detail in Luke and Acts.

The Lord's ascent is a triumphal one to the priesthood of Melchisedec as promised by Psalm 110:4 and Hebrews 5:6. Christ referred to this prophecy relative to His identity as the son of David (Mark 12:37). The position of the "right hand of God" is not physical, for God is Spirit. It signifies that the glorified and ascended man Christ has been invested with all the power and glory of the indwelling Spirit of God

Verse 20. Mark shows the straightforward actions of the expanding church by summarizing the activities of the apostles and early Christians. They went and preached everywhere, obedient to the instructions, and the Lord worked with them, confirming the Word with miraculous signs.

Notes

[1]Cole, 262.
[2]*Pulpit Commentary*, 248.